Squanto

Squanto

A Native Odyssey

Andrew Lipman

Yale

UNIVERSITY PRESS

New Haven and London

Published with support from the Fund established in memory of
Oliver Baty Cunningham, a distinguished graduate of the Class of 1917, Yale College,
Captain, 15th United States Field Artillery, born in Chicago September 17, 1894,
and killed while on active duty near Thiaucourt, France, September 17, 1918,
the twenty-fourth anniversary of his birth.

Published with assistance from the Mary Cady Tew Memorial Fund.

Yale University Press books may be purchased in quantity for educational, business,
or promotional use. For information, please e-mail sales.press@yale.edu (U.S. office)
or sales@yaleup.co.uk (U.K. office).

Set in Bulmer type by Integrated Publishing Solutions.
Printed in the United States of America.

Library of Congress Control Number: 2024930909
ISBN 978-0-300-23877-8 (hardcover : alk. paper)

A catalogue record for this book is available from the British Library.

This paper meets the requirements of ANSI/NISO Z39.48-1992
(Permanence of Paper).

10 9 8 7 6 5 4 3 2 1

To Dad, in memory

Contents

Squanto

Introduction

SQUANTO LAY DYING ON A LOW-SLUNG bed lined with pelts, in a house so close to the Atlantic that he could probably hear surf in the distance. His body glistened with sweat while blood trickled from his nose. The village healers prayed and chanted over him, offering him medicinal herbs and roots, but they could not give him much hope. They had seen these symptoms before. The sick man had to translate his grim prognosis for his English companions, who called the mysterious ailment "an Indean feavor," implying it was a disease that only locals suffered from.[1]

Those colonists are best known today as "Pilgrims," a name they did not call themselves. Squanto, who was also known as Tisquantum, had been their translator for twenty months when he fell ill in November 1622. It had been two years since the *Mayflower* arrived on American shores and one year after the so-called First Thanksgiving, a diplomatic visit that was not actually a feast of thanksgiving. As Tisquantum's condition worsened, the colonists' prayers became more urgent, for they saw this man's very existence as an act of providence. One described him as "a speciall instrument sent of God for their good beyond their expectation."[2]

While his life was not long—Tisquantum was probably in his thirties when he died—it was eventful. He grew up in Patuxet, the place now called Plymouth, Massachusetts. In 1614, eight years before he died, an English explorer captured him and twenty-odd other Wampanoag men to sell them into the Mediterranean slave trade. For the next five years his fate rested in the hands of Europeans. In Málaga, Spain, a Catholic priest briefly took custody of him, then English imperialists brought him first to the busy streets of London, then to a tiny Newfoundland outpost with a possible stop in Jamestown, and then to the original Plymouth in England before finally sending him home in 1619.

His return voyage had a tragic ending: he discovered that his home

1

in Patuxet had been abandoned. An epidemic had swept across the shore, killing tens of thousands, including almost all of his fellow villagers. In late 1620, a year after he came back, the most famous ship in American history sailed into Patuxet's harbor. Squanto met the English settlers as part of a Native delegation that came to make peace in the spring of 1621. He soon earned his reputation as "a spetiall instrument" when he started teaching them where to hunt deer and catch fish, how to plant corn, beans, and squash, and, most important, how to court allies and make peace. His translations helped them forge a partnership with the region's most powerful *sachem* (chief), a man who bore the title *Massasoit*. It can be translated roughly as "he who is great." Since Massasoit was an honorific title for his office and not his personal name, some modern Wampanoags refer to him as *the* Massasoit.[3]

The feast between these allies in fall 1621 marked a high point for the Patuxet man, a moment of triumph after years of painful exile. But it did not last long. Soon after the harvest, some Wampanoags started complaining to the Plymouth leadership that their new friend had ruthless ambitions. They alleged Squanto was demanding tributes from followers, bribing allies with gifts, and intimidating those who resisted him with threats that he could unleash the plague. The settlers were shocked. "They begane to see," Governor William Bradford wrote, "that Squanto sought his owne ends, and plaid his owne game." "Thus by degrees we began to discover *Tisquantum*," wrote the colonist Edward Winslow, disappointed that his trusted guide wanted "only to make himself great in the eyes of his Country-men."[4]

Upon learning of this scheming, the Massasoit demanded the colonists execute Tisquantum. But the settlers were fond of the man. Despite their misgivings about his behavior, they ended up sheltering him. As months passed, tensions between the Massasoit and Squanto gradually eased, and the great sachem relented in his calls for the translator's head. In November 1622, with this controversy seemingly behind him, the translator led the English on a trading mission that brought them to Monomoit, the place on Cape Cod later named Chatham, Massachusetts. It was there that he came down with his ominous sickness.

In his final feverish days, Tisquantum beckoned Bradford to his bedside. The dying man asked the governor "to pray for him, that he might goe to the Englishmens God in heaven." This confession of faith came as a surprise to the colonists. In their surviving writings, none mentioned him having any particular interest in Christianity before his death, though in his years abroad, Tisquantum had been inside churches and cathedrals, heard his share of sermons, probably learned to sing a few psalms, and perhaps been baptized by a Spanish priest. Yet his claim that he wanted to spend eternity with the English God seemed to indicate a drastic change in a man who had been plotting to become a powerful Indigenous leader just months earlier.[5]

Squanto took so many mysteries with him to his grave, the first being the exact cause of his death. Given the vagueness and suddenness of his symptoms, some historians have wondered—without any direct evidence— if he was poisoned. And that's hardly the only missing piece of the puzzle. What happened to him during those years of captivity overseas? How did he manage to return home when the other men taken with him had not? Why was he so willing to help the English after being captured by an En- glishman? Clearly he "sought his owne ends," but what exactly *were* those ends? What compelled him to make a deathbed conversion? Is it even possible to collect all the scraps of evidence now, four hundred years later, to come up with plausible answers to these questions?[6]

The following pages are just such an attempt. Using a broad range of evidence, I reconstruct an extraordinary life that ended right when many Americans think their story begins.

Squanto's legend is better known than his life. In American popular mem- ory, he belongs to the same rarified pantheon as Pocahontas, Sacajawea, Sitting Bull, Crazy Horse, and Geronimo, those famed Natives remem- bered as loyal helpmates or worthy opponents in the annals of the frontier. But whereas books about the *Mayflower* and its passengers could fill many shelves, there is none exclusively about Tisquantum—for adults, that is.

He has been the central character in over a dozen children's books and a supporting player in cartoons, television mini-series, and untold numbers of Thanksgiving school plays. He was even the subject of a live- action Hollywood film with a $20 million budget, *Squanto: A Warrior's Tale,* which Walt Disney Pictures released to mostly empty theaters in October 1994. Though schoolroom versions of his story sometimes differ in details, they share the same flaws. Most depict Squanto as a convenient figure whose main purpose was fulfilling the colonists' destiny. Even those that try to center his goals and feelings tend to omit the final year of his life when he was disgraced and died.

Outside of children's entertainment, plenty of writers have treated him with care in serious books about Plymouth Colony. Tisquantum reliably features in academic tomes, best-selling pop histories, and textbooks. The parts of his life that I expand on in this book—his time overseas and the events leading up to his death—are hardly a hidden history. The basic details of his exile and downfall have long interested scholars and have always been in full view in the firsthand accounts of early Plymouth.[7]

Still, there are good reasons no one has written a stand-alone study of him before now. The challenge lies in the sources. The standard primary texts leave many holes in his story. Some basic facts about the man one might expect to find in a biography are completely unknown: we don't know his dates of birth and death, we don't know the names of his family and whether he ever married or fathered children. No source can tell us concrete facts about where he was and what he was doing in the first twenty to thirty years of his life, and his whereabouts aren't always certain even after he appears in the historical record. The colonial papers have problems beyond their lack of detail. Although most English writers were genuinely curious about Squanto and his people, their ultimate motivation was to claim and rule Native land. They defined Natives by what they lacked: European technologies and the Christian faith. That colonial mindset was a constant ideological undercurrent in their accounts.

That is not to say that their letters, maps, illustrations, and books are useless—far from it. When read closely, staying mindful of the authors' intentions and blinkered perspectives, these texts narrate early encounters while illustrating patterns of everyday Wampanoag life. We cannot forget that the best sources were written by men who consulted closely with Wampanoag people. Three writers in particular—the explorer Thomas Dermer and the colonists Edward Winslow and William Bradford—relied on Tisquantum as their primary guide. Much of the information they recorded about local practices and politics came directly from him.

Over the following decades, dozens more bilingual Natives served as uncredited co-authors for the most reliable and valuable texts from this period, hence why we cannot dismiss English sources as mere propaganda for their colonizing project. Other European sources can illuminate his time overseas—including two recently uncovered deeds from a Spanish archive that reveal new information about Tisquantum's captivity. All these accounts become more reliable when they are tiled together into a mosaic of evidence, emphasizing consistent details recorded by more than one observer. Quoting from these sources often requires taking a moment to consider the values held by fervent Protestants from Stuart England and how their worldview shaped their perceptions. It's only when we account for the colonists' warped lens that we might be able to see Squanto's world more clearly in their writings.[8]

Within a couple of decades of Tisquantum's passing, New England missionaries began to learn his language so they could preach to Natives in their own tongue. Soon they began to print translated scripture in Wampanoag and many converts learned to write in a transliterated version of their own language. These documents have allowed thousands of modern tribal members to speak it today, thanks to the Wôpanâak Language Project. Founded in 1993 by Jessie Little Doe Baird, a Mashpee Wampanoag citizen who became an MIT-trained linguist, the program has brought the long-dormant language back to life. The work that Baird and many other teachers do today is a continuation of a long practice of Wampanoags preserving their ancestral traditions, agriculture, medicine, architecture, dance, music, crafts, and clothing.[9]

Wampanoag experts in their own living language and culture offer insights that deepen our understanding of the society that raised Squanto. When considering their past, these educators draw from a multilayered archive consisting of oral traditions, writings, sacred objects, and monuments in the land itself. These historians have deep personal and political stakes when interpreting the early colonial period—unlike me, a non-Native historian writing with an outsider's perspective, telling *a* story with an academic tool kit, and not telling *their* story. Still, no matter how knowledgeable they are, careful Indigenous experts never insist that they have definitive information about events that transpired four hundred years ago. When interpreting specific figures like Tisquantum or the Massasoit, Wampanoag scholars also turn to the same written records used by non-Native researchers.[10]

Additional information comes from archaeologists who have excavated sites across the region for decades. Even the smallest pieces of evidence—beads, pottery shards, pipe stems, seeds, animal bones, even strands of DNA—can be illuminating, especially when they offer fresh explanations for matters that no other source addresses satisfactorily. The complementary work of atmospheric scientists working with fossilized pollen, tree rings, and ice cores can explain larger climate and ecological dynamics shaping this story.

Material findings reveal compelling truths whether they confirm or challenge other sources, though they seldom answer difficult questions on their own. There are ethical concerns with how some of this evidence was discovered. A few digs cited in this book predated the passage of the 1983 Massachusetts Unmarked Burial Law and the 1990 federal Native American Graves Protection and Repatriation Act (NAGPRA), laws that address the handling of Indigenous human remains and cultural objects. Though many of these objects have since been repatriated, far too many bones and belongings of Tisquantum's people have been lost. And some artifacts may still be secreted away in archive basements across New England.[11]

Together, textual, linguistic, cultural, archaeological, and environmental evidence create a vibrant palette with which to paint a new picture of a man too often rendered as a caricature. Each body of knowledge about Squanto's world has its strengths and shortcomings, so this methodology is best described as the "more the merrier" or "all of the above." When sources are sparse, I use the conditional tense or words like "perhaps," "likely," "possibly," "probably," and "maybe" to indicate concrete information is lacking, or I pause the narrative to weigh the possibilities.

Caveats like this might set off alarms for readers who believe that historians are somehow breaking the rules when they speculate, but those critics have an incorrect understanding of what we do. No matter how many sources exist about a subject, scholars always find gaps in the record and questions that cannot be answered conclusively. In some ways, the combination of approaches in this book can resemble the work of paleontologists. For many species, they have never found a complete skeleton in the fossil record, just a few fragments. Nonetheless they try to reconstruct the frame, organs, flesh, diet, and behavior of a creature from the past. They do this by drawing on the insights of multiple disciplines: from their deeper knowledge of animal anatomy, their comparative study of the fossils of related animals, their understanding of the fossil's geological, climatological, and ecological contexts, and their close examination of the bones themselves, making inferences from wear and injuries to reimagine the life of their subject.

Their work, like ours, is never complete and changes with new information and theories—just look at their renderings of lumbering reptilian dinosaurs from fifty years ago compared with the agile bird-like species they depict today. Visitors to natural history museums seldom complain about the speculation of paleontologists; they accept it as a necessary part of the pursuit of knowledge about the past.

Of course, history is hardly a science, so this analogy is far from perfect. We look for meanings, not just material facts. The written word is usually our primary evidence—in this case, the incomplete colonial documents serve as the partial skeleton, as they are the frame of the narrative that supports the contextual information from other sources and approaches. Whether writing about peasants or presidents, historians attempt to enter the headspace of people they never met who lived through things they did not witness, which is a kind of intellectual make-believe.

Without a search for the reasons behind Tisquantum's actions, without an informed attempt to account for the missing pieces of his story, this book would not be history. It would just be a dreary list of the uncontested things we know about him and the other Natives and Europeans he met. That's all you get if you dismiss the open questions because it might require some inventiveness to answer them. There's a reason "story" is part of the word "history," after all. In many languages, they are the same word.[12]

Like an early modern Odysseus, Tisquantum was wily, worldly, and seldom in full control of his own fate. By the time the Plymouth colonists embarked on their ship, the man from Patuxet had seen more of the globe than most Europeans had. After being taken as a slave, he crossed the Atlantic four times, visiting at least two kingdoms (Spain and England) and two colonies (Newfoundland and Virginia). Even before his capture, he had already crossed paths with famed figures like Samuel de Champlain and John Smith. It is even possible he met Pocahontas when they were living mere blocks from each other in London at the same time.

In his years overseas, Squanto accumulated a reservoir of information about the English. By acquiring their language, he learned about their intentions, their strengths, and their weaknesses. His hard-won knowledge elevated his status among both colonists and his fellow Wampanoags, but in his career as a go-between, he seldom seemed divided in his loyalties. Those years abroad did not weaken his ties to his own people, nor did they lead him to identify more with his captors; rather, like most Native former captives, he demonstrated his fierce attachment to his home and his own kin. It was only in his last months on earth that he showed any interest in making a deeper connection with the English beyond strategic friendship.

My biggest revision to scholarship on Tisquantum and Plymouth is my contention—supported by documentary and archaeological evidence— that he and his surviving kin established a seasonal village across a narrow brook from the English settlement in the summer of 1621, just as he was performing his famed acts of generosity toward the settlers. This small, mobile Indigenous community was his supporting constituency when he began his ill-fated political machinations.

It changes the standard picture of the settlement's first year, where the village is typically imagined as an isolated group of colonists aided by a single Native consultant. In Plymouth's first summer, the English were in constant contact with a mirroring Wampanoag community led by Tisquantum that stood just a few yards away from their houses. This reappraisal also corrects the common misconception that the returning captive was Patuxet's sole survivor—"an outsider, an alien, one without a people," as a recent pop history described him. Many writers have framed him as a lonely actor who single-handedly assisted the colonists for his own self-interest. In this retelling, his actions appear in a different light. He is best understood as a figure who was motivated by communal concerns *and* his personal ambition.[13]

When Squanto "sought his own ends," he saw the English as helpmates to his people, returning the favors he had offered them. By aiding the newcomers, he never intended to create an exclusively English place but rather planned to bring his old village back to life alongside a band of useful new neighbors. His vision was grounded in age-old Wampanoag ideas about kinship, condolence, reciprocity, and spirituality, but when putting his plan into motion, he defied some of the core rules of Indigenous politics. His brash and deceitful attempts to challenge the traditional structures of power would lead to his undoing. In his struggles, we can find echoes of an old question from Homeric literature: after years at sea, can a homesick wanderer ever truly go home again?[14]

This book is not a traditional biography. It's a study of a person and his world—a portrait set in a larger land- and seascape. The opening chapters that explore his cultural upbringing before he appeared in the historic record are critical to interpreting his better-documented actions later in life. The interludes on pivotal side actors and far-flung locations help explain why he was taken and how he found his way home. Filling in the backdrop of his times allows us to perceive Squanto in silhouette, but these sections are intended to be more than just scenery. The places he saw and the things he learned would inform his decisions before and after he returned to Patuxet.

A wider frame also helps us see what is—and what is not—exceptional about his story. Contrary to the *Mayflower* legend, the New England settlements were not born from a single ship. The English families that came to squat in Patuxet were never a stand-alone band of dissidents that stood apart from their mother country. Their colony is best understood as one node among many in an emerging network of English plantations, fishing stations, and trading ventures. This budding empire connected Mediterranean ports, Atlantic islands, and Indigenous harbors on North American and Caribbean shores. Squanto and the Pilgrims are indeed important in both Native and colonial history writ large, but their encounter is best viewed on an appropriate scale: as one episode among many early Indigenous encounters with Europeans.[15]

Tracking Tisquantum and others like him as they pinballed around the Atlantic basin reveals the many transatlantic conflicts and ambitions that created the colonial societies of North America. Exploring the politics of the Wampanoags and their neighbors introduces us to a complicated Indigenous world that was changing for decades before the settlers arrived. The resulting narrative provides a more global saga than older, narrower accounts that followed the English families on their voyage west.

This narrative of Squanto's life and times is divided into three parts. The first, "Home," illuminates the most obscure part of Tisquantum's story: his childhood and young adult years. This part of the book is more ethnographic than biographic, as it is grounded in what we know about the daily life, material culture, language, religion, social structure, and government of the Wampanoag society that raised him. The result is a composite picture of a typical boy growing up in Patuxet, not quite a depiction of the real young man. This section also introduces the dynamic and sometimes dangerous Indigenous political world that Squanto navigated, both as the colonists' translator and as a politician in his own right.

"Away," the second part, looks at his captivity from several angles. It begins with the related stories of other Native men taken before him. Not only did their experiences foreshadow his ordeals, but their respective kidnappings are best seen as a single connected process. The man from Patuxet remains an opaque figure in his time overseas, but we can still explore the diverse places he encountered, while seeking to understand the means and motives of the imperialists who were trying—and often failing— to colonize North American shores.

The third section, "Home Again," narrates his homecoming, from his return in the late summer of 1619 to the day in November 1622 when he died. In a close rereading of the colonists' accounts, Tisquantum emerges as a distinctive, if still elusive, character. It was in this momentous period when his personal challenges and contradictions became most clear. Only at the close of this section, when we take stock of everything we can know about him from cradleboard to grave, can we arrive at provisional answers to the questions that loom over his final days.

The final chapter on the Patuxet man's "afterlives" traces his shifting place in American memory and popular culture. In the four hundred years since his death, Squanto has been reimagined by generations of storytellers, museum interpreters, writers, preachers, playwrights, painters, sculptors, filmmakers, and actors—Native and non-Native alike. In both life and death, he was many things to many people. Much like his real-world counterpart, the fictionalized Squanto was put to work, cast as helper, hero, villain, or victim in narratives of national origins.

In this book I aim to do justice to the real person, but myth busting itself isn't the main point; there are better reasons to learn about this past than seeking a cheap feeling of superiority over your grade school teachers. Debunking the narrative that he was a happily welcoming indigene is about as easy as tipping over a cardboard cutout. It takes a little more work to explore his culture, to retrace his travels, and then use this information to reconsider a misunderstood man.[16]

To follow his journeys across the Atlantic and home again, first we have to rewind to roughly thirty years before that fever took him, to a time before any European had set foot in Patuxet, when Tisquantum was still in his mother's womb.

PART ONE

Home

ONE

Infancy

OUR FIRST GLIMPSE OF SQUANTO'S childhood comes from a simple sketch. Drawn by the explorer Samuel de Champlain, it illustrates the Frenchman's 1605 visit to Patuxet. At the center of the frame is a protected harbor with Champlain's ship at anchor. As a group of stick-figure men greet his boat at the shore, another party rows a canoe toward them. The village is rendered in a wallpaper-like pattern of eight repeating images of square cornfields surrounding dome-shaped houses, with small stylized trees spaced evenly between the houses. It's a figurative illustration, never intended to be true to life, drawn cartoonishly with no consistent scale. As a window on the past, it offers a rather clouded view. Yet it represents an actual moment that Squanto witnessed: the day the visiting sailors called, July 18, 1605. It's possible to enhance and animate this sparse black-and-white picture, to imagine how his home looked on a typical summer day, in color, in motion, and filled with people.[1]

Had Champlain arrived in January instead of July, there would have been no houses or people in his drawing, just open clearings and empty fields. This community followed a semi-sedentary pattern of settlement, which meant relocating to other camps during peak hunting and fishing seasons. The village at Patuxet was where they raised plots of maize, beans, and squash, the crops that were the caloric base of their diet. The cycle began each year after harvest, when the villagers retreated through their network of paths to sheltered winter lodging sites, leaving the harbor a hushed and unpeopled place.[2]

When the winter thawed into spring and right before fish started spawning, the harbor came stirring back to life. Hundreds of dome-shaped houses started popping up around the bay—a much denser settlement than the one depicted in Champlain's sketch. The sachem, or chief, raised the largest house in a central location. The residents of Patuxet can be

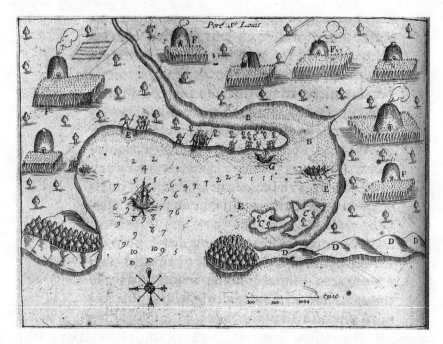

Samuel de Champlain's illustration of his 1605 visit to Patuxet harbor, which he called "Port St. Louis." Courtesy of the Beinecke Rare Book and Manuscript Library, Yale University.

described as *Wampanoag,* or people of the dawn. In this context, the name "Wampanoag" does not refer to a single political body but rather to the language and culture found in and around Patuxet. The peoples of the dawn consisted of more than a dozen culturally similar, closely related, and often allied communities whose homelands lie within the modern bounds of southeastern Massachusetts and eastern Rhode Island. At planting time, the two thousand villagers at Patuxet were a sizable fraction of the esti-mated total Wampanoag-speaking population of twenty to thirty thousand souls.[3]

The French sketch included wisps of smoke rising from houses, a reminder of the daily smells in Patuxet. Along with the ever-present wood-smoke came whiffs of the most popular local dishes: roasted and boiled fish, fowl, squash, and chestnuts, corn cakes cooked in hot ashes, corn and bean stew flavored with oysters and venison, and, on special occasions, bear haunches or fatty cuts of whale meat. The air carried pungent aromas of fish being gutted and game being dressed, while the earthy stench of latrine pits and trash heaps lingered further away at the town's edges. All the people in the sketch are men, since only men greeted Champlain. They cautiously kept him and his crew confined to the shore.[4]

If the Frenchman had been allowed to wander the village's lanes up to the stands of crops, he would have found himself surrounded by women. On a summer day, the fields and houses buzzed with chatter between mothers and grandmothers, the cries and shouts of children, and the rhythmic knock of wooden pestles hitting mortars, as women ground parched corn into flour. Men could be found there too, tending to their children, smoking their pipes, restringing their bows, or playing games of chance. Also living in the town was these people's only domesticated animal, a breed of dog that looked like a husky or a wolf.[5]

Down by the shore, men were busy at the waterfront, where they detangled their lines near hefty oceangoing dugouts that stuck out like fingers into the water. Europeans claimed that Indigenous men from the Northeast were tight-lipped and taciturn, an observation that had a bit of truth to it. Men who spent much of their time stalking prey or waiting for fish to bite surely valued silence, and the protocols of Indigenous diplomacy demanded that speakers choose their words carefully and listen attentively. But context mattered. Those same sources also mention men's casual gabbing and joking when at home in their villages, where they excelled in "merry jests and squibs [sarcastic remarks]." Most enjoyed talking about "hunting, fishing, and warfare," and "the young men will chat to each other about the girls."[6]

The cliché that small towns are hotbeds for gossip is seldom wrong; Patuxet was no exception. Besides the ordinary discussion among men and women about children, courtships, marriages, and quarrels, there would be more weighty news coming from other villages. Crowds regularly gathered to listen to visitors with reports of murders committed, battles fought, and alliances made among peoples nearby and further afield. News of these happenings were valuable intelligence that could put Patuxet on war footing in an instant.[7]

At night the harbor grew quiet, except on holidays and other occasions when villagers' singing and dancing punctured the ambient background noise of calling owls and chirping crickets. Above, a clear sky revealed the luminous clouds of the Milky Way. At daybreak, the sun rose above the far tip of Cape Cod, which was visible on the eastern horizon, a three- or four-day walk by land but just a few hours away by canoe. To the west lay more villages, fields, and woods. Natives had long shaped the ecology of the surrounding forest with seasonal burning, a spectacular event each fall when smoldering fires lit up the woods with an orange glow.[8]

Burns made the forest floor spacious by clearing out leaf litter, allowing the rapid growth of berry and nut bushes. The resulting man-made landscape attracted herds of white-tailed deer, a favorite source of meat and skins. Between stands of old-growth trees, the land was pocked with holes, created by a receding glacier, which had become ponds and marshy bogs laden with wild cranberries. There were no major rivers close to this site, only minor streams like the spring-fed brook that came tumbling down the harbor's central hill toward the sea and gave the place its primary name: Patuxet meant "at the small falls."[9]

That freshwater source that colonists later called Town Brook was the center of daily life. Among the hundreds of people who flocked to the brook to bathe, wash clothes, and fill vessels was a woman who had been coming here well before she gave birth to Tisquantum.

Although we know nothing specific about Tisquantum's mother, we do know what a typical Patuxet mother looked like. She wore her long dark hair in braids, had brown eyes and an olive complexion, and stood a couple of inches taller than most English women at the time. Usually wearing a deerskin mantle that covered her torso, she also wound crisscrossing leather strings up the length of her legs and wore bone and shell beads fashioned into delicate necklaces and bracelets, and embroidered into patterns on her garments.[10]

She probably grew up here at the small falls, while perhaps Squanto's father did not. Relationships between people from different villages were common. Tribal members and scholars believe that traditional Wampanoag communities were at least partly *matrilocal* and *matrilineal,* meaning that when a couple married, the woman's husband typically entered into her household and kinship network and their offspring were considered members of her family, not his. Some later land deeds and colonial accounts indicate that planting lands and houses could be considered women's property.[11]

Matrilocality and matrilineality are not the same as *matriarchy,* a society where women dominated the political sphere. There is a broad popular myth that many Native societies were matriarchies or had parity between genders, but when it comes to Squanto's people, there is little evidence to support such claims. It is true that male colonial authors had a blind spot around women's experiences, and they tended to project Western European ideas about gender onto Indigenous societies. But modern people can be just as guilty of foisting their own values on people from the past.[12]

In Patuxet, gender relations and marriages centered on principles of reciprocity rather than equality. Both men and women led Wampanoag governments, making them neither pure matriarchies nor patriarchies. On matters of landed property and power within families, Native women could possess rights that colonial women lacked. But in other ways, the dynamics between men and women resembled those of the English at the time: male leaders were far more prevalent than female ones, most women could not join male-centered political deliberations, and some men used force to discipline their wives. Questions about sexuality and gender also defy easy answers. The sources are too thin to determine if anything resembling "two-spirit" identities were part of Patuxet's belief system before contact.[13]

Tisquantum's mother's exact relationship with his father is, of course, unknown. For the purposes of this composite of a typical family, we can assume they were married when Tisquantum was born, though not necessarily when he was conceived. Some Native mores around sex and marriage were a little looser than those found in England at the same time. Premarital sex was not just permitted, it was encouraged. They considered divorce a routine way to resolve an unhappy marriage without shame and allowed either women or men to initiate a separation. Still, they considered adultery—especially when it was committed by a woman—to be a serious transgression that could be punished with public beating and humiliation.[14]

If Squanto's parents were in their first marriage when they had him, their courtship probably began in their teens; if one or both were older, they likely entered the marriage with children from a previous partner. Blended families were common. High-born male sachems often had multiple wives, but most ordinary marriages were between one man and one woman. Tisquantum did not come from a sachem's family, so his parents' marriage was almost certainly monogamous.[15]

Their wooden house, called a *wetu*, was home to two or more families, usually related through the women's lineages. Tisquantum's mother and her female kinfolk who shared this house did the bulk of home maintenance. They assembled it, repaired it, transported it, and spent considerably more time inside it than their husbands did. Their wetu had an oval floorplan centered on the hearth, with a frame made from long bent saplings and walls arching into a rounded ceiling. It had no windows, just a single low doorway, roughly three feet high, with a hanging flap as a door. A chimney hole, also outfitted with a flap, doubled as a skylight. The exterior shell was made of two layers of bark shingles or thatched with bundled dried grasses. Inside, the curving walls were ringed with sleeping platforms that the women lined with woven mats, skins, and furs that served as mattresses and bedclothes.[16]

More than just a shelter, the portable building provided valuable storage. Tisquantum's mother kept watertight baskets secreted under beds or hanging on hooks, each packed with provisions of tobacco, cornmeal, jerky, dried beans, dried fruits, and medicinal herbs. Adding to the household clutter were "wooden bowls, trays and dishes, earthen pots, handbaskets made of crabshells wrought together." In the arching rafters hung hunting prizes: hooves, antlers, and bird claws, the raw material for arrowheads and jewelry. Though snug and efficient, these dwellings had drawbacks. Smoke from the hearth filled the air and coated every surface, and they were prone to infestation by mosquitos, lice, fleas, and other hungry critters. But the fact that they were completely disassembled and repaired at least twice a year had the added benefit of shaking off accumulated ash and evicting whatever pests had joined the household.[17]

When she was pregnant with Squanto, his mother kept busy as her belly grew large. Depending on the time of year, she would take trips deep into the woods to harvest nuts, berries, and herbs; she would hunt and trap small game; and she would hike along the nearby shore with children in tow. As their first teacher, she showed her young helpers which muddy flats held the most clams and how to pick up lobsters without getting pinched.[18]

At points in the growing season, tending to crops took up much of her time, while cooking and childcare were her main duties year-round. Craft making represented her most skilled work and took years to master. Patuxet women's artisanal work included shaping clay into earthenware, fashioning skins into clothing and shoes, and braiding grasses into baskets and mats. Women who were not pregnant had an additional place where they rested once a month: the small wetus tucked away in the woods where they stayed during their periods. A cultural taboo forbade women from interacting with men while they were menstruating.[19]

Some Englishmen were aghast at seeing Native women working late into their pregnancies. In early modern England, women confined themselves to bed as delivery neared and for a month after giving birth. Not this new mother. She was up and walking with her son just days after delivery. But her health was not a given. Oral traditions described pregnancy as a fraught period, a time when displeased spirits threatened the lives of fetuses and mothers alike. Thus she obeyed taboos around certain foods, places, and animals as she carried the child to term, while praying to the spirits who looked over mothers and infants. Her reward was a swift delivery and a healthy newborn.[20]

Soon after the baby was born, his mother bathed him in water treated with medicinal bark and herbs, then regularly rubbed his skin with ashes, oils, and fats. Skin anointment was a universal practice for children and adults alike, though additional decorations like face paint and tattoos were reserved for grown men. Colonists had trouble making sense of this skin care regime. Some didn't care for the gamey smell of animal fats; others thought these lotions dyed the skin. Early English settlers believed the local children were born with pale white skin just like theirs and that regular anointing plus sun exposure stained their skin, giving them a tanned complexion. The reality was simpler and more practical. His mother "greased and sooted" her son to moisturize his skin and protect him from insect bites and sunburns.[21]

Going about her day with her new son, Tisquantum's mother relied on a versatile child-carrying device, the cradleboard. Found across the Indigenous continent, baby boards took many forms. Some tribal communities use them to this day. Hers was made of a piece of hardwood approximately two feet long, one foot wide, with a pair of straight legs at both ends, making a kind of H-shape. The two upper prongs were attached to a strap that could be slung around her forehead, shoulders, or chest, or it could be hung from a tree branch or a hook inside a house, turning the cradle into a rocking swing. The bottom fork acted as legs for leaning the board against a hard surface.[22]

To ready the carrier, his mother used a beaver skin as the swaddling fabric and placed a pile of cottony fluff from cattails and milkweed at the board's base. She placed her son on his back, with his legs folded up to his torso and his bottom resting on the absorbent plant fibers that served as a disposable diaper. She wrapped the waterproof beaver pelt tightly around the baby. With his knees bound close to his chest, she secured him on the board with leather strings that ran through holes along the board's edges and crisscrossed the swaddle like laces on a shoe. The newborn was a small bundle filling out his board month by month.[23]

Swaddling restricted the baby's movement in early months, which had little effect on his progress to walking, but it might have had a lasting influence on his posture. Wampanoag adults customarily sat in a distinctive pose with their buttocks resting on the ground, their feet tucked against their haunches, not unlike the position they were carried in as babies. One early explorer observed that the men he met "sate downe in a manner like Grey-hounds upon their heeles." Colonists noted that locals seemed comfortable sitting "their legs doubled up, their knees touching their chin," with one remarking that it was "as rare to see an Indian sit on a stoole at home, as it is strange to see an English man sit on his heeles abroad." Perhaps Indigenous people picked up this way of sitting in early childhood, when they graduated from the board but were still used to having their knees pulled close to their bodies.[24]

As he outgrew the swaddle, Tisquantum hit all the milestones of infancy: sitting up, teething, eating solids, crawling, standing, and walking. Prepubescent boys sometimes did not wear any clothes at all during warmer months; girls also went mostly nude with just a small loincloth over their privates. We don't know much about how exactly parents viewed their children's development, but we can learn something by looking at how they cared for children when they died. The people of Patuxet believed birth and death were mirroring moments when a soul passed to and from its earthly form.[25]

In Native graves across the coast, bodies often rested in the "fetal" or cradleboard position. Some buried corpses were covered with a dusting of red ochre, perhaps as a symbolic reference to the blood of childbirth. In societies that bury their dead with goods, the age at which the mourners start adding possessions to the graves of children offers clues about how they understood their children's evolving personhood.[26]

The smallest graves contained only bones. They stood alone, distant from the burials of adults that were placed close to homes. Anthropologists suggest that the lack of grave goods indicates that when infants died, their journey in death was seen as a mere visit to the spirit world. According to this theory, unlike a more mature soul, infants needed no goods or clothes because they would soon return to the world of the living in the body of a new baby.[27]

From toddler age on, Wampanoag children were buried with shell necklaces, toys, and medicine bundles. In one instance, a small boy, estimated to be three years old, was buried with a tobacco pipe. Children weren't allowed to smoke, so this gift suggested that he would continue to mature in the afterlife. When they assumed their children were bound for the land of the dead, parents planned to be reunited with them in the future. These toddlers were buried in the same woven shrouds that covered adult corpses, and they often rested alongside adults, further evidence that the bond between parents and children continued to the next life.[28]

In the 1910s, amateur archaeologists uncovered a paired grave in Wellfleet, Massachusetts, on Cape Cod. A woman and child rested together, with their knees pulled up to their chests and their heads back-to-back. The woman lay on her side facing west; the child faced east. Between their heads, where their skulls almost touched, their mourners had placed small carved stone effigies with faces: one was larger, heart-shaped, and had pronounced nose and lips, the other had a smaller, less defined, immature face. Their positioning and the paired effigies suggested an eternal kinship.[29]

The early Plymouth settlers found another such burial on the Cape in 1620, wherein a young toddler-aged boy rested alongside a man who was almost certainly his father. Draped on the child's body were "bound strings and bracelets of fine white beads" along with a toy-sized bow and other "odd knacks." A nearby grave of an adult man and small child was even more elaborately adorned. The contrast between bare graves of infants and the toy-packed burials of older children suggests that about the time the boy began to walk and speak, his parents viewed him as having crossed an important threshold.[30]

This transition likely came around his first birthday, when he received a name. A century after the colonial arrival, the writer Samson Occom, a

Mohegan from eastern Connecticut, described the traditional naming rite of the Montauketts from eastern Long Island, which likely bore a close resemblance to how Patuxet parents named their children. Families invited relatives and friends from near and far, circulating gifts for the joyous celebration. After the parents announced their child's name, the visitors joined in calling out the child's new name.[31]

Among Tisquantum's people, it was a repeating practice: the initial title given to a person was by no means the last. Later in life, when the boy was grown, he explained these rites to the Plymouth colonist Edward Winslow. "All their names are significant and variable," Winslow wrote, "for when they come to the state of men or women, they alter them according to their deeds or dispositions." It is therefore a given that the boy was *not* called Tisquantum by his parents and that his later title was one of his own choosing.[32]

Winslow's remark that appellations were "variable" hints at why colonists alternately called the grown man *Tisquantum, Squantum, Tisquanto,* and *Squanto.* As I will discuss further in the next chapter, Squanto/Squantum was also the name of a spirit. If that is indeed the origin of the name Squanto—a complicated question that linguists have not settled— then the name Tisquantum could have been a variation to help distinguish the mortal from the god. The prefix *Ti-* doesn't appear in any other recorded Wampanoag word, making its significance utterly obscure.[33]

Whatever the origins of his name(s), this ambiguity is why "Tisquantum" and "Squanto" appear interchangeably in this book. He clearly answered to both. And it was no coincidence that the boy received his initial pre-Squanto name around the same time he became verbal. Word by word, phrase by phrase, his education in Wampanoag—both the language and the culture—began.

TWO

Education

TISQUANTUM'S LANGUAGE WAS "hard to learne," colonists complained, as it was "very copious, large, and difficult." The Patuxet man later became proficient but never perfectly fluent in their language, so he probably had similar gripes about learning English. A quick look at what makes Squanto's tongue so distinct from ours offers tantalizing clues about his upbringing. The question of how language shapes culture and vice versa is a knotty problem: linguists never stop debating this topic. Still, there are patterns in Wampanoag grammar and vocabulary that shed light on the core values held by the people at the small falls. And some quirks of the dialect can help us grasp the challenges and advantages Squanto faced as a bilingual go-between. At times he would appear to stumble over concepts that stubbornly resisted full translation, and at other points he seemed to leave crucial words untranslated.[1]

Wampanoag is one of the forty-odd languages in the Algonquian family, one of the major language families of North America. These tongues have an impressively ancient lineage. The earliest ancestor of Algonquian dialects emerged seven thousand years ago in the center of the continent, two thousand years before the first Indo-European language—the ancient ancestor of English—arose on the Eurasian steppes. At the time of European contact, Algonquian speakers' homelands were vast and sprawling. Their languages could be heard in the shadow of the Rockies, along the windswept northern plains, around the woodsy shores of the Great Lakes, and across the rugged northeast Atlantic coast.[2]

Since English colonists often settled alongside Algonquian speakers, American English has collected many (somewhat distorted) loan words from their dialects, for example, *chipmunk, hickory, pecan, powwow, pumpkin, raccoon, skunk, tomahawk,* and *toboggan.* Thousands of Algonquian place-names can be found in places as far-flung as *Connecticut, Michigan,*

Saskatchewan, and *Wyoming.* Words with roots in Algonquian dialects can be eclectic, not just related to nature or the land. The anthropological concept of a symbolic *totem* is a corruption of the word *doodem,* meaning clan or kinship group. *Mugwump,* a term for political fence-sitters and the nickname for a faction of Gilded Age Republicans, came from a word meaning warrior or leader, while *caucus* possibly derives from a *cawcaw-wassough,* a gathering of elders.[3]

Mohawk, a nation in what is now upstate New York and Quebec and a colloquial name for a hairstyle, originated with the neighboring Lenape Algonquians as a term for the foes they called *Mhuweyok,* or "man-eating monsters." Mohawks, who speak an unrelated non-Algonquian language, actually call themselves *Kanyékeha:ka,* or "people of the place of the flint." *Tuxedo* is an Americanism coined after the first stateside appearance of the dinner jacket in Tuxedo Park, New York—a place whose name derives from the Lenape *Ptukwsiituw,* or "place of the wolf clan members."[4]

The obvious phonic gap between *Ptukwsiituw* and *tuxedo* illustrates how some sounds, or phonemes, that Tisquantum learned to make as a toddler were rather distinct from English ones. One frequently used example was a distinct vowel that sounded like the *oo* found in c*oo*l, m*oo*dy, or an owl's onomatopoetic h*oo*t. The first colonists to put the language in print struggled with how to render it. When the minister John Eliot set out to publish the Bible in Wampanoag in the mid-seventeenth century, he asked his printer to cast a new piece of type with the character ꝏ. Today, some writers also express this sound with the digit 8; in this text, which uses the most common American English renderings of most Native words, the vowel appears as either *ou* or *oo.* The vowel is found in both the name of a modern state in the Northeast (*Mâswachoosut*) and the word for a wide-antlered beast (*moos*).[5]

As the boy began to master the language's phonemes, he also started to pick up the elements of Wampanoag grammar. Tisquantum learned that nouns could be animate or inanimate, similar to how Romance languages sort nouns as either male or female. While those European languages switch the article, as in *le/la* in French, or *el/la* in Spanish, Wampanoag words change their plural endings: *-ak* or *-ag* endings for animate plural nouns, *-ash* for inanimate ones. A solo man is called a *waskeetôp,* an animate noun, and men collectively are known as *waskeetôpâak.* An inanimate boat is a *mishoon;* a fleet of them are called *mishoonash.* The *-ak/-ag* ending is also found in the very word *Wôpanâak/Wampanoag,* as it refers to a group of people, while examples of *-ash* appear in common Native foods, for example, the vegetable *askutasquash,* which colonists shortened to *squash,* and the bean and corn dish *msickquatash,* or *succotash.*[6]

Sometimes this distinction is intuitive. Humans, animals, and some plants are animate. Most plants, minerals, and objects are not. As with any such rule, there were exceptions that the child would have to master. For instance, body parts, whether attached to a living person or not, are always inanimate. Most natural features, like mountains and rivers, are considered stationary, but the earth itself is classified as mobile. The moon and stars are also animate, but the sun is inanimate even though it also moves through the sky.[7]

The rules for sorting nouns shouldn't be read literally as a primer on whether something had a "spirit" or not. It was never that simple, as Wampanoag speakers saw the spark of life in many things that were, in a grammatical sense, inanimate.[8]

As Jessie Little Doe Baird, the linguist who brought Wampanoag back to life, explains, "The language is polysynthetic, where you start with a piece that carries meaning and then you inflect that meaning by adding a system of prefixes, suffixes, and fixes to complete a phrase." For Tisquantum, learning to speak was a bit like working with blocks in a Lego set: new words would be formed by combining interlocking parts of speech in ever more elaborate yet economical ways. As Baird puts it, "Usually, one word in our language is really a whole sentence in English." Outsiders who learned the tongue were impressed by its density of meaning. Eliot, the bilingual missionary, praised Wampanoag's "elegancy," and the linguist Edward Sapir characterized the words in Algonquian dialects as "tiny imagist poems."[9]

For example, to attach a thing to a place, Wampanoag speakers use *-ut/-et,* a preposition-like suffix that linguists call a "locative." Translated roughly as "at or near," the locative is easy to spot in *Patuxet* and the names of places nearby: *Acushnet, Amagansett, Cohasset, Connecticut, Manomet, Mattapoisett, Massachusetts, Nantasket, Nantucket, Narragansett, Nauset, Pamet, Pawtucket, Sakonnet, Shawmut, Woonsocket,* the list goes on. This Algonquian grammar and geography are still inscribed on the New England landscape.[10]

Another ending is unlike any preposition in English: the "absentative." It does exactly what it sounds like: it indicates the noun is lost or absent. When attached to living beings, this ending indicated they were dead or missing. It was especially useful because Wampanoags and their neighbors had a strict taboo around speaking the name of the dead, especially when the person had died recently. Colonists who innocently made this mistake learned it was "a thing very offensive to them." Saying the name of the dead on purpose demanded restitution in the form of a gift, and naming a dead sachem was a grave transgression, punishable by death. The absentative made for a convenient work-around, which was plainly visible in colonial translations of Native speakers who mentioned "the former sachem," "the said sachem," "the old sachem," and "he that was sachem"—all translations of the absentative. Both the locative and absentative endings let speakers place a noun in space or memory, indicating either where something was or if something wasn't.[11]

Assembling words gets more intricate with pronouns and possession. A list of all the ways that the boy's parents would have referred to him and other children gives us a sense of this linguistic architecture. The root word -*neechan*-, meaning "child," could become rather stretched out depending on whose child(ren) the speaker was referring to and whether the speaker was addressing one or more people, or excluding the persons addressed (marked ex.), or including them (marked inc.):

child	neechan
my child	nuneechan
our (ex.) child	nuneechanun
our (inc.) child	kuneechanun
your child	kuneechan
your (pl.) child	kuneechanuw
his/her child	wuneechanah
their child	wuneechanuwôwah
my children	nuneechanak
our (ex.) children	nuneechanunônak
our (inc.) children	kuneechanunônak
your children	kuneechanak
your (pl.) children	kuneechanuwôwak
his/her children	wuneechanah
their children	wuneechanuwôwah

What makes these words so distinct from English isn't their ballooning length but their specificity. English speakers have no pithy linguistic bypass to indicate whether a pronoun like "our" includes or excludes the people being addressed, but in Wampanoag culture it's part of a pattern of describing interpersonal relationships with pinpoint precision. A colonist who learned a similar Algonquian dialect marveled that its speakers "more carefully distinguish the natural relations of men to each other, than we do, or perhaps any other nation."[12]

Family terms could be both exacting and elastic. If young Squanto had a sister, he might refer to her as *neehtat,* which meant "my sibling of the opposite sex" and thus could mean "brother" if his sister used it for him. *Neehtat* could never have the genderless meaning of "my sibling." He could also call her *neetukusq,* but that was inexact, as it could mean "my sister, kinswoman, or close female friend." If he called her *numusees,* he would identify her as "my older sister," but if he mentioned *numuseesôn,* he meant "my late sister." In still other contexts, kinship language could become loose, vague, and metaphoric. Some words for siblings could also apply to cousins, and animals, plants, and spirits could be referred to as family members as well.[13]

The social importance of these bonds was obvious to outsiders. "Their affections, especially to their children, are very strong," the colonist Roger Williams observed with a note of disapproval. From his perspective, "this extreme affection, together with want of learning, makes their children sawcie, bold, and undutifull." Another Englishman noted the locals were "great lovers of their children and people" and how "very indulgent they are" to their offspring.[14]

These remarks tell us more about colonists than Natives, as the prevailing parenting theory in seventeenth-century England emphasized strict discipline, even for young children. Careful onlookers also noticed that as Indigenous youth matured, they reciprocated their parents' and grandparents' love with respect and were "always obedient unto the elder people." Squanto's friend Winslow agreed; he witnessed youngsters politely performing tasks for the aged even if the elders were strangers. Respect for predecessors applied to the dead as well as the living. Squanto's people were "carefull to preserve the memory of their families," as each generation taught the next lengthy genealogies that stretched back for centuries.[15]

For Wampanoags, it wasn't just that family mattered but that most matters—political, spiritual, agricultural, environmental—could be understood through the lens of family. Tisquantum came to think of the ties of kinship as so capacious that they extended far beyond his mother's wetu, outside his extended family, beyond Patuxet, across species, and even beyond the visible world into the afterlife and the spirit realm. The intertwined relationships between humans and nature, between mortals and gods, and between the living and the dead formed his worldview and would become central themes in his life story.[16]

Claims of kinship in Patuxet were not necessarily about blood or even affection; they were about mutual obligations. When young Squanto learned to call an unrelated person or spirit his uncle or his grandmother, it was more than a term of endearment. He was identifying him or her as a person he had responsibilities toward and a person who had responsibilities toward him. When we unpack these ideas about obligation and reciprocity among peoples, plants, and animals, we can see why some simplistic stereotypes about Native peoples and nature—"they live in harmony with the earth" or "they are at one with nature"—have a grain of truth in them, at least in describing how Algonquian-language speakers *imagined* their relationships with their environment.[17]

That's not to say that Tisquantum's people were perfect environmentalists, incapable of exploiting or degrading the natural world. It would be equally silly to claim that because his people put an emphasis on kinship in their language, their families never suffered from strife—grammar is not a blueprint for behavior. Much like everyone else on the planet, Native peoples have faced ecological crises of their own making both before and after the colonial arrival. Denying the complexity of this history perpetuates "the pristine myth" that before Europeans arrived the Americas had been only lightly touched by human hands. That misconception, first created by European explorers, has long served as a justification for Indigenous dispossession. It erases millennia of hunting, foraging, fishing, trading, farming, irrigating, mining, mound making, deforestation, and town building that transformed North American ecology in countless ways. Natives' practices of land use could increase, sustain, and decrease the biodiversity of their environments depending on the time and place—hence why New Agey platitudes about "harmony" cannot possibly capture the realities of a whole continent.[18]

While being careful not to idealize Native cultures in unrealistic ways, scholars still convincingly argue that some age-old Indigenous ideas and traditions offer profound insights into ecological processes and can inform modern sustainable practices. Today, many scientists and activists looking to restore or protect endangered landscapes draw inspiration from traditional tribal peoples like the Wampanoags and their neighbors, seeking to emulate the principles of reciprocal kinship that Tisquantum learned as a boy. It's best to look at the intricate details of his people's beliefs about nature rather than paint with a broad or heavy brush.[19]

When his Patuxet elders taught Squanto about his relations in the natural and spiritual worlds, they were not speaking about an idealized, sentimentalized family. They were talking about a realistic one. These metaphoric family members could be loving and giving, but just as often they could be touchy, withholding, quarrelsome, and spiteful. When plants, animals, and spirits took on these anthropomorphic personalities, it helped their human relatives interpret their behavior. After all, these villagers relied on wild animals for much of their protein. They typically did not trade crops or other foods on a large scale over long distances. They were therefore dependent on their own farming and the nearest flora and fauna for survival. Scarcity was a lethal and ever-present threat. It makes sense that they would think of their relationships with local species and deities as intimate and emotionally fraught bonds that needed lots of work to maintain.

These ideas formed the core of traditional Wampanoag religion, which scholars typically label as "animism," a belief system that views non-human beings and objects as having souls. His people's faith centered on a versatile word: *manitou*. Often translated as "god," "creator," "spirit," "magic," "divine power," or "medicine," depending on its context, manitou can mean all of those things but also none of them. It defies full translation. Manitou was an invisible transcendent force that could take on many forms.

All Algonquian-language speakers use the word "manitou" or a close cognate and see the earth itself as thrumming with spiritual energy—as evidenced in place-names like *Manitowoc,* Wisconsin, or *Manitoba.* Along with being a descriptive word for land, the term applied to things that weren't obviously magical or sacred to outsiders. An eloquent speaker had manitou; a skilled basket maker had manitou; a well-made axe had manitou. Colonists noted Natives used manitou to describe "any excellency," but to see this as a separate and more secular definition misses the point: they viewed excellence itself as a manifestation of the divine.[20]

That said, manitou or *manit* sometimes *did* refer to gods, named deities with personalities and specific powers detailed in oral traditions. One colonist counted thirty-seven manitous among the nearby Narragansetts. Often appearing in the form of animals or else as visions in dreams, these potent and capricious beings could be contacted through gifts, prayers, dances, and songs. Some of these figures in oral traditions could also be described as cultural heroes, the beings that gave their world its shape, like Maushop, the giant who lived in the sea and created much of the Wampanoag coastal landscape.[21]

Colonial sources that explore these beliefs can sometimes hinder more than help our understanding, since so many English colonists belittled Native religion. Missionaries in particular liked to infantilize their potential converts, reducing their sacred practices to a childlike fear of punishment. In more sensitive accounts, other colonists acknowledged that these believers had subtle and mature relationships with their manitous, shaped by feelings of gratitude, respect, and ambivalence as well as fear.[22]

English Christians were quick to seek out Native versions of God and Satan, opposing avatars of good and evil. Winslow, who likely asked Tisquantum about these matters, named the creator figure Kiehtan, the positive figure, and Hobbamock as his opponent. Others reported that the Patuxet man's namesake was one of their major spirits. "The god they love they call Squanto," wrote the explorer Christopher Levett about the Wabanaki people of present-day southern Maine, adding, "the god they hate they call Tanto." But when the colonist Francis Higginson asked the nearby Massachusett people about their religion, they told him about the same duo, only with reversed spiritual polarities. "The good god they call Tantum," he wrote, adding, "their evil god, whome they fear will do them hurt, they call Squantum." Still another source, John Josselyn, reported that southern Wabanakis saw "Squantum" as a benevolent figure who "will do them no harm" and considered a spirit called Abbamocho or Cheepi as the malicious "devil."[23]

This confusion can be cleared up pretty easily. Neither Wampanoags nor their neighbors saw these spirits as purely good or evil, and neighbors who believed in the same god might see that figure in different lights. For example, the manitou called Squanto might have got his name from the clipped version of the phrase *musquántum,* "he is angry at or with." A purely literal translation of *musquántum* might be "bloody-minded," as it derived "from *musqui*, red, bloody, and *antam*, minded, proposing, or having in mind." This theory—which is debated by linguistic experts—tracks with the account of Squanto/Squantum as a wrathful figure. If true, it does not contradict the testimonies of his kindness. Even Christians could understand that being afraid of a god did not make the deity evil—as theirs too was both an angry and loving one.[24]

Long before anyone called him "Squanto," the boy learned that he inhabited a spiritually charged landscape. Supernatural power could be found everywhere, in most every being and thing, so his education was infused with religiosity. His elders did not just explain how to do things but also why they did things that way through sacred allegories that linked the everyday to the workings of manitou. Learning about language, family, gods, history, animals, and plants were all one connected curriculum.

In summer months, the boy spent his days playing with other children on wooden watching platforms that their parents built among Patuxet's corn-fields. These play structures kept him occupied and visible as his mother worked. A gathering of loud children in the midst of planting grounds had the added benefit of scaring away birds that came pecking at the crops. He'd learn that one bird in particular deserved respect, not unlike that he owed his elders, because this bird was also an educator.[25]

Many generations earlier, before Tisquantum's people grew corn, the Crow had come with gifts of a corn kernel and a single bean and dropped the seeds in the soil, teaching the boy's ancestors to grow the crops together. The Crow was a messenger of the powerful manitou Kiehtan, or maybe it was Kiehtan in disguise. Kiehtan was the creator, the god of corn, and ruler of the land of the dead, a place also known as the Southwest.[26]

The Crow myth reflected a verifiable historical event—the introduction of maize agriculture to the Northeast, which hit its stride six centuries before Tisquantum was born. The seeds had indeed come from south-westerly places. They originated thousands of miles away in a land that is now part of Mexico. Some elders told a more literal version of the story, one that agreed with the archaeological record which indicated that neighboring peoples to the south taught Tisquantum's ancestors to grow corn. The Crow was a mythic stand-in for those historic teachers while also serving as a metaphoric connection to the origin place of corn itself.[27]

Nearby Munsee Lenapes from the lower Hudson told a Dutch colonist that when they died and went to the Southwest they learned to sing (and perhaps speak) like crows—meaning every time they heard the bird's caws, they were hearing songs from the afterlife. Like all manitous, the Crow could be a caring and choleric relation. The bird was at once a symbol of life in the corn-giving myth and a symbol of death in stories of the afterlife; crows left seeds in their droppings and they were scavengers often found feasting on carcasses. Many other animals could be messengers from gods, but the Crow was one of the first that Tisquantum learned to recognize.[28]

The Crow's gifts, the kernel and the bean, also had lives of their own. His mother planted the seeds together with the carcass of a spawning spring fish to act as a fertilizer. Famously, Squanto instructed colonists to do the same, a moment that has inspired a bit of a scholarly debate. In the 1970s, an anthropologist argued that the Patuxet man actually borrowed a European farming technique that he picked up in his time overseas. The Wampanoag historian Nanepashemet soon pointed out the problems with this thesis: it rested on dubious textual evidence. In the 1990s, an archaeological dig on Cape Cod uncovered fish remains in a Wampanoag planting ground dating to before the contact period, further evidence that Squanto was following a long-standing Native practice. It was a smart planting strategy for refreshing tired soil: fish bodies set in moist spring soil decomposed rapidly, providing ample nutrients for the seeds. To people steeped in animistic thinking, there was clear logic in the idea that the remains of one living thing could summon the life of another.[29]

Maize sprouted right away. A tendril exploded out of the kernel, becoming a stiff green stalk that shot skyward to thrive in the light, casting out leaves as it grew. The bean's shoot broke the soil's surface soon after the cornstalk. The tip of the beanstalk started making "a loopy circle dance" in the air until it found something to curl around: the cornstalk. The bean's vine spiraled around the cornstalk's leaves, growing a bit slower than its support, so the stalk was strong enough to carry its green pods, which hung like ornaments off the towering corn plant.[30]

Growing slowly at the feet of these stalks were companion crops of pumpkins and squash. Their broad leaves and bulbous fruits fanned out around the stalk's base, keeping the soil moist and serving as sturdy barriers to pests and weeds. By summer, the corn started to ripen, as the green kernels turned red, orange, yellow, blue, and purple. On a hot midsummer day, a cornstalk can gain up to six inches in height, growing so rapidly it makes an audible rustling sound. As he outgrew the playing platform, Tisquantum would be put to work helping the adult women tend to these fields. It wasn't easy. A Narragansett man raised in a traditional village in the nineteenth century would remember late in his life "how I hated as a child, to pull the weeds" along "rows and rows of corn."[31]

Among many Native peoples, these crops are known as the Three Sisters. The metaphor imagines the three as mutually supportive siblings, with a birth order matching their rates of growth. Corn is the first born and the most ambitious sister, reaching for the sky. Beans are the middle sister, emulating the eldest by circling around her. Squash is the voluptuous youngest sister who goes her own way. Some Indigenous legends about the crops feature the Three Sisters personified by manitous in human form—the maize spirit standing tall with hair like cornsilk, her younger sisters clad in green and orange.[32]

In colonists' papers, however, there's no mention of Squanto's people calling these crops "sisters." This absence could reflect a local quirk, though far more likely the English simply failed to record Wampanoag beliefs around their staple crops. Whether or not Tisquantum grew up explicitly thinking of these plants as "sisters," he was raised to think of them as beings who had reciprocal relationships with each other and with the people who tended to them. As these crops were so closely associated with women, it's not much of a leap to suppose that he thought of them as female too.

In fact, all children had a social role that could be seen as more feminine than masculine. In an early encounter with armed colonists, a group of Native boys told colonists "neen squaes," meaning "we are women." It was not a literal claim that boys were considered the same as women and girls. After all, Wampanoag parents used different words for daughters and sons, and they even gave them gender-specific toys and grave goods. The boys meant to clarify in a tense moment that they were noncombatants like their mothers were, but there was also a larger truth to their statement. All prepubescent children belonged under the umbrella of "women" in that they spent much of their time contained within the women's social sphere, and that the early stage of their lives was a formative one.[33]

The act for which Squanto became most celebrated—teaching the

Mayflower passengers how to grow and harvest corn—was a spiritually significant women's task based on women's knowledge.

The next stage in Tisquantum's upbringing began a few years before puberty, as he started to drift out of his mother's daily orbit. It probably started gradually with small milestones, for example, when his father, uncle, or brother made him his own child-sized bow and arrows, taught him to swim long distances, or handed him an oar, expecting him to join in the strenuous paddling when crossing over to Pamet or Cummaquid in their oceangoing dugouts. He'd begin to learn how to use fire and stone axes to hollow a massive tree into a canoe, along with the painstaking art of assembling a featherlight birchbark canoe, and the delicate science of knapping a piece of chert into a razor-sharp blade or arrowhead. As years went by he'd learn the more advanced methods of hunting and fishing: how to pluck fish from streams with his bare hands or how to set a spring trap strong enough to hoist an adult deer off the ground. As with the tanning, weaving, sewing, and pottery-making skills that women learned, these skills took years to master.[34]

As he followed the general education that all boys received, adults took notice of his abilities—not just his skills as hunter and fisherman, but also his strength, his stamina, his talents as a speaker, and his overall character. At some point, they identified young Tisquantum as one of the "most forward and likeliest" to become a community leader chosen for his abilities and temperament. Edward Winslow called men of this rank *pniese*, but Winslow must have partially misheard this term, as he was the only source to use it and there isn't a "pn-" consonant sound in the language.[35]

When we look at political texts written by literate Wampanoags decades after Winslow, the term that best matches is *atoskauwou*. Colonists translated the plural *atoskauwoag* as "lords," "nobility," "rulers," "great men," or "chief men," but perhaps the most helpful translation was of a sachem's declaration that referred to "my council or chief men." Both "warrior" and "councilor" describe the role well. Theoretically any boy could become one of these leading men, though only a fraction of them were tapped to join this order. Chosen for their physical and mental abilities, councilors were a distinct part of a larger body politic. They served under sachems but held a higher status and larger set of community responsibilities than the ordinary villagers.[36]

While Squanto never explicitly described himself as an atoskauwou or councilor, the mere fact that he went to negotiate with the captain who kidnapped him is dispositive evidence that he was one of Patuxet's chief men at the time of his capture. In fact, every named Wampanoag man who appeared in the colonists' early writings was either a sachem or one of the atoskauwoag, as these were the community leaders worthy of the responsibility of dealing with the English.[37]

Winslow described the regime for training these chief men as an extreme toughening process, focused on "great hardness," requiring the boys to "abstain from dainty meat, observing divers orders prescribed." It was an apprenticeship of sorts, a yearslong regime of conditioning that featured rules, rites, criticisms, and encouragement, becoming ever more demanding as the child entered adolescence. Once he set down his toy bows and started to fire with real ones, he'd be drilled on the fundamentals of tracking, trapping, shooting, and field dressing. As he started to sprout up in height and his voice began to change, he stopped going naked in warm weather and started wearing a man's loincloth on a belt made of snakeskin. He'd get his own fire-starting flint, which he would carry everywhere in a leather bag he wore around his neck. His teachers would instruct him on the many ways of reading his environment, such as how to identify animal scat or how to interpret portents in the sky.[38]

Finally the day came when his educators deemed him ready to embark on a final series of tests. The stakes were high. If he failed, he'd let down the men who had invested years in training him, many of whom were relatives. Being raised in a culture where family responsibilities meant so much, he might fear disappointing those women and men who had devoted years to his education, ever since his tiny face peeked out of his swaddle.

There was a good reason to brave the rites ahead of him. If he passed, he would no longer be considered a boy or even an ordinary young man. He would be elevated into an exclusive new rank that would give him his first taste of power.

THREE

Manhood

THE BLINDFOLD WAS TIGHT AROUND his head, making it impossible to recognize the path. As he walked, Squanto followed the voice of a man who led him deep into the bare winter woods. His guide was most likely his father or else an uncle, older brother, cousin, or family friend. They pressed on for miles, heading for a remote corner of the forest, far from the paths, creeks, ponds, and beaches where the boy had spent his childhood. Late in the day, after night fell, his mentor left him. When he took the blindfold off and his eyes adjusted, the only things the boy could recognize were the stars in the sky. He carried with him tools of survival: his flint, his bow and arrows, his hatchet, and his knife.[1]

For the following weeks, the teenager lived alone, fending for himself in this unfamiliar part of the country. He wasn't merely hunting and foraging to survive—a challenge at any time and anywhere—he was doing it during a North American winter that was more frigid than most modern ones. The boy grew up in an era of global cooling we now call "the Little Ice Age." Stretching from the 1500s to the 1800s, this climate event had dramatic effects on both sides of the Atlantic. Thanks to data from ice cores, tree rings, buried pollen, and historic crop yields, we know that Squanto lived during the absolute coldest decades of this climate event: temperatures reached their nadir in the late sixteenth and early seventeenth centuries.

During this period, the polar ice caps started creeping southward. Shifts in the jet stream triggered devastating droughts and sent ocean storms spiraling on unpredictable tracks. Winters could last five weeks longer than they do now. During frequent deep freezes, the topsoil hardened like cement and ice covered ponds, lakes, rivers, and even brackish estuaries.[2]

These were exactly the conditions the boy had just spent years preparing to endure. His first priority would be shelter. He would either build a small one-man wetu or seek a convenient overhang to make into his home. In places or moments that the soil was still soft, he would be on the lookout for groundnuts, an edible tuber that was particularly sweet in early winter. A good haul of these starchy roots would give him much-needed carbohydrates to supplement the rest of his diet, which would be heavy in proteins and fats. He'd also search for still-flowing streams to catch frost-fish, a species that spawned in December. Deeper into the season, he would go ice fishing on ponds. If he was near the coast, he would regularly dig for clams.[3]

Snowfall was usually a welcome gift. A fresh blanket muffled his ap-proach when stalking game and revealed animal tracks, giving him an ad-vantage when setting traps. The most common trap he'd make would be snares on spring-loaded branches. These had a loop of rope set to catch the paw of a passing woodland creature and then snap into the air, leaving the prey dangling until he came back.[4]

When snow piled high, white-tailed deer found it harder to browse for food and run away, and their resulting fatigue and slowness made them easier targets for the young hunter. No doubt his winter trial had hard stretches—days that passed without a single catch or kill, or storms so in-tense they kept the boy in his improvised shelter, waiting out the weather. In good times and bad, he would reach out to manitous with prayers for help and mercy, while keeping an eye out for their avatars and omens in the landscape and looking for their guidance in his dreams.[5]

As spring neared, his mentor came to find him. Together they re-turned to Patuxet for planting season and a break from his ordeal. Yet there were more tests to come. A few weeks later, when the first sprouts of corn plants cast out their leaves, so did many potent herbs. Squanto and the other teenagers approaching manhood first fetched "the most poisonous and bitter" species, including the toxic flower of *Veratrum viride,* a plant colonists called "Indian poke." Each boy then had to drink a tea made from these plants and try to hold the concoction down. If he purged, he had to drink again. He was forced to swallow and purge repeatedly until his vomit "seem[ed] to be all blood" and he could "scarce stand on [his] legs," but he could hold the elixir in his stomach. Colonists believed this severe rite was intended to make the trainee immune to common toxins. One more physical test remained. The boys had to run through a gauntlet of men holding sticks they used to strike them on the shins, then cross a rough patch of brush filled with thorns and brambles.[6]

After their run, the young man and his fellow cadets limped on weak and bloody legs back to Patuxet, where the sachem waited along with the whole village to greet them with song and dance. More than a celebration, it was also an inspection. The gathered crowd would be looking at each teenager to see "if he has been able to stand it all well, and if he is fat and sleek," if his resourcefulness and hardiness were great enough to merit his becoming both warrior and councilor. It was at this same rite that the young man likely received his new name, which possibly was Tisquantum, or else the name that preceded it; women also took on new names when reaching this same threshold.[7]

The main account of this ceremony claimed that the young men who passed the tests were then considered eligible for marriage. Women of the same age were going through their own rites of passage, becoming ready for marriage or upon marrying. When transitioning into womanhood, they cut their hair and wore a head covering that one colonist described as "a redd cap made of lether." Although it's not clear whether Squanto married or fathered children before his captivity, it's a given that he was sexually active. That was an expected part of young romances.[8]

Many other benefits came with crossing the threshold into manhood. He would be allowed to take his first drag from a pipe, as only men could grow and smoke tobacco, a sacred substance. This was also the stage when the boy—who had a child's short haircut—started growing his hair out. Adult men wore their hair short on one side, perhaps to avoid it catching in bowstrings, while letting it hang long on the other, with a decorated scalp lock at the top of their heads that could be braided and fashioned with jewelry. As Tisquantum's facial hair started coming in, he'd pluck or shave off stray whiskers; Native men's beards were typically quite sparse and they preferred their faces to appear hairless. Soon he might get his first tattoos or brandings. According to English accounts, some Wampanoag men sported black ink on their cheeks in the shape of sacred animals, while others had lines of scarred tissue from deliberate burns with hot metal along their arms and chests.[9]

In addition to being a hunter, fisherman, warrior, and suitor, the young man was also an athlete. The most popular sport in Patuxet was a game that the English likened to football. Sometimes played among men within a village or else "towne against towne," these games could stretch on for days. Flat stretches of beaches served as the playing pitch, with the opposing goals set a mile apart. The ball itself was "no bigger than a handball." It could be kicked into the air or wrestled over in scrums. Given the vast distance between goals, hours could pass without any scoring. When the light began to fail and it came time to halt play, the players would "mark the ground they win and begin there the next day." They kept score in objects, each goal being worth a sum in furs or *wampumpeak,* prized and sacred shell beads. Women and children gathered as spectators, singing songs and dancing to celebrate feats on the field.[10]

Sports gave him a chance to measure up against rivals, and the game itself helped keep peace between neighbors. Although each side donned body and face paint to play, everyone set their weapons aside before the action began and exchanged warm greetings with the other team. The most detailed account of the game marveled at the sportsmanship of the players: "the goale being wonne, the goods on the one side lost; friends they were at the footeball, and friends they must meete at the kettle." A rare account of a 1667 game between the nearby Niantics and Mohegans that turned violent was the exception that proves the rule. When reporting to colonists that a Mohegan sachem had brutally beat two men on the ballfield, the opposing Niantic players noted it was "contrary to our laws" to bring malice to a match.[11]

Well after crossing into manhood, Squanto awaited a final step to confirm his new status as an atoskauwou: a revelation of Hobbamock, a powerful god with healing powers. This manitou could visit him in a dream or else appear in one of his many forms: "a Man, a Deer, a Fawn, an Eagle, etc. but most ordinarily a Snake." Being contacted by Hobbamock was a rare honor, granted only to the most holy and brave: the shamans known as *powwaws,* the village's greatest fighters, and the sachem himself.[12]

While women could be sachems, it is far more likely that Patuxet's leader was a man. This sovereign drew his power from dynastic legitimacy. He descended from a line of past sachems and he was connected by blood and marriage to other sachems in the region. His wetu was the largest house in the village, with a footprint up to a hundred feet long, built more like a longhouse than a traditional wetu. Inside its walls lived the sachem's extended family, including at least one of his multiple wives and the youngest of his brood of children. The sachem invited visitors to lodge in his beds and also welcomed the community's orphans and widows into his

Portrait of a Native sachem by an unknown artist, ca. 1700. Courtesy of the Rhode Island School of Design Museum.

household. The man himself stood out wherever he went: he wore elaborate beaded belts along with necklaces, bracelets, and earrings carved from shell and bone, he draped the rare pelts of black wolves and mountain lions around his shoulders, and he wore soft luxurious coats woven out of turkey feathers.[13]

With the trappings of the office came responsibilities. Not only did the sachem provide for the neediest in his community, he presided over the ongoing cycle of village events: namings, coming-of-age rites, funerals, and ceremonies of war. And he did not govern alone. Along with his councilors, he turned to the village powwaws, or holy men. (Colonists coined the term "powwow" to describe ceremonies led by powwaws.) Some sachems also had the power of shamans, who led dances and feasts to sway the favor of manitous for favorable weather and victory in war, tended to the sick, and made prophecies about the future. These healers joined the sachem and his top men in regular meetings to discuss public affairs, and this combined body traveled with the headman whenever he made diplomatic visits to other sachems. A powerful sachem's entourage could easily number over a hundred men.[14]

Whether at home or abroad, Native politicians spoke to each other in a formal, lyrical style. The best orators gave long speeches that featured rhetorical questions, call-and-response, rhyming, metaphors, and anaphora, the poetic device of starting successive sentences with the same word or phrase. Speakers sometimes punctuated their points by laying down speaking sticks or strings of wampum beads; wooden tallies served to outline their arguments, and the precious beads demonstrated the sincerity of their words.[15]

As a new member of this group, Tisquantum might have chimed in on occasion, but he took his cues from his seniors, as building consensus was a common goal for all. "The younger men's opinion shall be heard," noted an Englishman who witnessed these meetings, "but the old men's opinion and councell imbraced and followed." This assembly didn't just advise the sachem; they curbed his power. Sachems, an observer noted, "will not war or undertake any weighty business" without the approval of their councils.[16]

The sachem and his top men followed a higher code of conduct. Colonists described the fighters among them as though they were knights straight from the pages of a medieval romance. The "men of great courage and wisdom" possessed "the greatest stature and strength, and yet are more discreet, courteous, and humane in their carriages then any amongst them scorning theft, lying, and the like base dealings, and stand as much upon their reputation as any men." The best warriors claimed to be almost superhuman because of their association with Hobbamock, the healing manitou. Accounts claimed "one of them will chase almost an hundred men," and that their protecting god could "preserve them from death, by wounds, with arrows, knives, hatchets."[17]

There were obvious parallels between this masculine ethos of true words with bold deeds and the European concept of honor. Men in Patuxet, like their English counterparts, connected their outward conduct to their inner devotion to gods, which made the work of maintaining their reputations of the utmost importance. Of course, not every man who claimed to follow this code lived up to it. They continued to test each other for evidence of a weak or insincere character, constantly monitoring how each responded to rumors or threats and how they behaved in battle. Councilors and sachems alike could be quite sensitive to slights or unkind words. In honor-based Indigenous societies like this one, a man's "face" was "continuously reaffirmed yet constantly at risk." Rivalries between high-status men were "simultaneously egalitarian, in that only equals may contest honor, and competitive, in that honor is never secure."[18]

Patuxet men's concern with their honor went hand in hand with their culture of condolence. Any report that a family member, friend, or ally was dying would bring visitors flocking to pay their respects—even more so when the person was "especially of note." When a loved one perished, it began a somber, lengthy process of public grieving. Close kin and friends gathered "to lament and bewaile the losse" with keening cries, while painting their faces black "for a longer or shorter time according to the dignity of the person."[19]

Sharing grief meant sharing grievances. When a family member died at the hands of another man, the public rites of mourning served as rallying cries for revenge. Young men like Squanto knew that taking up arms for the dead was an essential pact between family members—whether they were genetic relatives or merely addressed like them. "They hold the bond of brother-hood so deare," one Englishman observed, "that when one had committed a murther and fled, they executed his brother; and 'tis common for a brother to pay the debt of a brother deceased." Hence why his people had such complex terminology for relatives—and even when used metaphorically, these words carried the expectation of reciprocal liability.[20]

We can see this logic at work in a speech given by the Narragansett sachem Miantonomi in 1642, which was soon after translated into English. Looking to form an alliance of different nations, some of whom had recently been enemies, he declared to his gathered audience of sachems and their councils that they were his "bretheren," imploring them to raise arms against colonists, and "say brother [*neemat*] to one another." In both the Wampanoag and Narragansett languages, *neemat* was used by a male speaker to refer to his male sibling. Its simplest translation is "my brother."[21]

Often, as in the case of Miantonomi's speech, the truer meaning of *neemat* might be closer to "I am my brother's keeper." Asking unrelated men "to say *neemat* to one another" was, in essence, asking them to take a mutual oath.

Like members of any political class, Squanto and his fellow leading men could be swayed by charisma, driven by ambition, sensitive to slights, and prone to envy. Conflicts could simmer for years or flare up rather suddenly. If a murder, a slander, or any other transgression offended a sachem and his council, it laid the grounds for armed conflict, but negotiation came first in the form of sachem-to-sachem summits, which were supposed to prompt gestures of contrition and restitution. A dispute between villages tested those elemental pacts between individuals and families to defend each other's honor. If left unresolved, one of these quarrels could lead to open war.[22]

As the threat of bloodshed rose, Natives surrounded their largest towns with wooden palisades to shield noncombatants, and appointed scouts to raise the alarm if a hostile party approached. If their village site felt too exposed, a community at war might decamp to wetlands, which gave them additional cover. On the eve of combat, the sachem, powwaws, and councilors joined in presiding over the pre-battle ceremonies. Those who were ready to fight formed a ring, with their families gathered around, to witness their transition into the role of warrior. In instances witnessed by colonists, the men proudly presented their weapons and laid out a symbolic deerskin that served as center stage. They kept a steady beat by pounding on the earth with hands and sticks, they took turns dancing with flaming torches, and they sang to summon manitous to their side. Each fighting man stepped forward and gave a solemn speech that demonstrated his lack of fear, his loyalty to his sachem and his kin, and his willingness to slay his foes.[23]

Once clad in body paint, the warriors planned their campaigns with the sensibilities of seasoned hunters, relying on stealth and the element of surprise. Their targets were enemy fighting-age men. Women, children, and the elderly were taken captive and spared from any grave bodily harm, though their captors sometimes forced them into slavery. Across the continent, many Native powers adopted people taken in war, incorporating them into their families, or else held them as low-status slaves. In most recorded instances, the Native people of the coastal Northeast ransomed

captured noncombatants during peace negotiations, though these hostages were often treated as slaves during their captivity. Accumulating prisoners was a deliberate strategy. The more that were captured, the more
pressure on the other side to surrender. As one scholar put it, this form
of captive taking was "a quintessential element of war, and a fundamental
opportunity for peace."[24]

Attacks were intended to be speedy and frightening operations,
more like strikes than battles. Fighters sometimes made loud, haunting
cries as they approached the enemy. Once engaged, each side showered
the other with three-foot-long arrows tipped with razor-sharp heads that
could puncture bones and impale a man clean through his torso. When
they clashed in hand-to-hand combat, men brandished heavy ball-ended
clubs to brain their enemies. Whether launching an assault or repelling
one, Native men quickly fled as soon as they ran out of arrows or lost their
numerical advantage. If a warrior could not slay any more foes, his next
priority was to avoid capture. It was disgraceful for a fighting-age man to
fall into enemy hands.[25]

Centuries later, the toll of war can still be seen in Native skeletons.
Burial sites near Patuxet from before the colonial period were found to
contain numerous individuals who died violent deaths. Archaeologists
have uncovered both male and female remains with arrowheads still embedded in their vertebrae and limbs, bodies missing heads, and individuals
who suffered fatal cranial blows made with blunt objects.[26]

Some of these injuries were postmortem. After their enemy cleared
the field, the victors set upon the dead with knives and hatchets, cutting
off enemy scalps, heads, hands, and feet to bring back to the aggrieved
kin. Scholars have theorized that this act was intended to capture part of
the spiritual essence of the man killed, which fit with the animistic beliefs
of men who also took hunting trophies. Allies sometimes circulated these
prizes to affirm their partnerships and obligations, believing that passing
along the body parts of slain foes served as "a meanes to knitt them togeather."[27]

In the most heated conflicts, warriors tortured their captive foes before executing them. One account described how nearby Pequot warriors
tied a colonial enemy to a stake, cut strips of skin from his body, ran hot
embers into his wounds, cut off his hands and feet, and watched him endure this agony for three days until he died. This punishing sequence was

intended to be a catharsis for the mourners while also giving the doomed man a chance to regain the valor lost in his capture by remaining stoic throughout every excruciating step in his execution. The tormentors made sure that the details of these bloody trials got back to their opponents.[28]

The initial English descriptions of Indigenous violence could be rather matter-of-fact. They too came from a country where spectators reveled in gruesome public executions and officials regularly displayed mutilated bodies in the name of justice. Some colonists dismissed their neighbors' internecine wars as trivial affairs since these conflicts were so brief and had small death tolls compared to European conflicts. But quick resolution was exactly the point. It may sound anachronistic to describe Native martial practices as "psychological warfare" or "reputation management," but these terms do capture some of the thinking behind these actions. Pre-battle dances, songs, body paint, battle cries, surprise raids, captive taking, trophy taking, and torture were all designed to strengthen the will of one side while terrifying the other. The point was to intimidate rivals so badly that they wouldn't dare engage in a new conflict or else to break their will with excessive force and hasten the end of ongoing hostilities.[29]

Outsiders were also slow to realize that while Wampanoags celebrated their best warriors, they held peacemakers in equally high regard. Their honor culture was supposed to foster respect among leading men and between communities, which is why slights and rumors were so serious— they eroded trust and threatened communal order. To keep rivals away from the brink of war, leaders constantly looked to repair rifts and cool hotter heads, which is exactly what village-versus-village sporting matches, acts of condolence, and elevated civil language in meetings were supposed to accomplish.

Symbolic gifts could also stop a conflict from overheating. A delivery of arrows was a clarifying action: tipped arrows served as a final warning while headless shafts were a sign of peaceful intent. Both kinds of arrows could serve as an opening overture for talks. Gifts of heavy strings of precious wampum beads could serve as a form of restitution when given with an apology for an unjust slaying. The final check against violence was the council itself, a body that could restrain a sachem set on war. It prized collective deliberation over individual whims, while establishing that the leader's power was not absolute.[30]

But as later events in Squanto's life will illustrate, even when threats and rumors were rampant, sachems and their advisors could be slow to act, seeking out better information and opening channels of communication before resorting to violence.

Growing up near punishing enemies in an age of unforgiving winters, Tisquantum knew there were good reasons for the training, sporting, hazing, and deprivation he endured as a teenager. To rise in his community, he proved he could live up to the expectations of his kinsfolk and meet the challenges of a dangerous world. If childhood had instilled those profoundly familiar values and shaped his animistic faith, coming of age had taught Tisquantum to live by the honor-bound rules of Wampanoag manhood.

The ideal leading man in Patuxet projected outer and inner strength. He was supposed to be a physically dominant individual who had mastered his tools and weapons, showed no fear in battle or under torment, and could survive on his own for weeks at a time. He was also expected to demonstrate deep compassion for the dying and their mourners and honor his obligation to kinsfolk. He spoke honestly and sought consensus within his community, all the while demonstrating his faithfulness to his sachem. He was supposed to become the embodiment of manitou in all its meanings—godly, fearsome, skillful, truthful, graceful, and powerful.

The Wampanoag political world entered an increasingly turbulent period just as the young man came of age. It all began when a parade of mysterious vessels made landfall near Patuxet in the decade before his captivity. These encounters were not "first contacts." The peoples of this shore had known about Europeans for generations. And not all the unfamiliar sailors were from Europe. Others were Mi'kmaqs, an Indigenous maritime power that was expanding its range at the same time the French and English started poking along the coastline. The region's sandy margins were turning into a fast-changing theater of engagement, as they became the focus of new kinds of commerce and conflicts.

FOUR

Dawnlands

WITH ITS EASTERLY VISTA ON CAPE COD and the Atlantic Ocean beyond, Patuxet greeted the rising sun. Wampanoags were not the only self-declared "people of the dawn," as the Wabanakis to the north had a name that meant the same thing; accordingly, they called their territories *Wabanahkik,* meaning "dawnland." Some present-day tribal members favor the term for the entire Indigenous coast from the Cape to Nova Scotia. As a title for Squanto's natal region, Dawnland is not a perfect one, for as we shall see, the peoples of this shore were not all on friendly terms, so they likely did not imagine their territories as a single place. Yet the name is clearly better than regional titles like coastal New England and the Canadian Maritimes since it comes closer to a Native perspective without imposing later nations on top of theirs, especially when pluralized as Dawn*lands* to reflect the multiple peoples who called it home.[1]

Over one hundred thousand souls lived in these Dawnlands. They all spoke related Algonquian languages. In the southern part of the coast, Tisquantum's people and their neighbors settled especially densely along the shore and fertile river valleys, forming a detailed quilt of territories. Wampanoags sat among three other cultural groups: Massachusett lands lay to the north, Nipmuc countries sat to the west, and to the southwest were the people called Narragansetts, their nearest enemy. The origins of the bad blood between Wampanoags and Narragansetts were obscure, but English sources indicated that it was deep, rancorous, and persisted well into the colonial period.[2]

While some neighbors were starkly divided by bitter grievances, unable to forget unjust murders or destructive wars, more were on good terms. Throughout the Dawnlands, many peoples in nearby villages intermarried and shared overlapping hunting, planting, and fishing grounds. Links across this region were strong and ancient, as evidenced by borrowed patterns in pottery and trade goods found in graves and village sites. Away from the coast, the landscape was stitched together by criss-crossing paths and rivers, and studded with storied meeting places, notorious battlefields, busy portages, secret refuges, and sacred landforms. When colonists attempted to scout this land, locals told them of a long river to the west (the Hudson) and an even longer river to the north (the St. Lawrence), and described one or more freshwater seas to the northeast (accounts of Lake Champlain and the eastern Great Lakes, jumbled together by colonists).[3]

Tisquantum was also, in a fuzzier way, aware of territory far outside his familiar temperate forests and glacial shores. When Patuxet's pow-waws spoke of the Southwest, the birthplace of corn and resting place of the dead, they were primarily speaking in myth and metaphor. But they were also incorporating accounts, passed along telephone-game style, of the places that lay to the southwest where maize had been cultivated for centuries before it came to the Dawnlands. Perhaps they heard of the massive sedentary farming towns centered around large ceremonial mounds that had recently flourished along the Mississippi River valley and the Gulf Coast, or perhaps the irrigated towns of clustered multistory adobe buildings on the Colorado Plateau, or maybe even the dense cities and towering pyramids of Central America.

Although it is impossible to say what exactly the young man knew, it is certain that he was aware of distant places and peoples in the interior. Scholars have pieced together ample evidence of sprawling and weblike trade networks and migrations that connected Indigenous communities across the Americas from the Atlantic to the Pacific, from the tropics to the arctic. Evidence of these routes is visible in the simple fact that Squanto grew up eating crops first domesticated in Mexico. And that's hardly the only proof. Archaeologists working in New England precontact sites have unearthed jasper from Pennsylvania, copper from the western Great Lakes, mica from Tennessee, and shells from the Florida coast, while artifacts originating from the Northeast have been discovered in sites deep in the Great Plains.[4]

Most seeds, goods, and stories passed through several sets of hands as they crossed the continent. But some just as easily could have been borne long distances by a single person. As reported in colonial records, Indigenous people regularly made overland voyages of a thousand miles or more, propelled by just their own feet and canoes. Lakotas from the Plains turned up at treaties held at Montreal; Shawnees from the Ohio valley followed the Mississippi to the Gulf of Mexico; Haudenosaunees from the shores of Lake Ontario waged war in the Carolina piedmont. Colonists marveled at these intrepid voyagers, who accomplished these long journeys without cumbersome provisions by relying on the hospitality of other nations and living off the land.[5]

Rather than adopt the outlook of English settlers, who envisioned the interior as a "desolate wilderness," or take the view of textbook mapmakers who leave empty space beyond colonial borders, we should remember the many thousands of people who moved confidently along far-reaching paths and across extensive watersheds to wage war and to make peace.[6]

No matter the extent of his travels, Tisquantum was well aware that he lived on a large and storied continent—a well-trodden old world, not a trackless new one.

The Patuxet man also knew that the sea itself was home to many travelers. The earliest detailed account of contact between Natives and Europeans in the southern Dawnlands came from the Florentine captain Giovanni da Verrazzano, who sailed in 1524, several decades before Squanto was born. Funded by the French king Francis I, he was seeking out the Northwest Passage, the European fantasy that there was a shortcut that led to the Pacific through the annoyingly massive bulk of North America.

Soon after he reached the narrows at the mouth of modern-day New York harbor, Verrazzano anchored off the biggest inlet of Aquidneck Island, today the harbor of Newport, Rhode Island. He stayed there for two weeks. It's possible some of Tisquantum's ancestors were among the crowds who flocked from nearby villages to see this exotic ship; and it's certain that the community at Patuxet heard stories of this encounter secondhand and laid eyes on the peculiar gifts the visitors left behind.[7]

Verrazzano was not the only navigator crossing these waters with dreams of redrawing the map of the earth. Giovanni Caboto (John Cabot) and his son Sebastian, Venetian captains who sailed under the auspices of King Henry VII, visited the northern fringes of the Dawnlands in the 1490s and early 1500s. A Portuguese captain named Estêvõa Gomes also poked around the Maine coast just a few weeks before Verrazzano did. Visits like these inspired the prophetic and surreal stories that young Tisquantum heard from his elders, tales about "great canoes" and "moving islands" that appeared in the summer months.[8]

Most sailors passing near these shores had no intention of discovering unknown passages to the Pacific. They were ordinary fishermen from the western fringes of Europe. Their motive was profit. They brought tons of dried-and-salted codfish back to their home ports. Cheap and rich in protein, dried cod kept for a long time, making it a popular dish among ordinary people. The fact that the majority of Western Europeans were Catholic, and thus abstained from eating meat on Fridays and during Lent, created another enduring source of demand for fish.[9]

Beginning by the 1490s, or perhaps earlier, Portuguese, Galician, Basque, French, Breton, Cornish, and English fishermen set courses for the Grand Banks. Unlike the highly publicized voyages of Columbus, these were clandestine affairs with sparse documentation. Fishing was a competitive business. Those who knew the location of the best grounds jealously guarded this information.[10]

Their destination, the Grand Banks, are essentially submerged islands. They stand south of Newfoundland at the open mouth of the Gulf of Saint Lawrence, a key juncture where continental runoff and deep ocean currents meet, perfectly positioned to act as a nursery for sea life. These flows carried nutrients into shallow waters warmed by sunlight, making these submarine plateaus an ideal incubator for the smallest forms of life. Soon after the end of winter, the banks bloomed with phytoplankton and zooplankton, microscopic plants and animals. This underwater pasture drew vast schools of cod, herring, and mackerel, along with pods of migrating whales. This marine life was so abundant that some mapmakers illustrated the Grand Banks as islands made of fish. The ecological cycle made spring and summer the ideal time for fishing, which set the schedule of ships arriving in these waters. Soon Native people associated the seasonal turn with the coming of "great canoes."[11]

A couple of decades into the sixteenth century, the banks were no longer a well-kept secret. When the Englishman John Rut sailed into Newfoundland harbor at the height of the 1527 season, he discovered more than a dozen ships hailing from port towns from the Basque country to Britain, "all a fishing." A recent study estimates that by the 1560s the European fishing fleet in North America was over a hundred strong annually. The combined tonnage of ships heading to the Grand Banks rivaled the total tonnage of hulls headed to Spain's and Portugal's colonies in Central and South America at the same time, though of course fish were not as precious as gold or silver. The summertime fishermen did their best to avoid the more heavily peopled mainland, favoring isolated spots on New-foundland's remote Avalon Peninsula for their onshore camps where they dried and salted their catch and lived in "huts like the natives." These were seasonal settlements, not permanent colonies.[12]

The northernmost Dawnlanders, the Mi'kmaqs, were among the earliest to barter with the fishing camps, using first sign language and then a limited trade pidgin made up of mixed Native and European words. Mi'kmaq home territories ranged from the Gulf of Maine to the Gulf of Saint Lawrence. They later would become part of a Wabanaki confederacy that united peoples across the upper Dawnlands, though no such union existed in the late sixteenth century. An inventory of items carried by Mi'kmaqs to a French outpost in 1583 included the skins of moose, deer, seals, otters, beavers, martens, lynx, and an assortment of red plant dyes.[13]

These exchanges started the slow trickle of foreign-made goods southward, into trading networks that connected thousands of villages on the continent's eastern side. By the time the boy from Patuxet was born, a smattering of these objects had made their way to Wampanoag country. Growing up, Tisquantum would have seen a fair number of things from the far side of the Atlantic: items made of European iron, tin, bronze, and copper started appearing in burial sites across the Northeast over the six-teenth century. (Native peoples in North America had long mined and worked their own copper, but it was comparatively scarce in the Dawn-lands.) By the time they arrived in the village at the small falls, these trade goods often looked nothing like the items that Europeans had swapped for furs. A single kettle, for example, could be broken into hundreds of pieces and completely reworked by Indigenous artisans into arrowheads, hooks, lures, and ornaments.[14]

Over decades of sporadic engagements, the Mi'kmaq people began to eye the Europeans' sailboats. Already seasoned mariners, the Mi'kmaq were accustomed to crossing stretches of open water in hefty dugout ca-noes, which they sometimes rigged with skin sails on poles. They quickly noticed the advantages European sailboats had over canoes—their large cloth sails on fixed masts could carry them farther with less effort, their daggerboards and keels made them more stable in ocean swells, and their wider plank-built hulls held more cargo.[15]

Mi'kmaqs were most interested in shallops, the auxiliary craft that

fishermen brought with them in the holds of their ships and used for setting nets and lines. The visitors made a habit of leaving these boats behind
over the winter to make more room for casks packed with salted fish. Upon
finding these spare vessels, Mi'kmaqs saw them as free for the taking.
Sources from as early as 1583 reported that they had taught themselves
how to sail the alien craft.[16]

Soon these Native pirates took so many vessels that some fishermen
started selling boats outright as trade items rather than leaving them to
be stolen. By the turn of the seventeenth century a veritable Mi'kmaq fleet
patrolled the coast north of Patuxet. European explorers came across them
in many places. One spotted a Native-operated Basque shallop off Nova
Scotia, another spied "two French shallops full of the country people"
near Penobscot Bay, while still another simply noted that the Mi'kmaq had
a fondness for French-made vessels, "which they can manage as well as
anie Christian."[17]

Drawing on advice from European mariners and learning by trial
and error, the Mi'kmaq became adept navigators who were comfortable
on the high seas, setting course to destinations hundreds of miles away.
They adopted the gear and clothes of foreign sailors while adding a distinctive Indigenous twist. They fashioned sails from both canvas and skins,
built their own bark-sided sailboats based on European plank-built watercraft, and even painted their sails with the image of a moose, a Mi'kmaq
manitou. When the Englishman Bartholomew Gosnold arrived at a spot
seventy miles north of Patuxet in 1602, he was greeted by a Basque-style
boat manned by eight Mi'kmaq men, one of whom was wearing shoes,
stockings, breeches, and a mariner's coat. While this captain wore the cos-
tume of a European mariner, his crew dressed traditionally with deerskin
mantles, sealskin leggings, and "their eie-browes painted white."[18]

By 1600, Mi'kmaqs had become a regional sea power and remained
one well into the 1760s. As one scholar puts it, they and their eventual
coalition of Wabanaki partners undertook "an extractive and expansionist
political project" that spanned the Dawnlands' coastal waters, based on
"punitive and plundering enterprises." Their adoption of European small
craft was similar to how Plains Natives approached European horses. Just
as new mounts transformed life for peoples west of the Mississippi, plank-
built sailboats exponentially increased these sea peoples' range for hunting, trading, and fighting, giving them a distinct advantage over those who
had yet to master this novel form of transportation.[19]

In military jargon, the new watercraft were "force multipliers"; in today's business-speak, they could be called "disruptive" technologies. Mi'kmaqs bartered with European seamen for new lines, sails, ships' biscuits, "and many other things," which soon enough included knives, swords, guns, shot, and powder. In 1607, one rising Mi'kmaq chief had started arming his shallops with French firearms, allowing him to launch a surprise attack on a community hundreds of miles away. Explorers across the coast heard similar tales of terrifying visits by Mi'kmaq sailboats.[20]

Unsurprisingly, the seafaring Mi'kmaqs swiftly became southern Dawnlanders' most hated enemies. They called them "Tarentines." The northerners usually came "in harvest time" to towns around Massachusetts Bay to "take away their corne, and many times kill their persons," seeking the crops to supplement their game-and-fish-heavy diet. The dreaded Tarentines also carried away captives as slaves and tortured Native men who resisted them. Later in the colonial period, Massachusett leaders confessed they were "much afraid" and regularly "came quaking and complaining of a barbarous and cruell people." Mi'kmaqs were, in their eyes, "war-like," "bloody," "deadly," "mortal enemies," and "the scumme of the country." Although we don't know whether these raiders ever hit Patuxet directly, they did strike nearby Massachusett villages. Many of these amphibious attacks were simultaneous with the arrival of a new wave of English and French explorers in the early 1600s.[21]

The looming presence of Native sea raiders near Wampanoag harbors created hidden dynamics in early encounters with Europeans. Squanto's people dreaded attacks from the north, but their feelings about these distant foes could have included envy as well as fear. Along with their unusual clothing and watercraft, Mi'kmaqs had an abundance of metal arrowheads, knives, and sometimes guns that were all more intimidating than traditionally made weapons. Such items were rare around Patuxet as they were available only from Indigenous trading partners at great expense. The arrival of ships gave Wampanoags a chance to eliminate the middlemen and deal directly with the foreign merchants, not just for weapons but also cloth, beads, brass, and other raw materials for jewelry. Perhaps they hoped that establishing a trading partnership could lead to a proper alliance. The resulting material and political advantages would help fend off Mi'kmaq predations and serve as a bulwark against threats from their neighbors the Narragansetts and another notorious nation from the deeper interior, the Mohawks.

These defensive and commercial motivations hint at why Tisquantum's people were welcoming to ships at first, a response that was by no means a given. From explorers' accounts, we know that in other places Natives' first reaction was to rain down arrows on the strangers or flee at the sight of them. By contrast, Wampanoag sachems all followed a similar canny and cautious gameplan. They made contacts in tentative stages, first sending a couple of men to intercept the mariners on the water before permitting them to come ashore. On land, a formidable party of armed men greeted the Europeans with furs, expressing their desire to trade. Though even when they were inviting, Dawnlanders remained vigilant: even when amity had been established, they never let visitors sleep ashore lest they attempt anything under cover of night.

Wampanoags might have also taken away lessons from the Mi'kmaqs' creative approach to new technology. The northerners illustrated that rewards could outweigh the risks of dealing with Europeans. Their offshore presence also serves as a reminder we should never see the meetings between ships and canoes as flat, two-sided affairs; there were always hidden dimensions. Just as Christian nations jousted among each other for access to America's coastal market in furs and goods, so too did Native powers.

The men who came in ships were clad in excessive clothing, a funny difference that inspired a common name for them: *Watâhkoonoag*, meaning "coat-wearers" or "coat-men." Squanto's initial sighting of these seafarers was probably one of three events from the years 1602 to 1605. The sources allow us to make out scenes of his home community learning firsthand about the ways and wiles of the coat-men.[22]

Although Wampanoags had long heard descriptions of ships and likely seen the small shallops manned by Native sailors, the first appearance of a multi-masted ship was a true revelation. A transatlantic craft of the day was an impressive sight. Its towering rig soared higher than any Native-built structure; its massive hull plowed through the seas; its billowing sails were larger than any skin or piece of fabric they had ever seen; its bow and stern were festooned with painted carvings in the shape of animals or people. In stories that elders told colonists later, they remembered that they once thought that ships were moving islands and described them as obviously possessing the element of manitou, speaking to a genuine feeling of awe.[23]

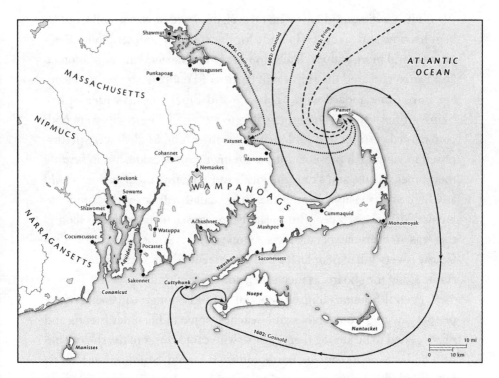

The southern Dawnlands, 1602–1605, with routes of Gosnold, Pring, and Champlain. Erin Greb Cartography.

Once ashore, the pink-skinned, hairy-faced visitors were also an object of fascination, as they expressed themselves in gestures, laughed, made music, shared food, and smoked tobacco with local sachems and their councilors. Although Tisquantum cannot be precisely placed at any of these visits, given how close each of these visitors came to Patuxet it is almost certain that the young man witnessed parts of these events, at least at a distance.

The earliest incident came on May 14, 1602—May 24 in our modern calendar. A ship entered the waters between Patuxet and Pamet. First it glided offshore for a while, while gulls began to crowd around it. Anyone close enough in a canoe would have plainly seen that the strangers were fishing, hauling in "a great store of Cod-fish." It was the men on this ship who named the curling tip of the bay's protective arm-shaped peninsula "Cape Cod." The vessel then cruised southward, making landfall near Cummaquid, a harbor just thirty miles from Tisquantum's home. There, one of the town's bolder councilors came to greet the ship.

The Cummaquid envoy met the visitors with a warm smile, but he kept his bow and arrow by his side for the entire encounter. Soon thereafter several more canoes, likely coming from Nauset, Pamet, Manomet, and Patuxet, neared the ship's rail. Parties of Wampanoag men and teenage boys came aboard with "Tobacco and Pipes steeled with Copper, Skins, artificial strings and other trifles to barter."[24] These gifts were both commercial gestures and diplomatic offerings. The English were predisposed to view such presentations as an invitation to trade, but in bearing their pipes, beads, and skins, the locals were treating them as they would any high-status visitor. Even if they had traded with an earlier, undocumented Mi'kmaq vessel or European fishing vessel, no one acted as though this was an everyday occurrence. As one of its crewmen recalled: "This Coaste is very full of people, for that as we trended the same Savagges still runne along the shoare, as men much admiring at us."[25]

Even if Squanto himself was not yet old enough to be one of the people gawking from canoes and beaches, some of his older friends and relatives had to be among them. Those who came closer to the ship would have laid eyes on its captain, Bartholomew Gosnold. Standing five feet, six inches tall, the thirty-one-year-old Gosnold came from a gentry family in Suffolk. After a brief stint as a student at Jesus College, Cambridge, he had become a privateer, and that experience at sea qualified him to serve as the leader of a new American expedition. Accompanied by a crew of thirty men and boys, Gosnold had left Dartmouth fifty days earlier aboard the bark *Concord,* with a mission to scout for a new English colony in the Americas, as earlier efforts at Newfoundland and Roanoke had failed.[26]

After a friendly brief exchange with the men in canoes, the *Concord* sailed outside the bay. It rounded Cape Cod and to the east of the peninsula reached a tiny island at the mouth of a wide inlet, which Gosnold named "Buzzards Bay." Dubbing their toehold "Elizabeth's Isle," the crew stayed there for a few weeks, meeting with parties of local Native men and continuing to trade. Gosnold directed his crew to build a small house on the island that he hoped would become a permanent trading outpost, but after they weighed anchor in mid-June, they never returned. Groups from the mainland, likely including men from Patuxet who had a convenient portage to Buzzards Bay, must have inspected the small house and its experimental plots of grain after Gosnold left. The structure and crops were obvious clues to the foreigners' aspirations.[27]

Englishmen came again the following year. That June, two ships sailed within the protected waters of Cape Cod Bay, this time dropping anchor off Pamet. They were the *Speedwell* and *Discoverer*, eight weeks out of Bristol. As their commander Martin Pring made Pamet his base, the news traveled around the bay. Soon Native parties of "ten, twentie, fortie, or threescore, and at one time one hundred and twentie at once" came to greet the visiting ship in canoes. Men from Patuxet were surely among the crowds. The English had brought a varied store of trade goods to distribute among the locals: colored hats, bolts of cloth, stockings, saws, pickaxes, spades, shovels, axes, hooks, and knives. Of particular interest to local men was the ship's boy "that could play upon a Gitterne [an early modern ancestor of the guitar] in whose homely Musicke they tooke great delight." To prompt him to play, the Natives "would give him many things, as Tobacco, Tobacco-pipes, Snakes skinnes of sixe foot long." They regularly broke out in song and dance while the young English musician strummed along.[28]

Pring, like Gosnold, was scouting a potential colony. To finance the voyage, he ordered his men to collect stores of sassafras root, a prized medicinal for "the French Poxe," meaning syphilis. He too attempted sowing European seeds, an experiment that was aborted when the Pamet locals started a controlled burn that engulfed the stand of alien plants. Not understanding that firing the underbrush was a regular part of Indigenous farming, the English took the burning as a menacing gesture.[29]

It may or may not have been intended as such, though Pring himself was hardly innocent of brutish actions. He tolerated Wampanoag men's visits to enjoy gittern music, but he was quick to use the ship's dogs, a pair of enormous mastiffs named "Foole and Gallant," to intimidate them. "When we would be [rid] of the Savages company," Pring wrote, "wee would let loose the Mastives, and suddenly with out-cryes they would flee away." Remaining wary of a Native attack and keeping their dogs close at hand, the English worried about overstaying their welcome. When a group of two hundred local men came marching toward their camp with uncertain motives, Pring decided it was time to sail back to Bristol.[30]

Tensions rose further during Samuel de Champlain's voyage along the coast in 1605. He was the explorer we can be most confident that young Tisquantum witnessed because he dropped anchor at Patuxet. Champlain was acting as the advance guard for the incipient French colonial project

Matthäus Merian, "Captain Gosnold Trades with the Indians" (Frankfurt, 1634). This
fanciful illustration was created by a European engraver with only written accounts as
his guide; note how it imagines Mediterranean-looking shrubs and cypress trees along
the Dawnlands coast. Courtesy of the Virginia Historical Society.

that was struggling to gain a toehold at the northern fringes of the Dawnlands. French fur traders had established an aborted colony at Tadoussac
(now in Quebec) on the Saint Lawrence River in 1599, and they tried again
at Saint Croix (now in Maine) and Port-Royal (now in Nova Scotia) in 1605.

When Champlain dropped anchor in Patuxet harbor on his trip
southward, a group of men who were out fishing intercepted his vessel,
had a short but pleasant encounter, then went ahead to alert the town. The
Frenchman noted that a tower of smoke started billowing into the sky,
which he assumed was announcing his arrival. No previous visitor mentioned the use of smoke signals. It was a possible indicator that ever since
things had gotten tense with Pring and his crew, the Patuxet community
was on heightened alert and had a mutual agreement among neighbors to
signal each other when an alien vessel approached.

Once Champlain came ashore, a group of "eighteen or twenty"—probably the sachem with his top councilors and powwaws—had gathered at his boat and "began to dance." Likely he was witnessing a traditional greeting for a traveler, so in similarly warm gesture, he offered the men "a few trinkets" as gifts, "at which they were quite pleased." The Frenchman admired the "good number of cabins and gardens" surrounding the harbor and made the first quick sketch of Patuxet, which was mentioned earlier. Champlain's visit turned out to be abrupt. Once he determined that none of the small estuaries by Patuxet were navigable, he lost interest in the bay and sailed away the same day.[31]

After departing the small falls, he stopped in a nearby Nauset harbor in the following days, where he set a bullying tone by letting his men harvest crops without asking. The locals responded by helping themselves to a French kettle, which triggered a violent standoff. The French began firing their muskets at the Nausets and took one man hostage. In revenge, Nausets murdered a sailor. Champlain summed up the disastrous affair with a stern warning to his readers: "One must be on one's guard among these people, and remain suspicious of them at all times without them noticing."[32]

The wariness was more than mutual. As Champlain's crew sailed away, they again saw columns of smoke rising from the coast as news of their deeds traveled from village to village.

Squanto, his sachem, and the other leading men doubtless spent hours considering these encounters, trying to make sense of the inscrutable coatmen. The visits had a worrisome trajectory. Gosnold's party had been consistently peaceful but had left a house behind, signaling ambitions beyond mere trade. Pring's men were alternatingly warm and menacing. Champlain's crew had insulted Wampanoag gestures of hospitality, and they took a man hostage, a clear act of war. Those who assumed the worst about the visitors could point to the last visit as proof that their suspicions were right. Though as time passed, others could cite Champlain's skittish departure followed by six years with no visitors as evidence that the Watâhkoonoag were only a minor concern.

The village leaders had more pressing concerns, not the least of which was the literal climate. The extreme cooling trend of the late sixteenth century brought droughts and stunted harvests that could lead to famine. In response to these challenges, villagers prayed and danced to sway the manitous of the fields and skies while perhaps also expanding their planting grounds and storage cellars as a hedge against bad seasons. Scarce resources could be the source of further instability, one more reason why the community's protectors remained alert to threats from all directions. They kept a watchful eye on Narragansetts to the southwest and Mi'kmaqs to the northeast. The waterborne Watâhkoonoag had been more troublesome than fearsome in their initial landfalls, but soon there would be no doubt about their darker intentions.

In the year 1611, when the English returned to their part of the Dawnlands, Tisquantum and the rest of Patuxet would start to see these sailors for what they were: scouts for a future invasion. Their nearest neighbors confirmed that the passing strangers were not just interested in swapping goods for furs. They were stealing men away.

PART TWO

Away

Sassacomoit and Epenow

MIDWAY BETWEEN WAMPANOAG AND Mi'kmaq territories lay a rugged land called Mawooshen. Today it's the Maine shoreline from Casco Bay to Penobscot Bay. Passing explorers marveled at Mawooshen's "high craggy cliffy rocks and stony iles" and trees that neared two hundred feet tall, describing this landscape as more likely to "affright rather than delight" Europeans. Though they hardly feared their own home, the Etchimens knew it was a challenging place to live. The forest here was more piney and less leafy, and the summers were so mild that the Etchimens did not raise many crops. Their primary diet was fish, game, and foraged plants. Like their neighbors to the south, they worried about fending off Mi'kmaq sea raiders while also remaining wary of the other foreign explorers and fishermen edging into their waters.[1]

Mawooshen was the home of an intrepid man named Sassacomoit, who lived among the Etchimen but may not have been one of them. An English source called him a "servant," meaning he might have been taken in a war as a captive and thus retained a lower rank than other men. Whatever his exact status, in 1605 he embarked on a nine-year ordeal that made him one of the earliest Dawnlanders to witness the lands of the coat-men firsthand.[2]

That spring, when a ship of Englishmen arrived in Mawooshen, a scene unfolded much like the Wampanoags' meetings with Gosnold, Pring, and Champlain. Sassacomoit was among the men who welcomed the visitors. He and four others were in the middle of a shoreside rendezvous where the captain offered them a meal, then "shewed them trifles to exchange, thinking thereby to have banish feare," and then "suddenly laid hands upon them." A struggle ensued: the men "were strong and so naked as our best hold was by their long haire on their heads." After forcing Sassacomoit and his companions into a rowboat, the kidnappers carried

them to their ship and weighed anchor. The abduction shocked the people onshore who witnessed it. Perhaps they wondered if the Europeans
would treat the men as they themselves treated enemies in war, subjecting
them to a drawn-out and painful death, a test of their mettle as men. Some
just assumed they were doomed. Two months later, when Champlain visited nearby, an Indigenous trader reported that the English had killed the
five captives.[3]

Thankfully, that rumor was false. They were still alive and aboard the
ship *Archangell* bound for England. The men taken with Sassacomoit included a sachem named Tahánedo and three others, Amóret, Skicowáros,
and Maneddo, all described as "gentlemen," which probably meant they
had a high social rank, the Etchimen equivalent of Patuxet's top men.[4]

Their captor, George Weymouth, was an experienced engineer and
navigator. Weymouth was scouting the Maine coast for a settlement for
English Catholics to escape persecution from the Protestant majority at
home. His brief trip sparked excitement in England, in no small part because of the valuable intelligence provided by their captives.[5]

Those five stolen men were the first of many. Over the next twenty years,
English sailors would enslave dozens of men from the Dawnlands. Squanto
was the most famous and consequential of these captives, but his fate was
inextricably connected to that of two taken before him: Sassacomoit and
a Wampanoag named Epenow. Taken in 1605 and 1611, these two crafty
men would meet while in captivity. Both were freed in the summer of 1614,
the same summer the man from Patuxet was taken. Parts of their ordeals
were so reminiscent of Squanto's experiences that many later writers have
confused (or, in some cases, intentionally conflated) their stories with his.
Their experiences provide a crucial backstory to how and why Tisquantum was ensnared, and they also introduce us to the ambitious, sometimes
bumbling cast of English adventurers and investors who made futile attempts to get a foothold in the Dawnlands in the decade and a half before
the *Mayflower* sailed.

First, though, we have to disentangle the threads of these captives'
respective lives. A number of authors have made faulty assumptions about
how many times Squanto was kidnapped and served as a guide. Part of
this uncertainty stems from the fuzzy memories of one elderly colonial
backer writing many years later who muddled his recollections of different

Indigenous captives, leading some to think that Squanto was among the men abducted from Mawooshen. Still others have speculated that the man from Patuxet was captured up to three times, theorizing that several other Native captives were actually Tisquantum by another name. But there is a simple reason that Squanto shouldn't be confused with any other captive: every colonist who met him, and thus heard his account in his own words, reported that he was kidnapped just one time. He never mentioned an earlier captivity.[6]

The writers who ignore the Patuxet man's testimony are victims of an exceptionalist mindset that plagues writings about Plymouth Colony. Claiming that he mingled with adventurers in Europe for *fifteen years* before meeting the *Mayflower* passengers frames him as a one-of-a-kind figure to match that extra-special group of colonists. The inflated version of his biography also rests on the unlikely premise that sailors kept taking the same man, as though he was the hero of a Hollywood action franchise who kept stumbling into remarkably similar situations in each sequel. That exact kind of screenwriter logic prevailed in the script for the Disney film *Squanto: A Warrior's Tale*, which inserted episodes from Epenow's story to pad out its retelling of Tisquantum's life.

These embellishments seem unnecessary considering how epic the verified details of his life already are. The notion that the captives with different names might be the same man is the product of a larger scholarly blind spot. Only in the last couple of decades have historians really grasped how common it was for colonists to enslave Natives, both in the Dawnlands and elsewhere in the Americas. We now know that hundreds of thousands more Indigenous women and men faced similar "reverse middle passages." Initiated by Christopher Columbus in the 1490s, the eastward transshipment of Natives occurred simultaneously with the much better known westward traffic in African peoples across the Atlantic.[7]

The first wave of people captured north of Mesoamerica rarely endured "chattel slavery," the typical experience of most captured Africans. On most occasions they were not taken as commodities to be sold and their status as slaves was never intended to be permanent or passed on to their children. But seeing them only as captives and not actual slaves isn't quite right either. After all, they were taken for their labor with no guarantee of freedom. For those who died on European soil, bondage turned out to be inescapable.

Nothing about this practice of enslaving locals before and during conquest started with the English. Kidnapping informants was an age-old military strategy used across the globe, and Native Americans were no exception. Across the continent, Indigenous powers had long captured enemies to aid with reconnaissance and translation. And well before Weymouth dragged those Wabanaki men onto his ship, Spanish, Portuguese, and French explorers had already tried abducting Natives in places they hoped to colonize. Lacking antibodies to many common European pathogens, Indigenous Americans were especially susceptible to deadly infections when surrounded by foreigners on their ships or shores. And those who survived the germy cities of Christendom often came home with deep resentment toward their captors.[8]

That was definitely true of the Dawnlanders taken and freed before Tisquantum. Much like the Patuxet man later would, these earlier captives played an outsized role in England's early attempts to found American colonies. They figured out how to exercise power while in bondage and when they were finally free. They discovered they could launch ships with their words and even decide whether a settlement failed or flourished. Above all, they demonstrated a burning desire to return to their side of the ocean, a drive that was obvious in the odysseys of Sassacomoit, Epenow, and Squanto. Much like the original return trip from Troy to Ithaca, each man's journey home was long and winding.

Aboard the *Archangell* in June 1605, Sassacomoit and the others were filled with dread at the sight of Mawooshen slipping below the horizon. They appeared frightened at first, though a sailor's account claimed they quickly accepted their lot: "After perceiving by their kinde usage that we intended them no harme, they have never since seemed discontented with us." The enslaved men reportedly became "very tractable, loving, & willing by their best means to satisfie us in any thing we demand of them, by words and signes for their understanding." Over the six-week passage, they conversed haltingly with James Rosier, an English Jesuit who was eager to learn as much as he could about their home country and language. In return, he began to teach them English.[9]

The *Archangell*'s destination was Plymouth, one of the main ports of the West Country. Located in Britain's southwest, the West Country is the foot-shaped peninsula that juts into the sea below Wales. Like the Dawn-

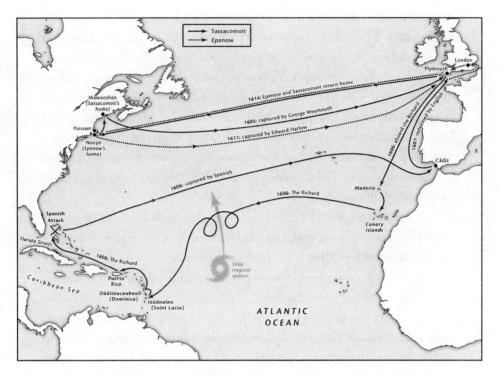

Sassacomoit's and Epenow's Atlantic odysseys, 1605–1614. Erin Greb Cartography.

lands, the region had a rockbound shoreline and an intensely maritime economy. Perhaps the stern coast on the way into Plymouth looked vaguely familiar to the captives, but everything else must have seemed impossibly strange: the gray stone church towers and windmills that were visible from miles away at sea; the forbidding new fort guarding the bay; the thicket of hulls and masts bobbing in the inner harbor; the timber-framed houses cramped in side by side; the yelling peddlers, clopping horses, and creaky carts passing over streets caked with manure; the surrounding green countryside crossed with hedgerows and dotted with beasts as tame as dogs.[10]

Why would people live like this, crowded into impractical heavy buildings on top of filth, unable to pick up their homes and make the most of the seasons? How could a town sustain itself without ample forests nearby to provide for them?

Plymouth's residents appeared stranger still. The captives had grown accustomed to sailors and their sturdy and striped clothes, so they would not be too aghast at the ordinary folks who gathered by the quay as they made landfall. But their jaws must have dropped when they first saw the local gentry. There were ladies with painted faces, red rouging on their cheeks and lips, walking on towering platform overshoes, their hair teased up into fashionable coiffures. Men were suited in doublets and breeches, heads adorned with waxed angular beards and mustaches, sporting decorative swords or rapiers at their hips, some still wearing the wide ruffled lace collars at their necklines that were starting to go out of style in London. The richest were clad in sumptuous velvet and fur-lined coats and gowns, their sleeves and breeches puffed with open slits revealing bright contrasting fabrics within.[11]

The captives would certainly recognize them as elites, as theirs too wore fine furs and sometimes sported feathered cloaks that had a gauzy effect similar to lace. But why would people who weren't even leaders wear such lavish costumes? Why would only women paint their faces, not men? The more they saw, the more questions arose. Why did men labor in fields doing women's work? The first weeks were no doubt full of surprises like these, as each encountered the unfathomable culture shock of leaving his woodsy village-scaled world of hunting and fishing and ending up a hostage in this heavily settled and partially denuded landscape teeming with so many kinds of coat-wearers.

Within months of arriving, they would meet one particular local gentleman, Sir Ferdinando Gorges, a major figure in English efforts to colonize North America. Sassacomoit and two others became his wards after the motive behind their capture—the idea of creating a refuge for English Catholics—changed soon after the *Archangell* returned. Just past midnight on November 5, 1605, a patrol in the cellars below the Houses of Parliament uncovered the Catholic saboteur Guy Fawkes and thirty-six barrels of gunpowder, enough to immolate the whole building and anyone in it. News of the treasonous Gunpowder Plot instantly made any pro-Catholic scheme politically toxic.[12]

Gorges, a Protestant, saw colonies as lucrative investments, not as harbors for religious minorities. After serving in several overseas wars as a young man, by the 1590s he had established himself as a leading citizen in Plymouth. Gorges took after wealthy swashbucklers from his home region: Sir Francis Drake, Sir Walter Ralegh, and Ralegh's half brother Sir Humphrey Gilbert. Famous in their own day, these wannabe imperialists were known as "West Country Men." They were hugely influential in shap-

ing the foreign policy of Queen Elizabeth I, prodding her to challenge
Spain on the high seas while expanding her realm farther across the Irish
Sea and Atlantic Ocean. But their dreams of American colonies came to
naught. Gilbert led a botched attempt to create an English foothold on
Newfoundland in 1583; Ralegh was behind the failed colony at Roanoke
in the late 1580s.[13]

Gorges was actually a distant cousin of Ralegh and Gilbert, though
he belonged to a younger generation. His connections across the southwest counties helped him get the ear of the most powerful man from the
region: Sir John Popham. Onetime Speaker of the House of Commons,
Popham served as Lord Chief Justice of England under Elizabeth and
then under her successor James I. Popham was rather busy in the winter
of 1605/6 soon after the Wabanakis arrived, as he ended up presiding over
the January trial of the terrorists behind the Gunpowder Plot. By the
spring, he and his son George, who shared his keen interest in colonial
ventures, welcomed the two other Native captives into their household.[14]

Of course, the five Wabanaki captives had no interest in colonies, but
they made the case for a return to their homelands. While lodged in the
spacious country homes of Gorges and Popham, Sassacomoit and the
others were eager to list all the Dawnlands' attractive qualities—friendly
people, "excellent" rivers, "pleasant" meadows, abundant furry animals,
"infinite" stores of salmon, "fresh water fish of all sorts"—mentioning everything they sorely missed in a transparent effort to convince these would-be
imperialists to bring them back. Their ploy worked. Both men being sold
on Mawooshen's promise, they set about getting royal support.[15]

Popham helped align Gorges's faction of pro-colonization merchants
in Plymouth with a like-minded group in London. In 1606, no doubt
prodded by his Lord Chief Justice, the king granted this body a charter
for a new joint-stock company devoted to the colonization of "Virginia,"
the English name for the American coast north of Florida and south of
Newfoundland. The charter permitted the London and Plymouth con-
tingents each to found its own colony funded by two separate pools of
investors, creating twin subcompanies under the umbrella of the Virginia
Company. The London Company aimed to settle in "the southern part"
of Virginia, specifically Chesapeake Bay, where they would soon establish
Jamestown; the members of the Plymouth Company had their eyes on "the
northern part," meaning the Dawnlands.

So began a new era in English colonialism. With its simultaneous attempts to plant northern and southern outposts in 1606, the parent Virginia Company initiated the first wholehearted scheme to overwinter in America since the Roanoke colonists mysteriously vanished sixteen years earlier. It was a far more structured plan than those doomed ventures led by swaggering knights from the West Country. Over the following year, the two pools of investors set about recruiting men for their founding expeditions, while also luring in more stockholders with promises of handsome returns.[16]

Sturdier legal and financial foundations in England, however, meant little in America. Jamestown's early years were a disaster. Poorly planned and staffed by self-interested and conflict-prone men, the colony continuously drained the coffers of the London Company for the better part of a decade. The first wave of settlers wasted valuable time panning for gold that turned out to be worthless mica or "gilded durt." They constantly clashed with their Powhatan neighbors. They starved and froze through successive winters that killed hundreds of colonists, including the unfathomably grim winter of 1610–1611 when some desperate settlers resorted to digging up and eating the dead. In 1609, the London Company's supply convoy ran straight into a hurricane. One ship sank with all aboard, and their largest and most expensive ship, *The Sea Venture,* wrecked off the isles of Bermuda. An early account written by a survivor of this shipwreck likely inspired parts of William Shakespeare's *The Tempest,* first performed for James I in 1611.[17]

Successful colonies weren't supposed to be fodder for drama. The Plymouth Company's northern scheme seemed to have better odds of a happy ending, thanks to the five captives who promised to serve as guides and win them local friends. By the late summer of 1606, the company had planned two staggered voyages to Mawooshen. Gorges funded one ship to make the initial exploratory return; Popham outfitted two more to follow up and bring over the bulk of the colonists.

Sassacomoit and one other captive sailed aboard Gorges's vessel, the *Richard*—though Gorges himself, who was always more of an armchair imperialist, stayed home. Leaving that fall and taking a longer southern route that followed prevailing winds, the *Richard* was waylaid by a colorful string of stop-offs and situations. The ship first resupplied at Madeira and the Canary Islands before making the Atlantic crossing. As it neared

North America, a passing tropical storm or hurricane blew it farther south, where Sassacomoit would first glimpse the Lesser Antilles, a chain of palm-laden islands that were thus far mostly untrodden by colonists.[18]

The *Richard* took on wood and water at the Kalinago (or Carib) isle of Ioüànalao, which Europeans called Saint Lucia. Ioüànalao was recently the site of a tiny English colony that folded quickly after conflicts with the local Kalinagos, who generally resisted any foreign intrusion. Soon there-after the men aboard the *Richard* redeemed a stranded Spanish mission-ary from Oüáitoucoubouli, another independent Kalinago island, known to Europeans as Dominica. When they stopped to deposit the friar on Puerto Rico, settlers rewarded them with live pigs and cattle for their good deed. They finally set off northward in the direction of the Dawnlands, crossing through the straits of Florida. While navigating those waters, they were surrounded by a fleet of merchant vessels from Santo Domingo. The approaching Spaniards bore a serious grudge. English privateers had been preying on their ships for decades in these waters. Upon spotting the *Rich-ard* flying English colors, they eagerly seized it as a prize.[19]

Sassacomoit did not surrender easily. After the Spaniards blasted the deck of the *Richard* with shot and leapt over the rail with rapiers in hand, he gave chase. He was following the same Indigenous rules of combat that Tisquantum learned: fighting men were supposed to avoid capture at all costs and always swear loyalty to their sachem. After he began "creeping under a Cabbin" to escape, the invaders started stabbing him with their swords. Sassacomoit cried out, "King James! King James! King James his ship! King James his ship!" He was "injured most cruelly in severall places in the bodie" when the Spanish marauders slashed his torso with their rapiers and ran one blade clean through his arm. Once the entire crew of the *Richard* had been captured, the Spanish beat the most uncooperative ones, took all their possessions, including most of their clothes, and di-vided them into two groups to be taken away as prisoners.

Perhaps Sassacomoit had a dark sense of déjà vu when he found him-self a captive twice over, this time on a ship bound to Spain while recover-ing from his wounds. He and the rest of the men were given a half-pint of water once a day and fed on cassava root and maggot-infested portions of salted beef. They arrived in Seville, where after several weeks of pleading their case before Spanish officials and being temporarily imprisoned, the men from the *Richard* were released to an English ship heading home.

Maneddo, the other Wabanaki man on the *Richard,* apparently died in Spain; Sassacomoit ended up back in England by 1607, where he would regain his health and remain trapped for the next seven years, spending at least part of his time with Gorges.[20]

The other three captives, Tahánedo, Amóret, and Skicowáros, had an uneventful passage west in a two-ship convoy. More than one hundred prospective settlers came to Mawooshen with them. Once arrived, the English freed the Natives and set about raising a fort along the Sagadahoc River. They soon found that the men they had cultivated as loyal supporters had become their biggest opponents. The ex-captives discouraged other Natives from trading with the English, preferring an alliance with the French, who continued to make trading visits along the coast. In one hostile encounter, Natives killed one of the settlers. Adding to their troubles, several buildings within the fort were lost to fire and constant infighting plagued the small settlement.

One leader, Ralegh Gilbert, the son of one famed West Country man and named after another, departed early. Another headman, George Popham, son of the main sponsor, perished in the unusually cold winter of 1607/8. It was a frigid year even by the standards of the Little Ice Age, giving the region a negative reputation among the English for "being over cold." Gorges would lament that "all our former hopes were frozen to death." The collapse of the Sagadahoc colony dampened English interest in the region for years. As Gorges put it, it became "a wonderfull discouragement" for future attempts to colonize the Dawnlands.[21]

This fizzled venture, the *Richard* fiasco, and the ongoing mess at Jamestown hobbled the Virginia Company's initial efforts. Passages westward were dangerous and costly: each ship could be lost to storms or imperial rivals, underlying the importance of making the most direct passage with the most seasoned mariners possible. Making things worse were repeated foolish decisions to arrive in the late summer or fall, which raised the odds of encountering a hurricane head-on and all but guaranteed the settlers would suffer from short supplies and poor shelter in the harsh American winters. The colonies were further compromised by their backers' habit of selecting prideful men who lacked the necessary experience in farming or leadership to help colonies get off the ground. Gorges bemoaned that colonies were staffed by "men more zealous of gain than frought with experience how to make it." And their assumption that kidnapped men would willingly become their helpmates was a dubious one at best.[22]

Figuring out how to manage these risks and correct these mistakes were lessons that some Englishmen seemed determined not to learn.

Not far from Patuxet, a tall and athletic man named Epenow was coming into his own as a sachem. Epenow lived on Noepe, a southern Dawnlands island that Squanto knew well. It was just two canoe rides and one portage away from Patuxet, and its landscape was similar—though its beaches were much better. In the present day, the seaside haven of Noepe is best known as Martha's Vineyard.

Sails appeared on the horizon in summer 1611, putting Epenow and his council on guard. The approaching ship had been funded by another English imperialist, one Henry Wriothesley, third Earl of Southampton, with Edward Harlow as skipper. An alumnus of the ill-fated Popham colony, Captain Harlow had seen firsthand how captives were crucial to any colonial venture. He or one of his crew produced an account of the trip that has since been lost.

The main takeaway from the two brief secondhand summaries is that Harlow's journey did not go well. His only discernible talent as an explorer was making enemies. After he had been misled by Native informants from Mawooshen, he arrived at Cape Cod in a foul mood. There he took several men hostage and then raided Nantucket, where he took at least one more man prisoner. When Epenow and another man named Coneconam came to greet Harlow, the English laid hands on them, netting at least a half dozen men in total before sailing home.[23]

Wampanoag peoples found these attacks alarming. The 1611 raid would sour their dealings with Europeans for a decade to come. The English were slow to realize the long repercussions of their actions; for them it was merely a waste of an expensive voyage. Rather than revive interest in the Dawnlands, Harlow's disastrous trip confirmed suspicions that the region was too troublesome to colonize. And he had unwittingly stranded the men he brought back in England.

If these captives couldn't be used as guides in America, they were, in the eyes of their captors, little more than mouths to feed. One common solution to occupy idle young men in Stuart England was to send them off to become soldiers. That apparently happened to Sakaweston, the man stolen from Nantucket. "After many yeeres in England," one account reported, he "went a Souldier to the warres of Bohemia." He joined the many mercenaries who fought on the side of Czech Protestants who rose up against the Holy Roman Empire in 1618, in a key theater of the Thirty Years' War. Whether he survived the fighting is anyone's guess, but since he appears in no accounts of return voyages to his home, Sakaweston probably died somewhere on the continent.[24]

Epenow also faced a surprising fate: he was bound for the stage. More than one writer attested he "was a goodly man of a brave aspect," "strong and heavy," and "of so great a stature," meaning that he was attractive, muscular, and, by the shrimpier standards of early modern England, rather tall. His figure was so striking that people would pay to see him. Wriothesley, the earl who sponsored Harlow's ship and was likely the kidnapped Wampanoags' first master in England, was also a lover of the theater; he's best known to scholars as one of William Shakespeare's main patrons. Perhaps he was the person who lent Epenow out to showmen who displayed him "up and down London for money as a wonder." The captive's looks and "sober" demeanor fit nicely with what many English expected an "Indian" to look like. Drawing in mobs of ale-swilling Londoners looking to kill a little time, he greeted his audience with a simple refrain of "welcome, welcome."[25]

Displays of Indigenous men were so commonplace in the capital that Shakespeare mocked the practice. In *The Tempest,* the character Trinculo made the wry observation that while Londoners "will not give a doit [a coin of little value] to relieve a lame beggar, they will lay out ten to see a dead Indian." In *Henry VIII,* when a rowdy mob gathered outside the palace to celebrate the birth of the infant Elizabeth, a porter dismissed them as "youths that thunder at a playhouse and fight for bitten apples," sarcastically asking if "some strange Indian with the great tool" caused the mob to gather.[26]

Given that Epenow and Shakespeare were connected through Wriothesley, and considering the timely fact that both plays debuted after Epenow arrived in England, scholars have suggested that the Bard witnessed Epenow's show and thus the Wampanoag inspired the allusion to "some strange Indian." It's possible, but the man from Noepe was hardly the first such celebrity. By the 1610s, nearly two dozen Natives had been displayed in England. Moreover, Shakespeare implied that these showcases were cheap entertainment. Fickle crowds soon agreed. Not long after it began,

Epenow's act had "growne out of the peoples wonder." No doubt he was more tired of the shtick than anyone else.[27]

With his brief career in show business over, Epenow's handlers sent him to Gorges's house in the West Country. There he lodged with Sassacomoit, the man from Mawooshen, who had been stranded in England ever since the *Richard* ordeal. They got to talking. "At the first," Georges observed, they "hardly understood one the others speech," but in time they seemed to be conversing easily.[28]

Their respective Wampanoag and Wabanaki dialects are distinct languages, but they sit close enough on a linguistic spectrum to be mutually intelligible, like Danish and Norwegian. Sassacomoit might have explained the old injury to his arm while Epenow perhaps shared his experiences in London. Gorges insisted that Sassacomoit, who was far more fluent in English, tell him "what he learned by conference between themselves." It's clear now that their conversations moved rather quickly to solving their shared predicament because Sassacomoit had quite the story to tell. He reported that his new friend's homeland held a glorious secret. It had mines filled with gold.[29]

In hindsight, the ruse seems obvious. But the two had been careful in shaping their pitch. From his adventures in the Caribbean and Spain, Sassacomoit knew how much the English coveted the precious metals of their main rival. He couldn't invent new reasons to return to Mawooshen, especially since the English had been there more recently than he had. Attributing this exciting new information to a man from a different corner of the Dawnlands solved that problem. Since he proved he could speak to Wampanoags, he assured himself a passage home as a translator. For his part, Epenow had already told his captors that he had friends in Mawooshen, also doing his best to seem as useful as possible.

The pair were convincing; Gorges persuaded Wriothesley to raise yet another ship. The earl had invested in the Jamestown colony after the Popham venture failed and he was starting to get impatient that Virginia had yet to produce any riches. Captain Nicholas Hobson took command of this reconnaissance voyage. Along with Sassacomoit and Epenow, Hobson brought with him Manamet and Wanape, two of the Wampanoags taken by Harlow. It's easy to imagine the captives sharing a knowing look when the ship they had commissioned weighed anchor from the Isle of Wight in June 1614.

When they arrived at Noepe weeks later, though, the crew started to catch on that something was amiss. At first Epenow played the part of a helpful guide, but when a party of his kinsmen were allowed to board the ship, something about the tones of their conversation in Wampanoag put the English on edge. Anticipating that it'd be difficult to restrain Epenow's bulky frame, they had made him don a shirt with long sleeves to serve as a kind of straightjacket if necessary.

The next day, the islanders arrived in a fleet of twenty canoes, their bows drawn and arrows trained at the ship, calling for Epenow's release. The sailors' attempts to grasp his sleeves did little to stop him from slipping over the rail with a splash. His kinsmen sent a cloud of arrows flying over the ship's deck. English musketeers returned fire, possibly killing several members of the rescue party. Although the sources on the voyage made no mention of casualties, a later report from aggrieved Wampanoags—translated by Tisquantum—accused the English of murdering several men and described a violent fight that loosely resembled this 1614 exchange of arrows and bullets.[30]

It was now clear that Wampanoag country held no El Dorado. Disappointed and embarrassed, Hobson cut his losses. His ship "returned as shee went, and did little or nothing, but lost her time." Before heading back, the English would have released Sassacomoit, though the exact details of his homecoming are unclear. Gorges obliquely mentioned that one of the guides died shortly after returning to his home, though it is unclear if that man was Sassacomoit or one of the other men taken in 1611.[31]

For Epenow and Sassacomoit, their return home probably wasn't easy. Scholars of slavery point out that the primary psychological trauma for the newly taken is "social death" or "natal alienation": the total erasure of their rights and status in their previous life. All the Dawnlands men who were taken to England, including Tisquantum, did not face the kind of degradation of their humanity that we typically associate with the enslavement of Africans in the Americas. For that matter, their ordeals were nothing like the form of captivity and social death they were more familiar with: the wartime enslavement of Natives by other Natives.[32]

Because they had been enslaved as intelligence assets, as providers of linguistic, cultural, and geographic information that could give the English a clear advantage on American shores, their captors didn't even try to assign them new names. Still, we shouldn't assume that these men were always treated gently while overseas, as regular beatings or whippings were an expected part of life for servants and all other lower members of the household in early modern England. They were each at the mercy of their respective masters' tempers.[33]

While not facing permanent social death, these men did suffer a loss of status and a period of estrangement from their birth culture; moreover, their families had come to think of them as *literally* dead. Those who had been married when they were taken would probably return to find their wives had new husbands. They might feel like strangers at first, when they were almost unrecognizable, costumed as they were in foreign clothes. Their social resurrection at home wasn't just about rejecting the garments and roles the English assigned them. It could also be a painful process to reclaim their former standing in a community when they weren't quite the same person they were when they left.[34]

The details of these homecomings are obscure, especially for Sassacomoit. His return in 1614 marked his exit from the historical record. His absence in any following sources suggests that if he did make it back to Mawooshen alive, he was content to keep his distance from Europeans for the rest of his days.

The only confirmed survivor was the man from Noepe, who reappeared in a letter by the explorer Thomas Dermer years later. Epenow came to relish telling the Englishman about his daring gambit to return. The sachem "laughed at his own escape, and reported the story of it" with obvious glee.[35]

SIX

Capture

IT WAS NEARING THE LONGEST DAY OF the year at the small falls. The fields of maize, beans, and squash planted weeks earlier were now flourishing. Squanto's daily life was occupied with all the usual concerns of grown Wampanoag men—spending much of his time with his wife and children, if he had started a family, checking in regularly with his large network of relatives in his community or farther away, readying his gear for his next hunting or fishing excursion, and tutoring the boys who would become the next generation of councilors and warriors. The year was 1614. It had been twelve years since Gosnold's ship first entered Cape Cod Bay, seven years since Weymouth's raid in Mawooshen, and three years since Harlow kidnapped Epenow and the others from Noepe, Pamet, and Nantucket. The same fate now awaited Squanto.

Sassacomoit, Epenow, and the others were headed home just as Squanto's captors came over the horizon. Tisquantum was actually enslaved before Epenow was freed, with his kidnapping and the release of the men on Martha's Vineyard transpiring within a few weeks and a few dozen miles of each other. In fact, the men who came to rescue the Noepe sachem from Hobson's ship were well aware of the recent abductions. When they got into that firefight with the sailors, they were, in part, avenging not just Epenow's captivity but also the taking of Tisquantum and twenty-some more.

The timing was no coincidence. Epenow and Sassacomoit repatriated themselves with an artful lie, but it had ironic consequences—their escape plan inadvertently led to the enslavement of dozens more. Their fabrications triggered a brief gold rush among funders who had long been hoping to strike it rich when investing in American exploration. The English explorers who came to Patuxet in 1614 were racing ahead of the ship that was carrying Sassacomoit and Epenow. They hoped to be the first to

78

get their hands on the Dawnlands' gold. Leading this prospecting voyage was a man of boundless ambition with a taste for adventure.[1]

Of all the contenders vying to be the next Walter Ralegh, none could match this son of tenant farmers from a small village in Lincolnshire. Baptized in 1580 with the most ordinary name in England, he nonetheless became the most famous John Smith who ever lived. Much like the fashionable clothing of his day, Smith's accounts of his exploits were puffed up and colorfully embroidered. His autobiography reads so much like a picaresque novel that some scholars once dismissed it as fiction. Historians have since established that while Smith had a narcissistic tendency to paint himself in the most dashing light, the essential facts in his tales were true. A literal man of the Renaissance, he was quick to demonstrate his wide range of learning in navigation, geography, languages, science, ethnography, theology, and history, most of which was self-taught. His love of knowledge was always intertwined with his love of power. Most of his adult life was a tireless campaign to claim "new" lands overseas for England, a passion that inspired his personal motto: *Vincere est Vivere,* or "to conquer is to live."[2]

Smith's early career resembled the experiences of captured Natives in that he too was a warrior and former slave with a knack for self-preservation. Working as a mercenary soldier, first in France then in Austria and Hungary, he earned the title of captain. In one bloody episode, he singlehandedly defeated three Turkish soldiers in combat and took their heads as prizes—a feat that men from the Dawnlands would approve of. (These events inspired his personal coat of arms, which featured the above motto and three severed heads; he would later name a cluster of three American islands "the Turks' Heads.") In that same conflict, Turkish fighters took him captive and put him to work rowing on galley ships; he eventually escaped bondage in 1604.

Upon his return to England, he befriended the colonial promoter and scientist Thomas Hariot and refashioned himself as an adventurer in the mold of a West Country man, drawn to the attempts to colonize the Chesapeake Bay. He claimed that when he was an early settler in Virginia, he was again taken prisoner, this time by the Powhatan people. In his telling, his life was spared by the "princess" Pocahontas. Some scholars believe this tale to be a fabrication, and others suggest he was misinterpreting a theatrical ritual that was intended to establish the benevolence of the powerful ruler Powhatan. Thanks to his dramatic telling of this episode— and later distortions by the good folks at Walt Disney Pictures—Smith is now indelibly associated with Virginia although he was there for only two years, never returning after his departure in 1609.[3]

He was living in England in 1614 when a company investor named Marmaduke Rawdon noticed that the captives' tall tales had stirred up a new wave of interest in colonizing farther north. Rawson hired Smith to lead an excursion that left two months ahead of the other gold-seeking ship. The adventurer listed the search for "Mynes of Gold and Copper" as his top goal. Smith later claimed he was not following mere rumors; it seems he retrospectively shaded the truth lest he admit that he too fell victim to the Native ploy. That distant glint on American shores was a powerful lure.[4]

Smith commanded two vessels and a crew numbering between forty and fifty, plus one Wampanoag man. His name was Tantum; he was one of the men captured by Harlow from Cape Cod in the raiding spree that also ensnared Epenow three years earlier. Details of his time overseas are scarce. A couple of scholars have proposed that Tantum was in fact Tisquantum by another name, but once again, the theory that Squanto was a Zelig-like figure falls apart under closer inspection.

Smith's account of Tantum established that he was taken before 1614 and that he asked to be returned to Pamet, the town at the far tip of Cape Cod, across the water from the small falls. Tellingly, the name Tantum gave for Patuxet was *Accomack,* which means "on the other side"—a detail that only makes sense if he wasn't from there. What's more, the Pamet man's name also contradicts the theory, as he borrowed his title Tantum/Tanto from the manitou whom colonists depicted as the inverse figure of the Patuxet man's likely namesake, Squantum/Squanto. Born on the opposite shore and named after an opposing spirit, Tantum clearly wasn't Tisquantum, but in a peculiar way, the earlier captive was the reversed mirror image of the later one.[5]

Rawdon and Smith probably planned on taking this man with them before they even readied their ships: not only could he be a translator but his knowledge of the shore made him a finer navigational aide than any chart or instrument. Smith surely made him a promise of freedom for his service to ensure that he would not undermine him the way the Mawooshen men had thwarted the Sagadahoc colony. Tantum certainly wouldn't have contradicted any excited speculation about precious metals in America, seeing as those rumors ensured his passage home.[6]

Another opaque figure sailing with Smith was Captain Thomas Hunt, his second-in-command. Clues in Smith's account suggest Hunt was heavily involved in Atlantic fishing and Mediterranean trading, had been on voyages to the Grand Banks before, and had perhaps dabbled in coastal trade with Natives in the northern Dawnlands. The little else we know about Hunt comes from his will, written in 1617. He was then living in the North Sea fishing village of Aldeburgh in Suffolk. He was married to a woman named Katherine and possessed a rather sizable estate, equaling over £500 sterling.[7]

Arriving near the rich coves of Mawooshen in April, Smith's small fleet began tracing its way down the coast over several weeks toward Patuxet. Smith set about charting the shoreline, creating the most detailed map of the Dawnlands yet. But there was a small problem of geographic nomenclature. "Virginia" was now closely associated with the Chesapeake colony that Smith had left, so he took it upon himself to end the practice of calling this other region Virginia's "northern part." This beckoning land, "this Virgin's sister," needed a name of its own, a name to make the foreign feel familiar by promising potential settlers that it was a lot like home.[8]

He called it "New England."

When Squanto heard the cry that sails were approaching, he grabbed his bow and arrows, then took a moment to apply some face paint, which men always wore to greet foreigners. He was waiting on the waterfront by the time the two vessels rounded the harbor's outer spits of land.[9]

Standing ready with his sachem and fellow councilors, he was there to witness a small boat paddling to shore and came face-to-face with Smith and Tantum. Hunt may or may not have been with them. The captain was a short, stocky man with brown hair and whiskers who looked a little dwarfish next to Patuxet's taller leading men. Squanto also sized up Tantum, a man he almost certainly knew before he had been stolen in 1611, seeing as Pamet and Patuxet were in frequent contact.[10]

It might have taken a minute to recognize him. Tantum was now dressed like the other English sailors. But when he began to speak in Wampanoag his old neighbors were no doubt eager to hear his story and

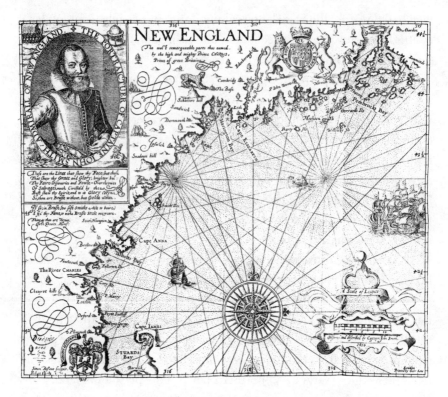

Captain John Smith's map of New England, 1616. Courtesy of the Beinecke Rare Book and Manuscript Library, Yale University.

to learn things that the captains didn't want them to know. Tantum was an effective emissary, and the strangers' initial overtures were well received. The Patuxet leaders treated Smith and his men with "much kindnesse," though there was obvious tension in the air. No one had forgotten Harlow's abductions three years earlier; the locals made sure to air their grievances over the raids, in a conversation translated by Tantum.[11]

The fragile peace soon broke. A vague "small occasion" provoked fifty Patuxet men—a group that must have included Tisquantum—to attack the English. The locals faced off with their customary clubs, knives, and arrows, and the visitors brandished their swords and fired their guns. Smith described this brief battle in a bizarrely offhand and passive way, as though his men had no active part: "Some [Natives] were hurt, and some slaine; yet within an houre after they became friendes." The sudden resolution to the violence was likely a defensive decision made by the sachem and his council. As the only bilingual person present, Tantum must have played a role in halting the fighting, but Smith did not reveal how the cease-fire came about in his terse account. The English left the small falls soon after making peace. As evidence of his gratitude, Smith returned his translator to his home across the bay.[12]

When the explorers left, the ramifications of this violent encounter were still sinking in. Tantum was the first Wampanoag prisoner to return alive, which must have stunned Tisquantum and everyone else. Just as Etichems did after Weymouth's raid, they were surely working on the assumption that when a man fell into the hands of enemies, he was doomed. Tantum had, by all appearances, returned from the dead. And just like Epenow, he had stories to tell. Even if no words passed directly between Tantum and Tisquantum that day, the returning figure must have made an impression on his counterpart. Named after a powerful deity, as was Squanto, the captive had found a way to return from the coat-men's land by virtue of learning their tongue, and he was now adept at smoothing over relations between newcomers and locals. It's not much of a leap to suggest that the resurrected Pamet man set an example that the Patuxet man would follow.

While Tantum had his long-awaited homecoming on the far side of the bay and the people of Patuxet buried the men who had died in the battle, the explorers sailed on, seemingly untroubled by the havoc they had wrought. The two captains seemed most bothered by each other, as they were "oft arguing" and butting heads. Perhaps because Hunt was the more seasoned mariner in these waters, he was quick to challenge his superior. Smith's rather high opinion of his own abilities no doubt made it hard to contradict him. They finally had a dramatic falling out midway through their journey. Later, Smith seethed over "the ingratitude of some, the malicious slanders of others, the falsenesse of friendes, the trechery of cowards, and slownesse [stupidity] of adventurers," then specified he was "chiefly" talking about "one Hunt." According to the explorer, his number two almost marooned him in an attempt to seize his charts of the region.[13]

Their disagreement was ultimately rooted in greed and competition. Smith alleged that his second-in-command was more interested in gaining a foothold in the ongoing fishing and trade in furs in the Dawnlands than in letting Smith and his backers profit from extensive mapping of the coast. Neither man had given up hope of finding gold—Smith tested soils

for mineral wealth everywhere they stopped. At an impasse, the two captains settled their differences with the simplest solution: parting ways.
Smith set a course back to England in August, leaving Hunt behind with
one of their two vessels, the *Isabella,* to catch codfish, then dry and process it for the voyage home. Still bearing a grudge against Smith, perhaps
feeling deflated by the lack of gold, Hunt thought of where he would be
taking the fish: to the Spanish Mediterranean. With that market in mind,
he realized that men made a far more lucrative cargo than cod.[14]

His first raid happened off Patuxet, where Hunt lured Tisquantum
and several others "aboard his ship to trade with him." He must have
made an extraordinary offer to give them "confidence of his honestie" as
they knew how dangerous it was to set foot on a strange vessel. It is tempting to guess at the bait: swords? armor? firearms? Maybe even a whole
pinnace like those sold to Mi'kmaqs? Whatever merchandise he dangled
in front of them must have had an immense upside to be worth the risk.[15]

Once the Wampanoags came over the rail, Hunt and his crew forced
them below decks—they had readied a compartment that could be locked—
and the vessel sailed off faster than any canoe could follow. The sailors
swiftly repeated the trick in Nauset territories on the inner arm of Cape
Cod, trapping several more men "under hatches." Likely the crew made
use of their fishing nets and lines to restrain and gag their prisoners, especially in the chaotic moments when they took on more captives. With
his human cargo secured, Hunt set the *Isabella* on an eastward course.[16]

A wooden ship at sea can seem uncannily alive. Riding each ocean swell,
the hull groans, taut lines whine and chatter, and sloshing water in the bilge
gurgles like an empty stomach, while wind inhales and exhales through
hatches.

These were the sounds Tisquantum and the twenty-odd other men
heard when they first clustered together in that fishy-smelling compartment, trapped in the belly of the beast. The newly enslaved were all men,
who could have ranged in age from their teens to their fifties; all were sachems, councilors, warriors, or powwaws in their communities. All spoke
the same language, but they came from two villages: Patuxet and Cummaquid. There could have been a feeling of general camaraderie in their
shared misery. No doubt most knew each other from inter-village sporting
matches and diplomatic meetings.

The captives might be allowed to keep their normal personal effects, carried in pouches around their necks: their pipes, tobacco, small medicine bundles, flints, and dried cornmeal. Within a couple of days, the last hints of paint on their faces and bodies would have faded. Without the oils and fats they used to moisturize, their skin could become painfully dry in the salt air. When their tobacco ran out, the heavier pipe smokers would endure a couple of uncomfortable days of nicotine withdrawal. As weeks passed, their hair, normally styled into elaborate braids and sometimes shorn along one side, would start to grow out, as would the stray whiskers on their face that they normally plucked.

It took roughly eight weeks to sail from Cape Cod to Málaga, Spain. The actual course would arch northward, carried along by the ocean's gyre of favorable currents and winds, with a likely layover in the Azores. Since Smith wrote multiple books covering all aspects of life at sea and detailed particulars of this specific expedition, we can know with reasonable certainty what conditions on this exact ship were like. The expedition's total workforce of fifty men was split between the two vessels. Hunt was master of the larger vessel, so he already had approximately thirty men aboard. The two dozen or so captives were only slightly outnumbered by the crew. The *Isabella* had a carrying capacity just shy of one hundred tons, with an approximate length of sixty feet from stern to bow.[17]

None of the crew agreed at the outset to sail on a slaving vessel. We know from records of the African slave trade that seamen universally considered transporting slaves on "floating dungeons" to be cruel and miserable work. Hunt would later claim that the captives damaged his ship—which, as we shall see, was most likely a ploy to get paid for selling them, but perhaps there was a moment early on when the Wampanoags attempted an uprising that defaced some part of the vessel. Eight weeks was a long time to keep the Wampanoags below decks and since Hunt wanted to sell them, he had an interest in keeping them healthy. Rather than impose conditions like those of the notorious Middle Passage, Hunt and his officers would be inclined to treat their captives more like passengers than cargo, though they would not have hesitated to whip any Patuxet or Cummaquid man who disobeyed, just as they would lash any misbehaving crewman. Hunt would have begun by letting them out to use the heads, the toilet holes at the bow that opened to the sea below. Bit by bit, perhaps using fresh air to reward good behavior, the captors and captives would build up trust in each other until the captain felt satisfied that his charges were pacified enough to share the weather deck with the sailors.[18]

The taken men would learn the seamen all had distinct roles to play. Hunt, the master, was in charge of navigation. He had two mates under him, one to command each watch. These four-hour shifts divided the sailors into teams: one worked while the other rested. Among themselves, the captives might have referred to Hunt as the sachem, as explorers noticed that some Natives made that exact analogy. The Englishmen seemed to lack powwaws, though, as Smith made no mention of a chaplain on any of his vessels. Still, the kidnapped men might notice how all the seamen bent their heads in prayer over their breakfast, sang psalms, and also recited another prayer at every change of watch.[19]

The ordinary sailors handled the helm, lines, and fishing gear, along with the drying, salting, and packing of their catch. Aiding them on most jobs were nimble ship's boys, who were usually the first to scramble up the masts to serve as lookouts, set the topsails, and untangle knotted halyards and sheets. On a larger ship, the crew included many specialists, including a carpenter to repair the hull and assemble shallops, a boatswain who maintained sails and ropes, a surgeon equipped with medicines and instruments, a steward who tended to the larder and galley, a cooper to fashion and fix casks, and a marshal in charge of discipline. In the pared-down crew that Hunt sailed with, seamen would likely wear more than one hat. Hunt would have charged his designated marshal and his mates with monitoring and punishing the captives.[20]

Over the next five years, Tisquantum would spend months at a time cooped up in wooden worlds like these. This voyage was his first time literally "getting his sea legs" and "learning the ropes," his first encounter with the sailors' diet of stale water, salted meat, and hard biscuits, and his first immersion in the routine of shipboard life. He would eventually make three more trips across the ocean, plus a couple more passages up and down the European and Atlantic coasts, logging at least twelve thousand nautical miles—a distance equal to half the world's circumference. When he made his final Atlantic crossing in 1619, no crewman would view Squanto as a mere passenger, as he would have spent more time at sea than many full-time sailors.[21]

This initial passage aboard the *Isabella* was where Tisquantum's education in English began. Atlantic crossings were often tedious, giving both crew and captives plenty of time to pass. Tantum's example of the usefulness of learning his captor's language was still fresh in the Patuxet man's mind as he and the other taken men started to converse with the sailors through pointing, gesturing, and repeating their words back to them, bit by bit creating a basic shared vocabulary.[22]

Later incidents in Squanto's life demonstrated he had a forward and confident personality, attributes that would have served him well on Hunt's vessel. Scholars don't know exactly why some people excel at picking up new tongues, but they believe a common trait of fast learners is their high tolerance for risk-taking. These aspects of his character might explain why he was the only Wampanoag taken from Spain to act as a translator, a choice that could not have been random. His fearlessness around the English and his abilities with their language were the two most likely factors that made him stand out from the others.[23]

Meanwhile, back in Patuxet and Cummaquid, the families of the stolen were inconsolable, crying out in sorrow and anger for days. They remained hostile toward visiting sailors for many years to come. A painful memory of the raid surfaced in the account of Plymouth colonists who met the aged matriarch of a family that had lost several young men when they went aboard Hunt's ship seven years earlier. Squanto, who was there to translate, told the colonists she had lost her sons, but given the expansive nature of kinship terms and the fact that she was quite elderly, she might have meant her grandsons. She was still so pained by her losses that she "could not behold us without breaking forth into a great passion, weeping and crying excessively."[24]

The cruel mystery of Hunt's intentions only added to the families' despair. They could hold out hope for the missing, as both Tantum and Epenow had returned years after their disappearance. But some of the men stolen by Harlow were never seen again. For years to come, the taken would exist in that ambiguous "absentative" state that Wampanoag speakers used for the missing or dead without breaking the taboo of speaking their name. If Tisquantum's mother was still living, she would tearfully refer to him as *nuneechanay:* "my late or absent child."[25]

Unfortunately, the grief-stricken families were correct to fear for their husbands, fathers, brothers, and sons. Of the two dozen taken, only one would return.

SEVEN

Spain

THE WEATHER WAS RELIABLY SUNNY and pleasant at the mouth of the Mediterranean in mid-October. On deck, Tisquantum and his fellow captives would have seen the Rock of Gibraltar, an enormous wedge-shaped headland standing fifteen hundred feet tall off the ship's port side. Its sheer limestone face formed the sharp corner of the European continent. To starboard lay the sloping coast of Africa, rising into mountains in the distance. Nothing was familiar about the shoreline that unscrolled in front of Tisquantum. His part of the Dawnlands was flat, sandy, and forested, surrounded by slate-blue water. The Andalusian coast was mountainous, rocky, and dry; a dull-green, beige, and brown land set against a turquoise sea. He and the other Wampanoags would glimpse small clusters of tiled-roof buildings set along foothills covered with grasses and scrub brush.

A day's sail past Gibraltar, they would get their first look at Málaga. The city sat at the base of a big hill. Winding walls zigzagged upward, leading to a handsome Moorish palace, called Alcazaba of Málaga, then continued up to an even higher fortress, the Gibralfaro castle. The two forts overlooked the harbor, and an intact Roman theater sat nestled in the hill's base. A boxy new cathedral, still under construction, rose out of the walled town center. Small fishing boats glided in and out of the harbor, their triangular lateen sails luffing and tilting with each tack into the wind. Also passing by were tubby high-masted galleons from points far away, smaller regional trading vessels, and galleys, the long and narrow oar-and-sail-powered ships that were still in active use throughout the Mediterranean.[1]

This land's deep history of conquest and commerce informed what happened after Squanto set foot ashore. A century before he was born, Málaga was a port in the Islamic Emirate of Granada. Spain itself was a fairly new nation, the product of a fifteenth-century matrimonial merger of

Málaga, ca. 1572, from Georg Braun and Frans Hogenberg, *Civitates Orbis Terrarum* (Cologne, 1618). Courtesy of the Library of Congress, Geography and Map Division.

Iberia's two largest kingdoms. Nine hundred years earlier Muslim powers from North Africa claimed the entire Iberian Peninsula. Fighting in fits and starts over the centuries, a long line of Christian kings clawed one province at a time out of the caliphate and into Christendom. Even before the fall of Granada in 1492 the co-sovereigns King Ferdinand and Queen Isabella and their clerical allies hoped to make their nation almost more Catholic than Rome itself.

Christopher Columbus's "discoveries" made Spain's rise possible. Once they arrived in the American tropics, Spanish conquistadors used the same strategies against Indigenous powers that their forebears had used against Islamic ones. These warriors laid siege to cities, overthrowing local rulers, intimidating locals with punitive violence, and replacing existing shrines and temples with cathedrals. When Spanish ships returned from the Americas, their holds were filled with gold, silver, and people. Indigenous wealth and labor transformed the upstart kingdom into a staggering global empire, which in turn made it Rome's most important ally during the religious schisms that roiled Europe during the sixteenth century.

In 1614 Spain was still indisputably the greatest power in the Americas, in Western Europe, and on the high seas. But Protestant nations were starting to close the gap. They had long looked at their Catholic rival's gains with burning envy and also righteous condemnation. Spain and England had negotiated a stable truce a decade earlier, as their mutual hatred had begun to mellow. They now had a straightforward, if still rancorous, commercial rivalry. The *Richard* affair in 1608 had been a tense moment, but a cease-fire in Spain's war with its rebellious provinces in the Low Countries the following year eased tensions. Peacetime also was a boon to the fast-growing communities of English traders based in the Spanish ports of Cádiz and Málaga.[2]

Although Thomas Hunt hoped to sell his trafficked humans in Iberia, technically it was illegal to hold or sell Native slaves on the peninsula, an exemption not granted to slaves from Africa. This policy stemmed from an earlier moral crisis in Spain's evolution as a colonial power, when holy men criticized the nation's mass slaughter and enslavement of Indigenous people. Prompted by the urgings of the Dominican friar Bartolomé de las Casas, the Spanish monarchy enacted sweeping reforms, known as the "New Laws," that outlawed most forms of Native slavery in 1542. The new policies did not free those already in bondage, and the overall enforcement of the ban was "contradictory and piecemeal."[3]

Over the following decades, enslavers relied on narrow reinterpretations, exemptions, and euphemisms to skirt the law or defy it. When enslaving Native people within Spain's jurisdictions, masters described their slaves as their wives, adopted orphans, or servants, framing them as part of their households. Or else they cast them as rebels and criminals, depicting them as prisoners of war or convicts serving out a sentence. Millions of Indigenous people under Spanish rule lived in these shadowy forms of bondage, which one historian calls "the other slavery," distinguishing it from the open, legal enslavement of Africans.[4]

The Spanish had complex relationships with the many peoples they called "Indios." In Málaga and the rest of the kingdom, Indigenous Americans, both free and enslaved, became a poorly defined ethnic caste, a subaltern group within a maturing global society. Seventeenth-century Spain had a "multicultural ethnoscape" that included numerous sub-Saharan African peoples, ethnic Jews, Berbers, Arabs, Turks, Kalinagos, Mayas, Nahuas, and even Tagalogs from the Spanish Philippines. Some of these people were enslaved, though most were not, at least not technically. Although the monarchy had laws that protected the rights of Indios, the Natives' advocates had to fight constantly to see that those laws were enforced. Still, many Indios unlawfully taken to Spain successfully sued for their freedom. Some of the protections offered to them were better than those given to enslaved Muslims who had been ensnared by a practice of forced conversion and servitude that scholars call "faith slavery." In at least a few instances, slaves from the Maghreb and the Middle East tried claiming that they were Indios in an attempt to be freed.[5]

The slave traders in Málaga primarily trafficked in people from nearer shores. Spanish and Islamic mariners regularly preyed upon each other's ships, taking captives for ransom or to sell into the lucrative cross-Mediterranean market for galley and household slaves. In the "traumatic cacophony" of dockside markets, the newly-taken would be paraded in front of buyers who inspected their bodies and teeth while their sellers shouted out their nationalities, ages, and occupations. A study found that the province of Málaga was home to ten thousand enslaved people in the sixteenth and seventeenth centuries. That very fact drew Hunt to the city: with so many slaves there already, it was a good place to unload twenty-five more.[6]

For centuries, historians have had only a foggy picture of what happened when Squanto and the rest of the captives on the *Isabella* arrived at the Málaga waterfront. A few vague sentences written by Ferdinando Gorges, John Smith, and the Plymouth colonists provided the only clues. But in 2012, Purificación Ruiz García, a Spanish scholar working in the Málaga provincial archives, came across two peculiar documents dated October 22, 1614. They were deeds for the transfer of twenty-five Native captives from an English captain to a prominent local priest. Although the name "Tomas Hunt" meant nothing to her, it was clear from the documents that something fishy was going on. When she returned to them eight years later, Ruiz was surprised to learn that she had found clues that could help solve a four-hundred-year-old mystery.[7]

These two documents both complement and contradict the sparse English accounts. They confirm a fact established by Gorges: Málaga's provincial governor and other local authorities had learned of Hunt's captives almost as soon as he arrived, and they stepped in before he had a chance to sell the men. The officials had "argued whether [the Natives] should be slaves" and seemingly reached a consensus that the captives should be converted instead, while living as servants in private homes.[8]

When asked to explain how the twenty-five men had come into his possession, Hunt gave a transparently false story. He did not disclose that he was on a voyage of discovery with Smith. Instead, the captain claimed that he had been fishing off Cape Breton—a part of Mi'kmaq territory, not Wampanoag lands—when the locals "came out to harass him with their armed canoes, hindering the fishing." According to Hunt, the assailants left him no choice but "to seize one of said canoes with twenty-five persons." "Even though he wanted to bring them back to land," the captain claimed that "he was unable to, so he was forced to carry them back on his vessel, not wanting to toss them into the sea out of Christian pity." Hunt's tale grew taller when he claimed that he planned to bring his captives back to England, but a series of storms had blown him off course and just happened to land him in one of the busiest slave-trading ports in Europe.[9]

The English sea captain was not fooling anyone. The terms of the transfer make it clear that he was selling the twenty-five Wampanoags as servants, but all parties involved were taking care to stay on the right side of the laws that forbid taking and selling Indigenous slaves. Hence why Hunt had to claim that it was the Natives' own fault that they were taken and that mere chance brought his ship to a place where he could unload captives for a profit. This particular kind of servitude matches the definition of "the other slavery": a scholar's term for the forms of gray bondage that Natives endured in Spain and its colonies. The transfer also resembled "faith slavery," the practice of Christians and Muslims enslaving each other on both sides of the Mediterranean.

The Wampanoags' new captor was Juan Bautista Reales, a priest from Iglesia de los Santos Mártires Ciriaco y Paula, one of the city's major churches. In the deed he pledged that he would "distribute" the captives "among Christian persons of good repute who would catechize them in the faith of Jesus Christ" so they might "receive the Holy Baptism." Reales's designated "virtuous and Christian" Spanish masters would be allowed to use their Native charges as servants for terms of eight years, after which, as long as the men had become Christians, "they will fully achieve their freedom." For handing over the captives, Hunt received "for each one of the said savages four hundred *reales*," or fifty Spanish dollars. Here the text was explicit—this was not payment for the men themselves but rather compensation for damage that Hunt's prisoners had supposedly inflicted on the ship and a reimbursement to the Englishman for the rations he provided the captives in their passage to Europe.[10]

The terms of the exchange gave Hunt plausible deniability against charges that he was an outright enslaver, and they also provided the Patuxet and Cummaquid men with some limited legal protections. The men could not be passed around as chattel slaves from one owner to another, and they each had a promise of freedom in eight years, or even sooner at the discretion of their respective masters. But the deal was hardly an act of Christian benevolence. Reales was a priest, not a friar: he had taken no vows of poverty. When he died in 1619, the cleric's estate included a town house in Málaga, four nearby farms, and part ownership of multiple warehouses and a sugar mill. Reales had played an active role in the expulsion of Muslim *moriscos* from Málaga years earlier, which had earned him the favor of King Philip III. The well-connected priest was also the father of three illegitimate children from two different mothers.

As Ruiz notes, one of the Spanish witnesses named in the document was the co-owner of Reales's sugar mill. She suggests that at least some of the men might have been put to work there. Or perhaps they could have been employed as field hands at one of Reales's farms. Given that Reales had a high social standing and many business interests around the city and province, he stood to gain from having close to two dozen servants, who were almost like free slaves, to "distribute" among his friends and partners at his own discretion.[11]

Even without concrete evidence of where the Wampanoags ended up, we can sketch out some of the likely experiences of those two dozen men. The first matter that would concern Reales as he acquired his bewildered charges would be their seeming lack of clothes. As Hunt would not have much extra clothing aboard, the bare-chested men would likely still be in their summer attire, which consisted of loincloths on snakeskin belts, moccasins, and not much else. Just as Spanish priests did when they tried to convert Native people in their American missions, Reales would give them breeches, shirts, and shoes to wear.

The Dawnlanders presented a challenge to Reales or any other devout Christian master who was concerned about their souls. Missionaries wanted their captives to have a general grasp of the Catholic faith before baptizing them. Initially they would rely on images, introducing the captives to iconic biblical moments, especially depictions of the Virgin Mary holding her infant son and scenes from Christ's Passion and his time on the cross. The men from Patuxet and Cummaquid might be surprised to see a mother without a cradleboard for her child and shocked to learn that the man enduring torture was not a fighter taken in war.

As their instruction progressed, they would learn the words to popular hymns and prayers. Once the converts were able to converse in Andalusian Spanish with some ease, true pre-baptismal instruction began. These lessons were "superficial" and "highly scripted," drilling the potential converts on the faith's most basic precepts: the single God, his three forms, his creation of the universe and humanity, the immortality of the soul, the existence of heaven and hell, Christ's virgin birth, his crucifixion, his message of peace, and his promise of salvation.

When the Dawnlanders' baptismal days came, each convert received a new name. Missionaries in the Americas liked to give Indigenous converts appellations that were "rich in Catholic association." The baptizing rite was not unlike the Wampanoag practice where adults could rename themselves after powerful manitous, especially after a significant life event or change in status. Following their christening, the converts would be ready for the next sacraments: confirmation, penance, and communion.[12]

At the time of this writing, Ruiz has begun combing through the two-hundred-odd volumes in the Málaga archives that could possibly contain evidence of the twenty-four Wampanoag men left stranded in Spain. She faces major challenges: the baptismal records of Reales's church, the Iglesia de los Santos Mártires, are lost. The fact that the men were never legal slaves means that there are no further bills of sale to recover. Still, she is optimistic that persistent archival digging may reveal the fates of some of those taken from Patuxet and Cummaquid. The only trace she has found thus far is an offhand mention of a servant in Juan Bautista Reales's household when his estate was in probate in 1619: a man named "Luis" who "pretends to be free." An inventory of the contents of the dead priest's house also mentioned a mattress that belonged to "Luis, free."[13]

If indeed Luis was one of the Wampanoags, these few words speak to his remarkable perseverance and his resemblance to his compatriot Tisquantum. For five years he had been trapped as a servant in a strange land, and now with his master dead, he had little more than some bedding to his name. Nonetheless, he knew it was illegal for Spaniards to treat him as a slave. By insisting that he was free, perhaps he held out hope that he would someday return to the Dawnlands.

Despite their own history of seizing Natives, some English imperialists were outraged when they learned about Hunt's actions in the Dawnlands and Spain. Smith cursed the captain for his "dishonest," "inhumane," and "vilde act" of slave taking, and Gorges called him a "devillish" and "worthless fellow of our Nation," though it is hard to see why what Hunt did was much worse than what Weymouth and Harlow had done earlier. Both Smith and Gorges were more than happy to benefit from the labor of abducted Dawnlanders, and they never voiced concerns for those who did not return home. Gorges kept Natives prisoner in his household for years at a time, repeatedly referring to some as "my Indian." Hunt's real crime was seeking personal profit by selling his captives as slaves rather than taking them to benefit shared English interests.[14]

The men who hoped to build England's empire were still in need of help. Outside of Jamestown, their only Atlantic colonies were a fledgling settlement on the previously uninhabited Bermuda archipelago and a tiny village on Newfoundland, the island European sailors had long called "Terra Nova." It was that latter colonial project, not the unrealized schemes in the Dawnlands, that first ensnared Tisquantum.

The timeline of Squanto's five years abroad is uncertain but not entirely unknown. The sources indicate that he "dwelt" for approximately "two year[s] or thereabout[s]" in London and spent at least the spring and summer of 1618 in Newfoundland (and possibly was there over the preceding year) and then was stranded in Plymouth, England, over that fall and winter before coming home in spring 1619. Therefore the maximum time he could have spent in Andalusia was a year and a half. The closest thing we have to a first-person account of Tisquantum's time overseas was the short summaries of his odyssey written by colonists who knew him, in which the only reference to Spain was that "he got away" from there: a hint that his stay was on the shorter side.[15]

At some point as early as October 1614 but no later than 1616, someone with an interest in the Newfoundland colony learned about Hunt's captives and assisted in Tisquantum's extraction from Málaga. The Spanish deeds provide new clues that could, with further research, explain what

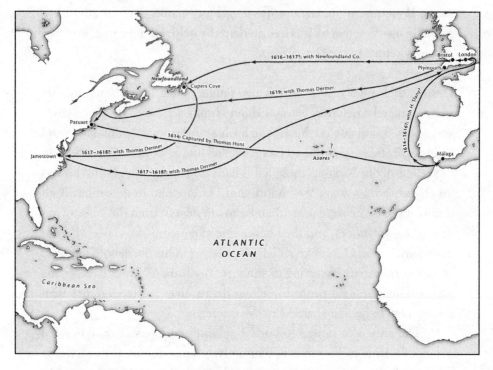

Tisquantum's Atlantic odyssey, 1614–1619. Erin Greb Cartography.

happened. Two English witnesses were named in both documents: "Enrique Loque" and "Joseph Toquer." Though their precise identities are not
yet known, they probably went by "Henry Locke" and "Joseph Tucker"—
or some other close cognates. They could have been Hunt's mates from
the *Isabella,* but more likely they were English traders living in the Spanish port who had been called upon to translate the negotiations between
Hunt and Reales.[16]

Those two Englishmen may have played a role in separating the
Patuxet man from the others. They could have alerted other English merchants to the existence of the captives (maybe even noting that one in
particular had a forward personality), or they could have acquired him
from the priest on the spot, while the ink on the deeds was still drying.
If they took custody of him immediately that October, then Tisquantum
never entered a Spanish household and had no exposure to the Catholic
faith. He could have been ferried off to London rather soon after arriving
in Málaga.

Again, the uncovered Málaga deeds shed a bit more light on this dimly understood moment. Hunt's lie that he took the men from Cape Breton Island, which lay just across Cabot Strait from Newfoundland, surely created a misunderstanding. The mistaken belief that the Wampanoags were from Cape Breton was almost certainly what prompted an Englishman—perhaps one of the English witnesses "Loque" and "Toquer," perhaps someone else—to acquire Squanto from Juan Bautista Reales or a subsequent master with the intent of sending him to Newfoundland.

Much like how fantasies of a gold mine led to Tisquantum's capture, another fib would change the course of his life.

Newfoundland was bigger than Ireland and half the size of Great Britain. As an early governor liked to point out, it also lay almost halfway between the Chesapeake and the Thames. The ancient home of the Beothuk people, this land had a long colonial history dating back to the eleventh century, when Norsemen led by Leif Erikson founded a short-lived settlement called Vinland at its northern tip. Fishermen from Europe's western fringes had been visiting Terra Nova since the days of Columbus, and it was "the one constant focus of English attention" in their first century of attempting to get a foothold on North America. The nearby Grand Banks were the heart of the booming transatlantic market in dried fish. The fishery's growth was tied to the Iberian Peninsula and the south of France, the biggest consumer base for salt cod. For the Mediterranean-based English merchants who hoped to dominate this traffic, there were fortunes to be made.[17]

In 1610, the brand-new Newfoundland Company sponsored a thirty-nine-man expedition, led by John Guy. The colonists planted themselves in Cupers Cove, a favorite inlet of fishermen in the southeasternmost corner of the island. Guy turned out to be an able governor, having learned from the mistakes of Virginia and the previously aborted Newfoundland colony. The well-provisioned settlement never faced a starving time. Its backers hoped their men would find some other profitable commodity, but ultimately fish remained the colony's only staple export. The company did not have an official monopoly on fishing, but its intent was to create a profit cycle where its sponsored fleet took the biggest possible share of the annual catch, peddled that fish in Lisbon, Cádiz, Seville, Málaga, Barcelona, and Marseille, then imported Mediterranean goods to the company's merchant investors in Bristol and London. In its early years, the tiny Cupers settlement was more of a base than a proper colony, an outpost meant to warn off any competing nation from claiming these shores.[18]

The colonists intended, but mostly failed, to trade with the local Beothuks. They rarely caught sight of them: by 1614 they had had only one brief sign language exchange. The settlers grew frustrated, not just because they hoped to profit from the fur trade but because they imagined the indigenes might uncover riches hidden deep in Newfoundland's unmapped interior. Reports from the failed colony from the 1580s speculated that the island held iron ore and silver in its soils.[19]

These elusive possibilities intrigued two officers of the Newfoundland Company: the brothers John and Humphrey Slany. The Slanys were typical of the enterprising businessmen who funded and staffed the overseas trading companies that started popping up in late Tudor and early Stuart England. Though they lacked the titles, estates, and fame of figures like Ralegh, Gorges, Popham, Wriothesley, and Smith, they could offer significant funding along with their valuable expertise in bookkeeping practices and the finer points of commercial law. Unlike the flamboyant knights and noblemen who dreamt of glorious acts of discovery and conquest, these backroom moneymen had a more grounded interest in the bottom line.[20]

The first born, John, lived in London, where his primary occupation was buying and exporting textiles. He served as the Newfoundland Company's only treasurer over its entire eighteen-year existence. The treasurer was the executive officer of the company, in charge of convening meetings of the council, appointing his own deputy, and writing correspondence to the colony's governor. John's younger brother Humphrey was the hands-on empire builder of the family. He had lived abroad in the Azores for a while, and he had traded extensively with the outlying islands of Spain and Portugal, across Mediterranean shores from Gibraltar to the Holy Land, down the coast of Africa to Guinea, while investing in both the Virginia and Bermuda Companies. One historian remarked, "There was hardly a trading venture of the period with which his name was not linked." Another ranked Humphrey among the more "audacious merchants of the time."[21]

As members of the company council, the Slany brothers had a hand in the 1610 instructions given to Governor Guy, advising that if the Beothuks were willing, Guy should appoint an Englishman to live with them to learn their tongue. Failing that, the council recommended that they recruit or capture a Beothuk man for the same purpose. A go-between would enable "farther discoverie" inland and ensure "a safe and free commerce with" Beothuks. Neither plan came to pass. Over the first four years, the colonists had yet to learn the name of a single Native and had hardly traveled more than three miles inland. The lack of a translator was a clear shortcoming.[22]

Humphrey, the brother who regularly passed through the south of Spain and had extensive contacts there, likely played a role in bringing Squanto into the custody of the Newfoundland Company. It could have happened either in Spain or in London. Whoever exactly "Enrique Loque" and "Joseph Toquer" were, they were likely tied to Málaga's English merchants and thus were known to Slany. From his involvement with the Virginia Company, Humphrey knew the prevailing theory that all the Indigenous languages of the coastal Northeast were related. Even when it later became clear that Squanto did not hail from Cape Breton, Slany still had reason to believe the Wampanoag might be able to speak to the Beothuks. This linguistic envoy could open up the fur trade in earnest, reveal whatever treasures the island's soil held, and transform the company from a glorified fishing concern into a more prosperous, diversified enterprise that exported pelts and minerals as well as cod.

Why would "Loque," "Toquer," or Slany want Tisquantum in particular? The simplest answer would be that he was the captive who was the most outgoing and capable of speaking to the English merchants. This theory fits with the ample evidence of Squanto's bold personality and the general profile of quick language learners. There were also good reasons why the English would take only one man: it was the cheapest, safest move. After all, Epenow and Sassacomoit ended up being stuck in England for several years at their captors' expense. While working as a pair, they'd conspired against their minders.

In time, when the Slany brothers learned Squanto's correct place of origin, they could get over their disappointment by considering the upsides. Men from Mawooshen and Noepe defied the English almost immediately because they had been returned from whence they came. A translator working outside his own homelands might be more loyal to colonists; taking him alone, without countrymen, would also speed up his progress learning the language. And should something happen to their asset, the Englishmen knew that there were more potential go-betweens in Málaga.

Moreover, the possibility of further rescues would be the most likely motivation for Tisquantum to volunteer himself and also prompt his compatriots to urge him on: the man who had the firmest grasp of the sailors' language and went along with them would be their best advocate to persuade a captain to bring them all home. If Squanto left Spain with any will of his own, it would have been on behalf of his fellow captives. That motivation aligned with his identity as a man bound by honor and obligation to the men he called *neematak,* his brothers.

Freeing them was a task he failed to accomplish, though surely not for a lack of trying.

EIGHT

England

WHEN SQUANTO JOINED THEIR HOUSEHOLD, John Slany was in his mid-forties and his wife Elizabeth was in her mid-thirties. Their London residence made quite the contrast to the cramped lower deck of a ship. Built of brick or in the timber-framed Tudor style, their townhouse would have multiple floors, glass windowpanes, and elaborate carvings on all the wood trim and furniture. Its cellar was stocked with wines, liqueurs, olive oil, currants, raisins, and dates; the interior air was freshened with cut flowers and dried herbs; a tapestry or two might have adorned the parlor walls.[1]

The Slanys' wardrobes held garments made of wool, linen, lace, silk, leather, fur, and whalebone, all tailored in the latest fashions, plus perfumes, potions, hats, heeled shoes, and jewelry adorned with gems and pearls. These luxuries came from John's involvement in the textiles industry and Mediterranean trade. He also collected rents from tenant farmers on inherited family lands in Shropshire and Essex. His houseguest would soon get some inkling of his line of work, since the lower floors of his house were also where he did much of his business.[2]

In Tisquantum's eyes, this smartly dressed man could appear to be an English atoskauwou, a prominent member of the ruling class. His townhouse in the Cornhill ward sat in the middle of London's emerging financial district. Standing almost next door was the Royal Exchange, a hub for dealing and trading. A few steps away was Cheapside, the city's main commercial thoroughfare. A couple of blocks to the north lay Guildhall, the seat of local government. John's uncle Stephen Slany was a longtime fixture there, serving as alderman, as sheriff, and finally as the city's lord mayor in 1595.[3]

Along with his position as the executive of the Newfoundland Company, John belonged to the prestigious Merchant Taylors Company, one

View of London, from Claes Visscher, "Londinum Florentissima Britanniae Urbs Toto Orbe Celeberrimum Emporiumque" (Amsterdam, 1616). ⊘Wikimedia Commons.

of the "Great Twelve" livery companies—powerful guilds that acted as private corporations, lobbying firms, charitable organizations, and, not least of all, social clubs. As a member, Slany had the chance to mingle with the king himself and other members of the royal family who came through the hall, plus countless other courtiers, noblemen, and members of Parliament. His own dinner table was frequented by similarly rich Londoners from his corporate and family networks.[4]

At the time the Patuxet man arrived, the Slanys were childless; their two sons had died as infants. Although he had no direct heirs of his own, John valued kinship in ways that his Wampanoag guest would admire. He

maintained close ties with his extended family, and in his will he made generous bequests to his siblings, nieces, nephews, cousins, and in-laws, passing along fine apparel, furnishings, and sums of cash, dividing up his ample real estate holdings among his closest male relations, and setting aside funds for the next generation's education.[5]

The Slanys belonged to the nearby St. Martin Pomary parish and they gave to the city's hospitals and almshouses that sheltered the poor. There's no explicit record of them trying to convert their captive, but given that every imperialist professed a desire to introduce Natives to the gospel, they surely would bring him along to St. Martin's on Sundays and to attend services on major holidays at St. Paul's, the Gothic stone pile atop Ludgate Hill. (Christopher Wren's Baroque cathedral replaced the medieval structure after the 1666 Great Fire of London.) The services in both churches were not that different from what the other Wampanoag captives might have witnessed in Spain. The mainstream Church of England kept much of the standard "smells and bells" of a Roman Catholic Mass, though they made many distinctions in their rites. Much like his brethren who were still trapped in Iberia, Squanto would likely have been intrigued by the iconography of the Virgin Mary with child and Christ on the cross.[6]

The willingness of these Christians to house the Patuxet man was hardly an act of charity since John was purposefully grooming him to serve his Newfoundland venture. It was not the first time Slany welcomed long-term boarders for business purposes. Like most prosperous merchants, he took in apprentices. These were young men of means looking to get into the textiles trade by serving as his assistant for a set term before beginning their own careers as merchants.[7]

After Squanto described his time in London to William Bradford, the colonist reported that he had been "entertained" (meaning "hosted") and "imployed" (meaning "put to use") by Slany. The word choices suggested the merchant treated him more like an apprentice than a servant. In the days immediately after he arrived, the Slanys might have tried presenting him as a private attraction for their fancy friends, piquing their curiosity about this "savage" from faraway shores. Squanto, like Epenow and others before him, might have begrudgingly played along. But the merchant and his wife would find they had stiff competition in drawing visitors to meet their "Indian." Another more interesting American had arrived in London around the same time Squanto did: the woman then going by the name Rebecca Rolfe who was, then and now, best known as Pocahontas.[8]

Billed as a "Virginian princess" and celebrated for her marriage to the Englishman John Rolfe, the twenty-year-old Pocahontas drew crowds in her public appearances at an inn or as a guest in the court of King James, where she watched a production of *Twelfth Night*. Her lodging in London was less than three hundred yards from the Slany residence, prompting scholars to wonder if the Patuxet man and the Powhatan woman crossed paths.

It's definitely possible. Her host in the capital, Sir Thomas Smythe, was part of Slany's professional circles. Both Smythe and Humphrey Slany were involved in the Bermuda and Virginia Companies. And the Slany brothers had a genuine reason to arrange a meetup: they were curious about the overall usefulness of their translator-in-training in all American colonies. They would want to know if their Wampanoag captive could understand the Powhatan language. They would be in for a disappointment. If those two Algonquian speakers met face-to-face, they would have to converse in English as their dialects are not mutually intelligible.[9]

We do not know how Squanto passed his days when he was in England. Outside the Slanys' door lay a cityscape that was considered chaotic and seedy in its own time. Soon after daybreak, the City of London came alive with vendors hawking wares and servants fetching groceries and water. The narrow lanes of cobblestones were awash with the contents of chamber pots and littered with the droppings of cart horses; teams of street scrapers could be found hard at work every day except Sunday. In colder months, dark smoke often shrouded the capital, as coal had recently surpassed firewood as the primary heating fuel for both household and industrial use. Stray dogs and robbers were common hazards at night, when pedestrians had to carry a lantern or torch to find their way along the unlit streets.[10]

Near his lodgings, Tisquantum would see regular public whippings at the pillory on Cheapside, and he might have joined the crowds of thousands that flocked to hangings of ordinary criminals at the gallows at Tyburn or to see pirates meet their end at the Execution Dock at Wapping. There was a similar young and rowdy element around the city's numerous brothels, taverns, and theaters, many of which stood on the opposite side of the Thames in Southwark. That is also where he would find the "gardens" where spectators watched dogfighting, bearbaiting, and bullbaiting. High above the stone arches of London Bridge, he would occasionally see severed heads of traitors mounted on spikes on the drawbridge tower. If the Patuxet man ever sought a reprieve from the urban din he'd find open meadows just half a mile north of Cornhill.[11]

The captive surely would want something to occupy his time and perhaps earn a bit of pocket money. Having spent his life crossing Cape Cod Bay and Massachusetts Bay in canoes, he would be particularly well-suited to operate a wherry, the rowboats that Londoners hired to flit around the city. There was only one span over the Thames River and the city itself was oriented around the riverbanks; a quick ride on the water was a lot faster and more pleasant than jostling across the congested bridge or through the capital's narrow streets. And there was constant demand for new hands: in the 1610s, the number of boatmen in the city was approaching twenty thousand.[12]

While this is merely a speculative point, there are good reasons to suspect that Squanto would be drawn to a maritime job. Wherries weren't that different from his familiar dugout and bark vessels. As the Mi'kmaqs demonstrated, Indigenous mariners could make the switch to European craft rather effortlessly. Not only did Tisquantum end up spending many months at sea in his years of exile, he also served as a coastal pilot for explorers and colonists once he returned to the Dawnlands. Later in the colonial period, many Wampanoags became whalers and seamen, preferring to work on the water if they could not continue their sustenance practices as hunters and fishermen. When the Patuxet man was stranded by the Thames, perhaps he made a similar choice.[13]

No matter what Squanto did outside the house, the work that most concerned John Slany was his progress in learning English. We actually know quite a bit about what the merchant sounded like because he was a contemporary of William Shakespeare's—Tisquantum was likely in England when the Bard died in 1616. Over the last few decades, theater scholars and linguists have carefully combed through archaic spellings, rhymes, and puns in the work of Shakespeare and his contemporaries. They have reconstructed a lost early modern version of the language for use in stage productions, called "Original Pronunciation" or "O.P."[14]

The four-hundred-year-old tongue that Tisquantum learned to speak can be at once familiar and peculiar to modern ears. Depending on the word or phrase, Stuart-era English can resemble Cornish, Yorkshire, Scottish, and Irish accents, with flecks of North American and Australian pronunciations as well. Actors and audience members alike sometimes compare it to the West Country accent that most associate with pirates from old swashbuckling movies. When Slany spoke, the way he said "reason" sounded like "raisin," "vice" sounded like "voice," "lines" sounded like "loins," while "whore" and "hour" sounded like each other and a bit like "o'er." This restored pronunciation can reveal hidden wordplay in early modern literature that has been lost over the centuries. The linguists who created O.P. caution that it isn't an accent, it's a "sound system" or "phonology" that was common to all early modern English speakers, who spoke with myriad local inflections.[15]

From the Patuxet man's perspective, one particularly vexing English phoneme was the consonant *r*. In present-day Britain, most speakers drop the *r* sound if it comes after a vowel, while most Americans outside the Northeast do not—think of how a Londoner might say "fathah" and "rathah" compared to how a Californian would say "father" or "rather." In Shakespeare's and Squanto's time, though, all Britons pronounced the *r* following vowels, often with a gruff "doggish" or pirate-like sound or a trill similar to how some Scots pronounce *r*. We can almost hear the roughly rolling letter tumble out of the mouth of Governor Bradford through his original spellings: "warr," "wher," "farr," and "ther," for "war," "where," "far," and "there."[16]

Both the *r* and *l* sounds were tricky for some Dawnlanders, who were reported to have "much difficulty" with them. Colonists who actually learned local tongues noted that the *l*, *n*, and *r* sounds changed in neighboring Algonquian dialects, with Wampanoags pronouncing *n* in some words that Nipmucs said with an *l* and Wabanakis said with an *r*. To some English ears, it sounded like their Native neighbors used *n* for *l* and *n* for *r*, "calling a Lobster a Nobstann." Similarly, the Plymouth settler Edward Winslow reported his Indigenous friends called him "Winsnow." When Squanto was first learning the language, he likely pronounced his hosts' surname as "Snany" and called his temporary home "Engnand." The *th* sound could also be a stumbling block, but perhaps he simply imitated those who pronounced *th* as *t*, like how many Irish speakers still do in the present. Given that Wampanoag had no phonemes exactly like *j* or *z*, perhaps when he was still a new learner, he referred to his hosts as "Chon" and "Enisabet."[17]

There's no indication that anyone in London took pains to instruct Tisquantum formally in English. He seemed to have learned mostly through immersion, which experts believe is the fastest way for anyone to pick up a new language. Though in their everyday exchanges with him, the Slanys would surely make an effort to improve his pronunciation and grammar, while explaining any words or phrases that puzzled him. Once he was proficient, the apprentice was ready to serve his master's company.[18]

That moment came in the spring of either 1617 or 1618 when Slany put Squanto on a Newfoundland Company ship bound for Cupers Cove. It would depart no earlier than May to make sure they were past the peak of iceberg season. The vessel would be laden with fishing gear, livestock, and

The settlement at Cupers Cove in the seventeenth century. From Daniel Woodley Prowse, *A History of Newfoundland from the English, Colonial and Foreign Records* (London, 1895).

provisions for the colony, plus a store of trading goods that Slany hoped his apprentice would peddle among the Beothuks in exchange for furs. After two months at sea, they neared Newfoundland's Avalon Peninsula. The captive saw a shoreline not unlike parts of the northern Dawnlands: it was rugged, windswept, and wooded in parts. When he came ashore in Cupers, he found himself in a small village of houses. Alongside the few meager cottages were pens filled with hogs. Beyond that lay fenced pastures where goats roamed. Close to shore were open-air sheds where fishermen dried and salted their catch for export to the Mediterranean.[19]

The fresh air and natural vistas must have appealed to Squanto after years spent in the claustrophobic confines of London. Perhaps for the first time in years he'd get the chance to fashion his own bow and hunt. But he definitely would not feel "at home" in this alien land; he once again had to adapt to being a stranger in a new community that was small and largely seasonal. The three dozen or so permanent English settlers were mostly men with a few women and children in tow. Hundreds more fishermen appeared over the summer months, setting up temporary camps across the shore and sometimes dropping by Cupers. The colony's new governor, John Mason, was there to welcome him, having no doubt heard of this envoy in letters from Slany. Few sources from Mason's term survive. All that is left is a single letter and brief tract by Mason himself. In both, he mentioned his intention of trading with the Beothuks.[20]

The islanders preferred the northern side of the island and were reluctant to approach colonists, much less conduct business with them. Then and now, outsiders knew very little about them. Whereas most Indigenous nations from the Northeast survive to this day, the last Beothuk died in the nineteenth century. We don't know how many people lived in Newfoundland before contact. Most estimates range from five hundred to one thousand, which would mean that the entire island's population was less than half the size of Patuxet. Archaeologists suspect that limited resources, especially the lack of major crops, checked population growth. If Tisquantum caught sight of any of them, the main likenesses he would see between them and his people would be how they looked: they had ethnic features vaguely like his and they made their clothes from tanned hides and painted their faces. They also had oval-shaped portable houses much like those found in the Dawnlands.[21]

Beyond that, the differences start to pile up. Beothuks did not farm. Their island's long winters and cool summers—plus the added effects of the Little Ice Age—made it near impossible to raise corn, beans, and squash. The locals were therefore nomads who lived off foraging, hunting, and fishing. The precious few words from their language that have been written down do not have many cognates in nearby dialects. Linguists believe that the Beothuk tongue belonged to a distinct spur of the eastern Algonquian family without any close linguistic siblings.[22]

When the man from Patuxet got the chance to explore the forested interior, he would discover a subarctic boreal landscape that was not nearly as biodiverse as his part of the Dawnlands. The only big game were caribou and bears; deer and moose were not native to the island. Newfoundland also lacked the wider range of "fall back" species that were common on the mainland. There were no porcupines, groundhogs, raccoons, squirrels, rabbits, or snakes, those smaller animals that Indigenous hunters turned to when larger prey eluded them. Beothuks instead mostly relied on seabirds, shellfish, fish, and marine mammals for additional protein and fat.[23]

Memories of Norsemen surely lingered in the islanders' oral tradi-
tions, giving them good reasons not to approach. The two surviving sagas
of the Norse colony indicate that encounters between the Beothuks and
Vikings were brief and brusque. Over the sixteenth century, Portuguese,
English, and French explorers captured a few men from the vicinity of
Newfoundland, but the sources are too vague to determine if those cap-
tives were actually Beothuk or one of their neighbors, the Inuit, Innu, or
Mi'kmaq peoples.[24]

By the seventeenth century, Beothuks refused to approach newcomers under almost any circumstance. The islanders, who had only rare contact with mainland Native peoples, did not have robust traditions of diplomatic politics or armed defense like the Wampanoags and Wabanakis to
the south, who lived in a more crowded and competitive landscape. For
these isolated people, the safest route was always retreat. Even after a band
of Beothuks had a rare and pleasant encounter with John Guy in 1612, they
decided their next exchange would be a faceless trade: they left furs hanging on a pole at the site of the earlier meeting.[25]

Once the man from Patuxet arrived, the new governor, Mason, tried
to repeat Guy's success and restart the trade. When his term was over, his
only remark on "hope of trade with Salvages" was a disenchanted comment
that he *could* subject his reader to lengthy details, but all that "may suffice"
was "Verbum sapienti," meaning: a word to the wise. His weary tone implied that Beothuks kept their distance while Tisquantum was in Newfoundland, though not for a lack of effort on the part of the English.[26]

Even if he did cross paths with Beothuks, any attempt by Squanto to
reach out as an interpreter had clearly failed. It was the many differences
between Native peoples, not the few similarities, that mattered. Tisquantum had little in common with these mobile bands who never raised crops
and spoke an almost unrecognizable language. The islanders might realize
that he was not English because of his skin tone or because the Wampanoag words he offered as a greeting sounded faintly familiar, but why would
they trust him? To them, the translator would have appeared to be one
with the colonists. He could speak their language, he was dressed in their
clothes, and he was clearly there to serve their interests.

There was no common Indigenous identity connecting the peoples
of North America at this time and there was no previous relationship between these two peoples separated by almost a thousand miles of coast-

line. Nonetheless, the Patuxet man's stay on the Beothuks' island offered him a number of lessons he would carry with him. The settlement at Cupers was, in essence, a preview of what he would later see English colonists attempt in his own home. Those weeks spent attempting to contact the Beothuks was his first experience observing Englishmen trying to make their way through wooded lands on unfamiliar shores. Although he might be as mystified by aspects of the Newfoundland landscape as they were, no doubt he impressed Mason and the others with his ability to track animals, find drinking water, improvise shelter, and forage for food. And they also had the chance to teach him about some of their technologies, especially their compasses, maps, gunpowder, and firearms.

Squanto's time in Cupers represented a moment of limbo in his Atlantic odyssey. Once again he found himself stranded in an unfamiliar place, but this time he was closer to home in more ways than one. Unlike when he was in Málaga and London, his understanding of his surroundings soon equaled or surpassed that of his minders. Though he was still a lone outsider in the community, his status had risen. With his growing command of English, he could make his thoughts known. Leading men viewed him not just as a curiosity but also as an authority. When he was helping these colonists in their clumsy attempts to find their way around Newfoundland, Tisquantum was starting to figure out his own way home.

NINE

The Angry Star

A DARK MOOD OF "INVETERATE MALICE" hung over Patuxet for years after Squanto's capture. The families of the taken had never stopped mourning, and any sighting of ships on the horizon filled them with anger and dread. The Dawnlanders' rage was evident when a French vessel came from the Acadia colony in 1616 to trade for beaver pelts. As the ship sailed near Cape Cod, a violent storm caused it to wreck by Pamet. The sailors scrambled ashore, recovering most of their rations and wares from their ruined hull. As they set up camp and tried to hide their trading goods, they considered how they could possibly be rescued. Unlike all the previous landfalls of European sailors, no locals came to greet them.[1]

News spread about this vulnerable group of mariners who had no way to escape. Grieving men from all sides of Cape Cod Bay—including, no doubt, Tisquantum's kinsmen—banded together. They were seeking blood justice for the men stolen by Harlow and Hunt. These avengers patiently stalked the sailors for days, waiting for the right moment. Then they attacked and killed all except five men. The survivors "wept very much" as they were separated. Each faction of the vigilante force brought captives back to its respective town, surely also carrying the severed heads and hands of those they had slain. Their prisoners were "sent from one Sachem to another, to make sporte with, and used them worse then slaves." Their masters only fed them "such meat as they gave their dogs." They ordered the Frenchmen to fetch firewood and water, which were degrading tasks for adult men.[2]

Soon thereafter a band of Massachusett warriors attacked another French ship captained by one Monsieur Finch. The ringleader later confessed their motive was robbery, not revenge—no European had ever stolen away their men. When Finch dropped anchor in what is now Boston Harbor, a party, pretending they wanted to trade, boarded with knives hidden in their belts. When their leader, Pecksuot, gave a signal, they slaughtered all aboard. Once they offloaded the booty, they set the ship ablaze. Fifteen years later, a colonist near Boston found a likely token from Pecksuot's heist when he dug up "two pieces of French money: one was coined in 1596."[3]

These two predations demonstrated that all the goodwill that the Wampanoag and Massachusett peoples had offered the coat-men from 1602 to 1614 was gone. Whether or not they could tell the difference between the French and English—and they probably could—most did not seem to care. The angriest had seen enough treachery from the Europeans. Everything they did to the French was a warning to any other nation of coat-men. If they dared come near, they were going to pay with their treasure and their lives.

In years to come, the Wampanoags' values of condolence and reconciliation won out over their fury. One forgiving sachem at Pamet received a blond-haired man as a captive and took mercy on him. He was kind to the man, permitting him to marry a Native woman. They had a son together, though *père et fils* died when the boy was just a toddler. Men from the *Mayflower* later opened their shared grave in their clueless weeks on the Cape. The grave revealed that his captors had come to accept the sailor into their community and honored him as a husband and father. They had given him a proper high-status burial. Lining his grave with boards and mats, they had dressed his body in his seaman's cloak and breeches. They doused his corpse with red ochre and included his personal effects to take to the afterlife: "a knife, a packneedle, and two or three old iron things." When the English found him, the Frenchman's skull had "fine yellow hair still on," and "some of the flesh" remained on his bones.[4]

Nestled with him, wrapped in a smaller shroud, was the skeleton of his son. The people who buried the child dressed him with "bound strings and bracelets of fine white beads." In a rather heartbreaking gesture, they made sure he had toys to play with in the next world: "a little bow, about three quarters long, and some other odd knacks." The Frenchman would not have thought to (or been able to) make such a toy for his son, indicating that his wife's male relations also took an interest in the boy's upbringing.[5]

Later, the Patuxet man also demonstrated sympathy for the plight of the enslaved French sailors. When he returned home in 1619, Squanto helped negotiate the release of the still-living captives from their masters. Perhaps he saw parallels between their ordeals and his own.[6]

Decades after the fact, other Wampanoags reconsidered the consequences of how they treated the Frenchmen. Their change of heart was informed in part by what happened soon after they attacked the sailors: a devastating epidemic hit the Dawnlands. Only then did they reconsider some defiant things the enslaved sailors said. One had a book with him that he regularly read—probably a Bible. When his captors asked him what it was about, he told them it said "there was a people like French men that would come into the Country, and drive out the Indians." In retrospect, it sure sounded like an accurate prophecy of what would come in the following decades. Another Native informant recalled that one captive (perhaps the same man with the book) cursed his captors "for their bloudy deede, saying God would be angry with them for it, that hee would in his displeasure destroy them." The locals scoffed at this, boasting "that they were so many, that God could not kill them." These stories reflected a common feature of Indigenous storytelling, in which events from the past were later interpreted as portents of the present.[7]

It was clear at the time that a furious manitou had unleashed his wrath. Starting in 1616, a terrifying sickness swept across the coast from north to south, likely coming from the fishermen who traded with the northern Dawnlanders. The first sign of infection was a painful all-consuming headache. Then came fever and an eruption of pockmarks all over the body. As patients deteriorated, their skin turned yellow, a sign of liver failure.[8]

Although the precise pathogen is unknowable, it has not stopped a number of doctors from making forensic diagnoses as though it were a puzzle to be solved or a medical school detective game. They have proposed a long list of candidates: smallpox, measles, yellow fever, influenza, chickenpox, bubonic plague, trichinosis, cerebrospinal meningitis, hepatitis A, hepatitis D, and, finally, in one of the most recent and esoteric diagnoses, leptospirosis complicated by Weil syndrome. Smallpox remains a prime suspect, but it's possible that more than one infectious disease hit the Dawnlands in waves, which would explain the various and inconsistent symptoms.[9]

This catastrophic event, called the "Great Dying" by some Wampanoag writers today, remains the most famous example of a "virgin soil epidemic." To Natives who had never encountered common European infections—and thus had no antibodies to them—every foreign infection acted like a novel virus. A pathogen that was benign to previously exposed colonists could be overwhelmingly lethal to Indigenous Americans. Estimates of the death rate among Dawnlanders range from 75 to 90 percent. The region's peoples shared a common practice of visiting to offer prayers and comfort when they heard a friend or family member was ailing; this culture of condolence only hastened the spread. When well-wishers started falling ill and the plague flared up in a new village, the Natives began to flee the outbreaks. But these refugees spread the disease further, as many of them were already incubating the infection.[10]

As an Englishman put it, "the Plague fell on the Indians with such a mortall stroake that they died on heapes." At the peak of the epidemic, entire villages were stricken, with no one healthy enough to nurse the others. The few who were recovered had to abandon the bodies of their loved ones, leaving them unburied. When the living fled the ravaged towns and campsites, scavengers came to eat the dead: ravens, crows, vultures, opossums, bears, coyotes, and wolves—and maybe even the Natives' dogs who had gone feral—all picked the bones clean. Over a decade later, colonists still came across clearings strewn with sun-bleached skeletons. The "sad spectackle" they witnessed seemed positively biblical. To one Christian writer, the bones evoked the skull-shaped hill where Jesus died: "It seemed to mee a new found Golgatha."[11]

The religious implications were even more foreboding to Wampanoags and their neighbors. The epidemic triggered a spiritual crisis across the Dawnlands that echoed for decades to come. The survivors wondered what sort of vengeful god could have done this to them. They were troubled to see that Europeans were spared: the obvious conclusion was that a frightful manitou with powers beyond imagination protected the coatmen while he punished Natives.[12]

Later colonists spoke to locals still searching for answers, trying to understand how their world had been so irrevocably changed. For some, it meant drifting away from manitous they once esteemed. Some confessed they had become "more and more cold in their worship to Kiehtan; saying in their memory he was much more called upon." Others noted that the Narragansetts, who had been spared in the epidemic, lavishly praised Kiehtan for preserving them. Perhaps Wampanoags needed to win back his affections.[13]

In the 1650s and 1660s, colonists spoke to "ancient Indians" who recalled that around the time the sickness hit Massachusetts Bay and Patuxet, they saw an omen in the sky. It appeared in the southwest, the direction of Kiehtan's house, the land of the dead. For thirty nights, the "blazing Starre" crossed the sky with a long bluish streak trailing behind it. It had to be a message from a manitou, perhaps the same one who sent the plague. The elders remembered that when they saw this eerie apparition, "they expected some strange things to follow."[14]

The "star" over Patuxet was a massive chunk of cosmic dust and ice, looping around the sun at the end of a voyage from the far reaches of the solar system. It was the third and largest comet spotted from earth in 1618, appearing in the night sky in early November. The comet grew brighter for a few weeks before breaking into pieces and dimming in late December. At its maximum shine, it was visible in the morning sky. Outside the Dawnlands, observers documented their sightings in Britain, Italy, the Holy Roman Empire, Persia, the Kingdom of Korea, Imperial China, and the colonial Philippines. Anxious theologians and natural philosophers in Europe published a flurry of tracts considering its significance and origins. The Great Comet of 1618 holds a special place in the history of astronomy: it was the first comet observed through a telescope.[15]

People across the early modern world considered comets to be omens; three in a row were an undeniable warning. A catastrophe could be imminent. England's King James I, who was facing both domestic unrest and new international tensions, tried to tamp down any alarm. When the Great Comet appeared, he quipped that the latest "blazing star" was "nothing else but Venus with a firebrand in her arse." As it started to inspire doomsaying broadsheets, he wrote a poem. The first three stanzas suggested the meaning of the comet was unknowable beyond serving as a vague reminder to repent:

> Yee men of Brittayne wherefore gaze yee so,
> Upon an angry starre? When as yee knowe
> The Sun must turne to darke, the Moone to bloode,
> And then t'will bee to[o] late to turne to good.
>
> O bee so happy then whilst time doth last,
> As to remember Doomesday is not past:

And misinterpret not with vayne conceyte
The character yow see of Heaven's heighte:

Which though it bringe the World some newes from fate,
The letter is such as none can it translate:
And for to guesse at God Almighties minde,
Were such a thinge might cosen [trick] all mankinde

The poem gives us a literal sense of the monarch's voice. One can "hear" his Scots-inflected O.P. in the ways he rhymed "bloode" with "good" and "conceyte" with "heighte." Both his verse and joke also captured James Stuart's distinctively crass and pompous personality. His chiding tone would seem hubristic a few months later when religious wars once again roiled the continent and his wife Anne of Denmark died.[16]

Closer to home, James faced ongoing clashes with dissidents who were, as he might put it, a real "firebrand in the arse" for the Church of England. In parishes across the kingdom, groups of fervent believers condemned official Anglican rites and doctrine. They referred to themselves as "the hotter sort of Protestants" as the word "puritan" had negative connotations even then—in Shakespeare's 1602 comedy *Twelfth Night,* the dour, fun-hating, and self-important character Malvolio was described as "a kinde of Puritane." Historians now reject this popular caricature, framing these "hot Protestants" as nonconforming and vibrant thinkers who were indeed censorious but were not always humorless.[17]

As this diverse movement was taking shape in the 1580s, the preacher Robert Browne began encouraging "hot Protestants" to break away from their Anglican parishes and form independent congregations. These "Brownists" followed Martin Luther's call for a "priesthood of all believers" by rejecting the top-down dictates of the national church. Their list of reforms was long: they wanted to do away with the profane costumes, rites, symbols, and imagery that they associated with the Roman Catholic Church. They especially objected to the Anglican Book of Common Prayer, believing that God's truth could only be revealed in the Bible itself. Like most puritans, their preferred text was the Geneva Bible, an English translation with copious annotations based on the teachings of John Calvin. This Swiss theologian preached that all humanity was depraved, but God had predestined a select number of souls to be saved from damnation.[18]

This stern doctrine appealed to an independently minded congregation of hot Protestants in the village of Scrooby in Lincolnshire, some of whom would meet Squanto when they became the leaders of Plymouth Colony. The Scrooby group shared Browne's distaste for episcopal hierarchy and subscribed to Calvin's view of God's will. They believed that all sworn members of their congregation were among the few "elect" or "visible saints," who lived godly lives as they followed their fated path toward salvation.[19]

Radical Brownists had been imprisoned and executed during the reign of Elizabeth, but many puritans hoped James I would support some of their proposed reforms when he took the throne in 1603. Their optimism faded once the newly crowned king called for all English Protestants to obey "one Doctrine, one discipline, one religion." He made his feelings on dissenters clear: "I will make them conform themselves, or else I will harry them out of the land, or else do worse."[20]

The king directed his church to stamp out dissenting views within the clergy. His bishops soon expelled as many as three hundred nonconforming ministers. Still, James's anti-puritan crackdowns were mild when compared with those of his predecessor, Elizabeth I, or his son, Charles I. At the parish level, ministers who survived the purge had "a fair amount of discretion to pick and choose among the church's ceremonial requirements." But in the view of the Scrooby minister John Robinson, the Stuart monarch had cast a "thick Antichristian darkness" over England.[21]

By 1607, Robinson and many others in the Scrooby congregation had seen enough. Fearing persecution, they made plans to move to the Netherlands, a haven for dissenting English Protestants since the 1580s. After a couple of failed attempts to leave and a brief stay in Amsterdam, the Scrooby exiles settled in the university town of Leiden in 1609. Many writers have since described the Plymouth founders as "separatists." In their own time, that label was a smear favored by their critics who saw them as a seditious lot. Centuries later, Yankee historians called them separatists as a compliment, seeing these "Pilgrims" as the freedom-loving progenitors of New England's Revolutionary spirit, whose voyage on the *Mayflower* was a kind of precocious declaration of their independence.[22]

Both these views distort the truth. In spite of their decision to start a breakaway church and flee the country, the Scrooby puritans "walked a fine line" by resisting Anglican liturgy while rejecting the positions of hardline separatists. When in Holland and later in the Dawnlands, their congregation artfully kept its distance from the Church of England while still professing their allegiance to the church's supreme governor, James I. They maintained ties with some Anglican ministers, they admitted members who had never explicitly rejected the national church, and they kept fellowship with many puritan-leaning Anglicans.[23]

After living in Leiden for the better part of a decade, the English expatriates grew discontent. Many were struggling to earn enough to live, working for mean wages as hatters, glovemakers, wool carders, and twine makers. Parents worried that their children were being corrupted by the profane temptations of Dutch society. Only adding to their problems, the Netherlands' climate of tolerance was turning chilly. A battle of rival theologies threatened to tear their national church apart. When sectarian riots broke out in the streets of Leiden, a mob of Calvinists mistook a sixty-three-year-old church member for an opponent and knocked him senseless with a cobblestone. Most concerning, the Dutch Republic appeared to be on the precipice of war; it was nearing the end of a twelve-year truce in their long war of independence from the Habsburg Spanish monarchy.[24]

By 1617, the congregation leaders—the church elder William Brewster and the minister John Robinson—started reaching out to officials in London and Virginia to see if they could migrate to Chesapeake Bay, while downplaying rumors that they were radical separatists. The idea that colonies could be refuges for religious minorities was hardly a new one. Almost a decade before Sassacomoit's captor George Weymouth floated the idea of letting Catholics found a colony in the Dawnlands, a hot Protestant named Francis Johnson made a brief attempt to start a settlement on the Magdalen Islands in the Gulf of Saint Lawrence in 1597.

The venture failed almost the instant it began. Johnson's expedition lost a ship en route and then faced stiff resistance from Breton and Basque mariners who were using the islands as a base for fishing, whaling, and walrus hunting. Once he made it home, Johnson and his supporters decamped to Amsterdam instead. In August 1618, when the Leiden group were still lobbying for approvals and funding for their migration, nearly two hundred members of Johnson's old congregation departed Holland ahead of them, bound for Virginia. Despite the fact that more English settlements in North America had failed than had succeeded, the far-off continent was starting to look like those exiled puritans' best option.[25]

As they considered their next move in late 1618, the "angry starre" glowed overhead. There is no explicit record of their reaction to the comet, but Leiden was awash in printed sermons from across Europe that declared it was God's signal that some world-transforming event was nigh. The rising threat of wars between Catholic and Protestant powers made these prophecies feel especially grave. To the Scrooby saints, even an ambiguous heavenly message added urgency to their plans to uproot their church and seek new soil where it could flourish.[26]

At some point between 1616 and 1618, when Tisquantum was still in New-foundland, he made a new friend. Thomas Dermer was an English adventurer and a colleague of John Smith, who once praised him as "an understanding and industrious Gentleman." In 1615, before Dermer came to Cupers, Smith hired him to be his number two in his follow-up voyage to New England, replacing the disgraced Thomas Hunt. It was a curious coincidence that Dermer, who eventually brought Squanto home, held the same position as the man who abducted him.[27]

Smith's planned return to the Dawnlands was ill-fated. The first time he and Dermer sailed west, a gale ripped off their ship's mast soon after departing. In their second attempt, they both were detained by French privateers and had to return home. With his funds exhausted, Smith postponed the voyage, though Dermer remained undeterred and eager to participate in colonial projects. At an unknown moment between 1616 and 1618 he arrived at Cupers Cove. It's possible that he left England in the same ship Tisquantum did, and it's near certain that Dermer was among the colonists who trekked into the interior with the Patuxet man to seek out the Beothuks.[28]

After those disappointing expeditions, Dermer was still thinking about New England's potential and saw an opportunity. It was obvious that Tisquantum's talents and knowledge were being wasted at Cupers Cove; he would make an ideal guide for another reconnaissance mission to his own homelands. The Patuxet man was thinking along similar lines. Like Sassacomoit, Epenow, and Tantum did before him, Squanto would have made the case for his return. The translator and the explorer shared a plan that was mutually beneficial, but their relationship wasn't merely transactional. In time, they formed a genuine personal bond. Dermer later credited his guide with saving his life, and one of the Plymouth colonists described the Patuxet man as the explorer's "honored friend."[29]

The patchy Newfoundland papers offer no explicit details on when the two started their partnership. However, sources indicate that Dermer brought Tisquantum to other Atlantic colonies in the years before they made it back to Wampanoag country. William Bradford reported he had been "imployed to New-foundland and other parts." Edward Winslow noted that the only Wampanoag who knew about the chief Powhatan in 1622 was "Tisquantum, who went in an English Ship thither" to Virginia. When we consider these two scraps of evidence together, it stands to reason that one of the "other parts" he visited with Dermer in 1617 or 1618 was Jamestown. Bermuda was another plausible stop-off on their way back to England.[30]

Details of the Patuxet man's time in Virginia remain a mystery. No surviving letters from the Chesapeake colony include him or anyone matching his description. Winslow's aside is so easy to miss that most historians who have written about Squanto failed to mention it. Indeed, the fact it was a passing remark hints that his stay was brief and seemingly insignificant. The Wampanoag wouldn't be of much use as a translator in Powhatan country, but Dermer could be interested in unloading the surplus of trade goods that were intended for the Beothuks. Squanto certainly had heard about Virginia before from Slany, Dermer, and maybe even Pocahontas. Still, no description could capture its unique character. There was a stark contrast between this fast-growing settlement along humid tidewaters and the modest fishing village at Cupers Cove.[31]

In the late 1610s, Jamestown was no longer on the brink of starvation. The settler population was approaching nine hundred strong and new plantations were popping up along the James River estuary. The colonists' relationship with the local Powhatan confederacy had stabilized temporarily. While Virginia had started to prosper, newcomers still remarked on the colony's "crooked" and "ruinous condicion." An account from 1617 painted a picture: most cottages were "decaying," the fort's palisades were "broken," the nearby wooden bridge was "in pieces," the main well had "spoiled" water, and ramshackle fences could not contain the "innumerable numbers of Swine" roaming the streets.[32]

Though their structures were in disrepair, the English had transformed patches of the surrounding countryside to suit their ample herds of cattle and sheep. Along with their grazing lands, the English had laid out extensive planting grounds along the James estuary where they raised

corn, tobacco, wheat, and barley in "great plenty." In contrast to the Beothuks, the locals here didn't shy away from the settlement. The Powhatan
people and their allies dropped by English houses on a daily basis. Many
spoke basic English and a few even owned firearms. For the first time since
being separated from his kinsmen in Málaga, Squanto was no longer an
oddity or the only one of his kind. Although he wouldn't have seen the
locals as *his* people, he'd recognize similar aspects of their language and
culture. The Powhatans' relations with the colonists were on the brink of
violently deteriorating, but in the time window of the Wampanoag's arrival, it might appear that they had happily profited from their friendship
with Virginians.[33]

This place was so unlike Cupers, London, or Patuxet, yet it combined elements of all three landscapes and societies. Tisquantum would
have seen fields of familiar crops that he used to eat at home alongside
pastures for sheep and cattle. Squarish stationary cottages sat not far from
portable houses much like his childhood wetu. As the site of colliding
worlds, this mixed-up, messy settlement could have seemed disorienting
to the Patuxet man. Though in retrospect, it could have been inspiring. A
couple of years later, when he helped a similar bicultural community take
shape by the small falls, perhaps he was remembering what he saw along
the James River.

Squanto was witnessing the birth of an empire; whether it would survive
its infancy was an open question. The combined number of English colonists in Newfoundland, Virginia, and Bermuda was smaller than Patuxet's
population before the plague hit. In 1618, their places on the map were
better marked in pencil than ink.

Back in England, Gorges, Smith, and other imperial boosters were
again mulling over their long-delayed and oft-revised plans for the Dawnlands. When Dermer first began pitching another scouting mission in letters from Newfoundland, he was met with a lot of enthusiasm. Tisquantum
himself lobbied for the return, telling them through Dermer that he hoped
"to worke a peace between us, and his friends, they being the principall
inhabitants of that coast." At first the explorer tried to depart directly from
Cupers, but Gorges "persuaded him first to goe for England." Gorges
became their most enthusiastic backer. Despite all the stumbles and false
starts of the previous two decades, he was still determined to launch a

colony—ideally in Mawooshen, where English mariners had established a regular presence as seasonal fishermen and traders.[34]

Since Tisquantum had been let go by the Newfoundland Company, he did not return to Slany's house in London. Instead he joined Gorges near Plymouth, where the adventurer's country seat in Devon had hosted a revolving cast of Native men for various stretches since 1605. It's likely that Squanto lodged in the same quarters Sassacomoit and Epenow shared years earlier. That winter, as the great comet shone bright in the West Country sky, he patiently anticipated his return. It was probably for the best that he did not know what awaited him on his side of the ocean.

PART THREE

Home Again

TEN

Homecoming

EARLY IN 1619 TISQUANTUM BEGAN HIS final Atlantic crossing on a ship bound for Mawooshen. Its initial destination was Monhegan, an island that lay twelve miles off the mainland. It had become a seasonal base for English fishermen who traded with the local bands of Wabanakis. Again, the Patuxet man faced a test of his patience. Once across the ocean he spent his first few weeks assisting the crew with trading and fishing, resulting in a lucrative haul of pelts and cod that netted them £2,100, which more than covered their costs and gave Gorges a fine return on his investment.[1]

On Monhegan, the translator had his first chance to meet survivors of the sickness that had swept across the coast in the previous years. Among them was a man named Samoset who spoke passable English, who would later greet the *Mayflower* passengers and introduce them to Tisquantum. Dermer would have welcomed the services of a second interpreter during the weeks they spent trading and fishing off Mawooshen; this was almost certainly when Samoset and Squanto first met. Through conversation with the Wabanakis who came to truck with Dermer, the Patuxet man learned more about the devastating epidemic, though he did not know for sure what had befallen his people.

After putting in his time dragging nets in the sea and haggling over beaver pelts to earn his keep, Dermer got to the real reason for his voyage. At the start of May, he took command of a small open-decked five-ton pinnace with Tisquantum and four or five others as his crew. They started retracing Smith's 1614 travels, hopping from harbor to harbor on a south-westerly course. Five years earlier the previous adventurer had found a coast that was thick with cornfields and villages. Now those "antient plantations" lay barren and the once-crowded land was "utterly void."[2]

In the heart of Massachusett country—presently Boston Harbor—

128

they stopped at fragmented villages ravaged by plague. The living showed
Tisquantum and his companions their healed-over sores and described
the pocks that covered the bodies of the dead. The translator no doubt
offered his old neighbors his condolences, but he also would have spoken
to them with some urgency as he tried to learn how hard the pestilence had
hit the small falls.[3]

Soon his worst fears came true. Dermer described Tisquantum's
traumatic return in a matter-of-fact tone: "I arrived at my savage's native
country (finding all dead)." That parenthetical aside about "finding all
dead" hints at the horrors he saw. Scattered among the abandoned fields,
hearth pits, and bare frames of deteriorating wetus, they found long bones,
pelvises, ribcages, and skulls.[4]

Those were the remains of most of his family. Those bones belonged
to the community that had raised him, to the many unrelated friends he
also called family, to the people he had once sworn to protect and defend.
It's hard to fathom the devastation he felt. Over the previous five years,
when he was taken to an Andalusian port, living in the heart of London,
seeking out the elusive Beothuks, stopping by Jamestown, boarding in
the Devon countryside, and during every shipboard passage in between,
he had been dreaming of this day. Now it had come and it was a night-
mare.

Stricken with grief, Squanto made his first priority finding fellow
survivors. He and Dermer set off inland to Nemasket, a river town that lay
a day's walk to the west. (It's unclear if any of Dermer's small crew joined
them; at least a couple would have stayed behind in Patuxet to watch his
bark.) As they drew near, the inlanders were no doubt alarmed at the unknown party of coat-men traipsing through the early spring woods. As
they faced off, Tisquantum would have shouted a greeting or gotten Dermer to discharge a firearm to keep them from releasing their arrows. Even
after he had identified himself as a Wampanoag in foreign clothes, their
arrival was a perilously tense moment. The Nemasket men were suspicious
of Dermer—he was, after all, an Englishman like Hunt and the others who
had been preying on their neighbors for years. Tisquantum engaged them
in a long discussion as Dermer stood by cluelessly, unaware that they were
negotiating over his life. Only later did he learn from his translator that
"they would have kiled me when I was at Namasket, had he not entreated
hard for me."[5]

Once he saved his friend's head, Tisquantum asked to get in touch with the most powerful sachems in the region. A messenger headed south to the coastal village of Sowams. It was the primary settlement in Pokanoket, a region of fertile peninsulas at the head of Narragansett Bay. The plague had hit this area especially hard. The messenger passed acres of fallow fields and ghost villages as he headed down the path between Nemasket and Sowams. When he arrived, he shared the news with Sowams's sachems, the brothers Quadequina and Ousamequin. The latter man still held one of the captured Frenchman as a servant. The sachems and their fifty-man council decided that bringing the European with them might serve as a sign of goodwill, and taking him with them they headed to Nemasket, curious to hear from the visiting Englishman and the long-lost Tisquantum.[6]

Ousamequin must have made an impression on Dermer when he arrived in Nemasket. An English writer described the great sachem "as proper a man as ever was seen in this country." Another declared him to be "a very lustie [healthy, vigorous] man, in his best years, an able body, grave of countenance, and spare of speech." The phrase "in his best years" gives a clue to his age: Englishmen saw their late twenties and thirties as their peak. The sachem typically wore clothes that were similar to those of his followers—deer leather loincloth, leggings, and moccasins. He wore jewelry and belts made from bone and shell, and he hung a heavy wampum necklace, a tobacco bag, and a large knife from his neck.[7]

One of the sachem's supporters later praised his character to colonists, informing them that he was "ruled by reason," and "he governed his men better with few strokes, than others did with many; truly loving where he was loved." When aggrieved families came to him seeking violent revenge, "he oft-times restrained their malice." He constantly looked for opportunities to cool hot heads and win new friends, intuiting that in the wake of so much death, alliances would be the key to the Pokanoket peoples' survival. Ousamequin's sound judgment and even temperament as a leader was the primary reason for his ascent as the mightiest sachem in the region, leading his people to bestow him with the honorific of the Massasoit, "he who is great."[8]

When the Massasoit, his brother, their French captive, and their fifty councilors arrived in Nemasket, they were eager to talk with both Tisquantum and Dermer. The brothers spoke to the foreigner through his partner,

beginning with typical clearing-the-air statements that often opened negotiations in Native politics. They explained the roots of their animosity
toward Europeans. Along with the abductions, they described another
hostile encounter with an English ship, where the crew fired muskets and
cannon at their men and killed several of their allies—an engagement that
could have been the firefight that ensued when Epenow escaped. Dermer
was skeptical that the sailors were English and that any such attack could
be unprovoked. Ousamequin and Quadequina insisted that their information was correct, pointing out that the Frenchmen agreed that the murder-
ous ship was English.[9]

No matter the exact truth of these past wrongs, the Massasoit and his
brother were there to make peace. They handed over their Frenchman to
Dermer. For that merciful act, Tisquantum would have instructed his partner to offer a lavish counter-gift with whatever trade goods he had with
him. The Englishman and the Patuxet man had a lengthy chat with the two
brothers. Dermer described the sachems as being "desirous of noveltie"—
no doubt eager to hear Tisquantum explain where he had been the last
five years and to gain better information about European activities in the
area. Not since Epenow's return had Wampanoags been able to learn so
much about the English in particular. Squanto surely had questions for
them about his family and relations, questions he had to have been asking
in Nemasket.[10]

The brief summit broke up with all on good terms. Squanto led the
Englishman and their new French companion to Massachusett country,
where they offered another ransom for the other Frenchman enslaved
there. As Dermer got ready to explore farther down the coast, he parted
ways with his translator at "Sawahquatooke." The exact place that name
refers to is unclear, but the most likely candidate in the region would
be Satucket, a small tributary river that snaked between Nemasket and
Patuxet, draining into the watershed of the Pokanoket territory. Tisquantum told Dermer he "desired (in regard of our long journey) to stay with
some of our Savage friends" who were living there.[11]

With the man from Patuxet now resting among friends, probably less
than a day's walk from the small falls, Dermer sailed off, first back to Monhegan then south to Virginia. The explorer's mention of what Squanto
"desired" was the only explicit description he gave of his translator's mental state in the midst of his painful homecoming. It spoke to Tisquantum's

exhaustion and his wish to be with his own people now that his "long journey" was finally over.[12]

The year and seven months that he spent back in Wampanoag country before he came to greet the colonists might seem like another blank spot in his biography. It's a moment that has eluded historians. Yet there are ways we can shed light on Squanto's activities between June 1619 and March 1621. First we have to comb the Plymouth papers for small but revelatory clues. If we compile that trace evidence alongside everything we know about his upbringing, a picture emerges that adds new dimensions to previous interpretations of his return.[13]

There's a clichéd epithet that writers often attach to Tisquantum: they declare he was the one person from Patuxet who survived. This popular factoid appears in countless history books and the rote articles about Thanksgiving that newspapers and magazines in the United States run every November. It's a claim that aligns with the common interpretation of him as a lone survivor without people of his own who thus put himself first, which is why he "sought his owne ends, and plaid his owne game."[14]

This image of the translator as "the last of the Patuxets" isn't entirely baseless: after all, Dermer wrote that he found "all dead" at the small falls, though he also observed that in many places where the plague emptied out towns, "a remnant remaines." Several English sources flatly declared that everyone from the village except Tisquantum perished. But those who spent the most time with him were explicit that a small number survived. When Bradford described him as "a native of this place," he added a caveat about the other survivors, writing that there were "scarce any left besids him selfe."[15]

The Plymouth preacher Robert Cushman also made a direct mention of refugees, stating: "Wee found the place where we live emptie, the people being all dead and gone away, and none living neere by 8 or 10 Myles." Although these settlers emphasized the abandonment of Patuxet, they simultaneously confirmed that a "scarce" number of people from the small falls had "gone away" but were still within a day's walk of their natal home. That rough radius would include the Satucket River, a clue that the "Savage friends" that Dermer left Squanto with in 1619 could have been a band from the small falls.[16]

Not only did Squanto reconnect with Patuxet's few survivors, he also had a living family. In a later chapter, Bradford mentioned "an Indean belonging to Squantos family" who made a dramatic gesture of his loyalty to his kinsman. During one of Edward Winslow's visits to Nemasket, he mentioned that the Plymouth colonists "went to the house of Squanto to breakfast." The revelation that he belonged to a household in Nemasket is a rather unambiguous indication that he had kin in that community; if he were a mere visitor, he would have stayed with the sachem. Furthermore, wetus were women's spaces where they fed all guests. Whoever served the English their breakfast at "the house of Squanto" was, in fact, welcoming them to *her* house.[17]

Together, these scattered mentions of his former neighbors, his household, and his family discredit the assumption he had no people of his own. The women at "the house of Squanto" could have been surviving female relations he knew from before he left. The other possibility was that the wetu belonged to his new wife from Nemasket and her kinfolk. No one mentioned her explicitly, but that was typical of male colonists; one scholar points out their spouses "were either absent from the record or they can be only glimpsed in passing references." Winslow, for example, wrote two books about his time in Plymouth in which he failed to mention either the existence or the death of his own wife. The same was true when they wrote about Natives; the only time individual Wampanoag women appeared in the early records was when the anonymous wives of Ousamequin, his envoy Hobbamock, and the unnamed sachem at Mattapoisett each made a brief cameo.[18]

Tisquantum just spent five prime years of his life as an outsider in foreign lands with few opportunities for sex, much less marriage. He returned to a community filled with widows. Wampanoag widowers, especially elite ones, did not stay single for long—the Massasoit was stunned when he found out that King James had yet to remarry two years after his wife Anne of Denmark died. Some historians have stated that Squanto was a bachelor as though it was an obvious fact, but that's a modern and anachronistic assumption that is dramatically at odds with what we know about his culture's norms and their most elemental value: kinship.[19]

Remember, his people had more than fifteen subtly different words to distinguish whose children they were discussing, one indication among many of how their language, social structure, government, and spiritual worldview put an extraordinary emphasis on familial connections. Then consider that Tisquantum was, both before and after his captivity, a man who sought prominence among his fellow Wampanoags. Once returned, he wouldn't just want to rebuild his circle of family and friends, he also would want to widen it. Indigenous marriages did not work like the typical modern nuclear family: constant cohabitation of husbands and wives was optional. So if Tisquantum married a woman from Nemasket, the fact she often lived in a wetu there would be completely consistent with a matri-local culture that obliged her to stay close to her kin. The English, coming from a patrilocal society, would just assume that her wetu was "the house of Squanto."[20]

True, this is a circumstantial argument that goes beyond the evidence. At the very least, we can confirm that upon his return, the man from Patuxet made contact with a small number of his former neighbors that were now living in or around Nemasket and he had family ties to at least one household within that community. Though the details of his reconnection with these folks are obscure, surely part of their reunion was about sharing their immense grief for all who were lost. The redeemed captive and the survivors would have so many questions for each other. He would want to hear their accounts of the plague and ask after relations and allies to learn who had weathered the epidemic. They would want to know what befell the other men taken with him, a matter that had weighed heavily on Squanto ever since he left Málaga. He was as close as anyone to his fellow atoskauwoag who went aboard Hunt's ship that fateful day, and he had been suffering from their loss in his years away. He would have no answers, only deep condolences.

Death and renewal would become central themes in Tisquantum's gradual reentry into his old world. We can think about this process as a form of "social rebirth." This is where the Patuxet man's experiences diverged most from those of the others taken before him. Sassacomoit, Epenow, Tantum, and the rest all returned to the Dawnlands before the epidemic. Since Squanto's pre-capture world had been all but annihilated, his struggle to reestablish himself would necessarily be longer and more fraught than that of the other men who found their way home. The fact that he first appeared to his former neighbors as the loyal guide to Dermer added to his difficulties. Many Wampanoags remained suspicious of him. His old neighbor Epenow, by contrast, had dramatically turned his back on his captors before they had a chance to set foot on his native soil.

The events of the next three years would show that whereas Tisquantum reconnected with old friends and relations, he faced persistent skepticism about his character. He did not, however, follow the man from Noepe's example and distance himself from the English. Having now seen the vast size of their homeland and the far reach of their settlements, he understood the seriousness of their imperial ambitions. These people just refused to leave the Dawnlands alone. So rather than disavow them, he turned to his skills as an interpreter of their language, culture, and intentions, leveraging his experiences as a captive into a potent new source of status and influence.

Once Dermer parted ways with Tisquantum, his nameless French companions became his guides and translators. Their open-decked vessel soon ran aground, and he lost most of the food and extra clothing he was carrying, leaving him with not much "besides hope to encourage us to persist." Everywhere they went, they found Wampanoags to be standoffish or openly hostile. Dermer knew exactly why his fortunes had changed: "it was by reason of our Savages absence."[21]

Near Monomoit at the elbow of Cape Cod's flexed arm, an angry faction of Natives took Dermer hostage. They demanded a ransom or else they claimed they would kill him, his crew, and the Frenchmen. The explorer handed over the hatchets he had saved in his near wreck as a trade for his life. Whether he was actually in mortal danger or if this was a mere shakedown is not clear. Somehow Dermer and his men got the upper hand, seized a couple of their would-be captors, and demanded their hatchets back, along with some food to help them survive on their way south. Finally a sachem—probably the Pamet leader Aspinet or the Cummaquid headman Iyannough—arrived to defuse the situation. Not only did the sachem redeem the explorer's merchandise, he brought the foreigners a canoe full of corn as a gesture of peace. Dermer's next stop in Noepe went a bit better. There he met Epenow, who was more than happy to tell the Englishman about his brazen escape.[22]

The explorer and his crew faced further near wrecks as they made their way through Long Island Sound and down the coast, where they found more Natives who wanted nothing to do with them. At one point, a group of disgruntled locals drew their bows and fired on his pinnace. When Dermer finally arrived safely in Virginia, one of the first things he did was close off part of the deck on his vessel so he'd be a bit less vulnerable to the elements and arrows on his next trip.[23]

He returned to Wampanoag country the following spring to trade for furs. Tisquantum heard reports of his return and found him to volunteer to be his guide again. But when they came to Noepe, something went wrong. A party of islanders set upon the trading party. They gravely wounded Dermer—ironically, his head was lacerated against the edge of the new cabin he had built to protect himself. They killed all his men, sparing only the explorer, Tisquantum, and one English crew member, who was able to fight off the attackers with a sword. The two Englishmen escaped, leaving the Patuxet man ashore. Once again, the translator ended up in the uncomfortable position of defending the lives of his new friends when they were threatened by his old neighbors. Dermer died soon after he returned to Virginia: the sources are not clear if it was due to his injuries or because he fell ill with a lethal fever.[24]

After the explorer's death, two of his letters recounting his Dawnlands exploits had a life of their own. They made their way back to England and into the hands of the imperial booster Samuel Purchas and his friend John Smith. The reports of an emptied coast only added to the region's appeal. Of particular note was Dermer's account of the vacant harbor at the small falls. Praising its "hardy but strong soyle," and calling it both "Patuxite" and Smith's name for it, "Plimoth," Dermer suggested that the next attempt at an English colony "might hear be seated." The letters added to a renewed enthusiasm in England to place a new colony between Jamestown and Cupers. In time, one of the two letters would be forwarded to the colonists after they arrived at the small falls.[25]

Meanwhile in Leiden, the congregation from Scrooby was still trying to find an investor to support their removal to North America. When they were in negotiations over the possibility of heading for Virginia, they received "heavie news." The other group of expatriated puritans who had left Amsterdam for Jamestown earlier that year had met a dreadful end. The hundred and eighty congregants had been "packed togeather like herings" in two ships. When their convoy lost its way, they were stuck at sea two months longer than intended. They ran low on fresh water and a deadly stomach virus started killing off passengers. Only fifty survived. The Leiden congregation mourned their co-religionists, though Bradford suspected that the leader of the Amsterdam group, Francis Blackwell, was doomed because he dishonestly groveled before Anglican bishops to get them to approve his voyage. Rather than take the disaster as a warning about the terrible dangers that might await them on the seas or on American shores, the Scrooby puritans comforted themselves that they might avoid such an awful fate since they would only set forth with "a good conscience" and "the Lords blessing."[26]

When their attempts to join the Virginia colony fell through, the church members who favored migrating entertained a proposal to head west under the auspices of the Netherlands, but Dutch officials rejected the plan. Finally an English textiles trader (and smuggler) named Thomas Weston came to their aid. He and a group of London-based investors were willing to support a new colony somewhere north of Virginia that would export fish, furs, and other commodities. They drafted a seven-year plan for the settlement to repay its backers, and by July 1620, the American-bound puritans left from the port of Delfshaven to London. Once arrived in the capital, they hired a substantial ship with a 180-ton burden. Neither Bradford nor Winslow thought the name of the larger ship was important enough to mention in their accounts of Plymouth's founding—it was jotted down in a colonial record only three years later. They also planned to sail west with a second 60-ton vessel named the *Speedwell*.[27]

The final months before they sailed were tense and bedeviled by logistical delays and contentious negotiations with Weston over the terms of their agreement. Among other issues, Weston had recruited more non-puritan colonists to join them, which was necessary to pad out their population but did not sit easily with the tight-knit group of saints. As weeks passed the would-be colonists worried that they were eating through all the provisions they had bought for the voyage and the coming winter.[28]

As they nervously awaited their passage, the Scrooby leaders were still considering where exactly their colony would be located. The Hudson River seemed like an agreeable spot, but they were trying to get acquainted with the geography of the larger region. The church elder Brewster had a copy of John Smith's 1616 *Description of New-England,* which included his detailed map. Writing with the intent of changing the region's negative reputation from the failed colony in Mawooshen, Smith made a hard sell to his readers, declaring of the place he had labeled "New England," "of all the foure parts of the world that I have yet seene not inhabited, could I have but meanes to transport a Colonie, I would rather live here than any where." His enthusiasm for the beautiful, temperate, and resource-rich Dawnlands would excite the prospective colonists and their backers alike. At some point in their preparations, Smith caught wind of Weston's plans and reached out to the group, likely proposing that he could serve as their captain or military leader. But the migrants already had a devout soldier willing to serve that role: Myles Standish, who had been living in the Netherlands since serving as a mercenary in the revolt against Spain a decade earlier. It's not clear if Standish joined the congregation in Leiden but he was definitely a fellow puritan. Smith was miffed to find his offer rejected, claiming the Scrooby church leaders told him "my books and maps were much better [and more] cheap to teach them, than myself."[29]

Surely they also felt that Smith, an Anglican who consulted his Book of Common Prayer every day, did not share their godly vision. To these Christians who distanced themselves from their national church and considered themselves "well weaned from the milke of their mother country," the title "New England" was not just an advertising slogan.[30]

It was their mission statement.

ELEVEN

The Treaty

THE *MAYFLOWER* AND *SPEEDWELL* WERE only hours from departing Southampton on August 5, 1620, when the second vessel started leaking badly, forcing both to return to port. Even after an attempted repair, the *Speedwell* was still "leakie as a seive." After weeks spent agonizing, the colonists decided they had to consolidate into the one larger, more seaworthy ship. They set off again on September 6. At first their voyage was sound enough, but within a couple of weeks, they sailed head-on into a string of "boysterous stormes." A disturbing crack appeared in one of the ship's central beams. Seawater came seeping in through leaks in the upper cabins.[1]

The situation was so dire that the crew considered turning back once more, even though they were halfway across the Atlantic. A few improvised repairs helped bolster their confidence, but storms continued to batter the ship. The seasick passengers endured days riding out rain and heavy surf while the ship made no forward progress. The only good news on the voyage was that the passenger Elizabeth Hopkins gave birth to a healthy son, appropriately named "Oceanus," and another woman, Susannah White, had a second shipboard delivery when the *Mayflower* was at anchor off the Dawnlands. Only one adult died in "all the periles and miseries" of this "sea of troubles."[2]

They anchored off Pamet, the outlying village at the curling tip of Cape Cod. They thought about sailing south to the Hudson River, one proposed place for settlement, but they found the extensive sandbars below the Cape too dangerous to cross, so they returned to Pamet. It wasn't just shoals that blocked their way: the land itself seemed hostile to their every step. The passengers' first American meal, a feast of large mussels plucked off the shore, gave them all food poisoning, and their initial run-ins with the Nausets ended with the locals fleeing.[3]

Walking through dense underbrush "tore our very armor in pieces," while Bradford got his leg snared in a Native deer trap. Days after dropping anchor, some of the men came down with cases of pneumonia that turned out to be lethal. A couple of weeks later, a late November cold front brought frigid air and six inches of snow. Bradford remembered their arrival in a famously grim and self-pitying passage, lamenting that "they had now no friends to wellcome them, nor inns to entertaine or refresh their weatherbeaten bodys, no houses or much less townes to repair to . . . what could they see but a hideous and desolate wildernes, full of wild beasts and willd men?"[4]

When heading inland, the English made a number of mistakes that easily could have gotten them killed. Near Pamet they came upon a Nauset farmstead and opened up a cellar filled with baskets of corn. The next day they came upon a small empty settlement and helped themselves to more corn and beans left by locals who had likely just fled upon hearing the English crashing through the forest. Realizing that these stores offered them their best chances of surviving the winter, they returned to the farm and dug up ten more bushels of corn. The colonists earnestly planned to pay the Nausets back, but of course the Nausets had no way of knowing their intentions. In their hunt for more corn, the English came upon a burial ground and opened up some recent graves, discovering the blond French sailor with his child and another buried child. Again, they knew that their actions would offend Natives. Still, their better judgment did not stop them from taking "the prettiest things" out of the graves they ransacked.[5]

Their offenses came back to haunt a group of men ashore days later, when alarming cries awoke them with a start in the middle of the night. They fired their muskets into the dark, and the noise stopped, leaving some to suspect it was only wolves. But the cries came again at the break of dawn. This time they could discern individual voices and words, revealing it to be a war song. To the English, it sounded like the advancing Nausets were saying "Woach woach ha ha hach woach." As arrows started whistling into their camp, the colonists rushed to throw on their armor and ready their firearms. One Nauset man, either a sachem or leading warrior-councilor, stood bravely in the path of musket fire surely confident in the protection of the healing powers of the manitou Hobbamock, firing his arrows right back at the English. The same man called off the attack with an "extraordinary shrike," and the Nausets withdrew.[6]

Retreat was, in the eyes of the English, a submissive move rather than a tactical one, so they concluded they had gained the upper hand. But to the Nausets, the whole point of their attack was intimidation and there was no shame in running away when outgunned. That's why they gave advance notice with their haunting battle cries and did not stay long after opening fire. In truth, both sides had effectively terrified the other. The loud report of gunfire alarmed the Nausets and gave them pause. Even after they had run the attackers off, the English were all too aware that "we could not so well discern them among the trees, as they could see us by our fireside."[7]

The only true moment of good fortune in their early months was when they arrived in Patuxet. The sight of empty land that had so devastated Squanto a year earlier was, in their eyes, evidence of God's providence. Much like Champlain, Smith, and Dermer before them, they immediately saw the virtues of a well-protected harbor with ample fresh water and open land, making it "a goodly land" and "a most hopeful place." The men began to build houses right away along a central lane, with the women and children still sheltering aboard the *Mayflower*.[8]

Although they finally had a base on land, their troubles worsened. As winter progressed, colonists started to die from exposure and scurvy. Half of the original 102 settlers perished in January, February, and March 1621. At times two or three people were dying a day, with so many sick that only a handful of adults were well enough to feed and care for them all. To save time, the living deposited the bodies in a common grave at the top of the hill overlooking the harbor, known as Cole's Hill today. Their raw settlement built on top of a ghost town was starting to look as though it would meet the same fate.[9]

In these early months, the nearby Massachusett and Wampanoag people kept their distance. The English set up a platform on high ground to mount their cannon, giving them an open prospect of Cape Cod Bay. Occasionally they'd scale the highest trees to get the best possible view to the west. Any sign of Natives put them on edge. A distant sound, the glow of far-off fires deep in the woods, even just the sight of smoke on the horizon repeatedly caused the men to ready their guns and wait for hours for foes who never appeared.[10]

Among the colonial leadership, a few men in particular considered themselves qualified to approach Natives. The first was Captain Standish, the seasoned veteran of war in the Low Countries whom the colonists had preferred over Smith to serve as their head of defense. Another man, Stephen Hopkins, was the only alumni of another colony, and thus probably the only man in the region who could approach Tisquantum with first-hand knowledge of what other English projects looked like. Hopkins had been aboard the *Sea Venture* when it wrecked off Bermuda in 1609. Also on the wrecked ship were two Powhatan men, Namontack and Machumps; Hopkins understood the value of having Native informants and had at least a passing familiarity with Indigenous diplomacy.[11]

Two more prominent settlers—Bradford and Winslow—also took an interest in Native relations. Bradford, who held the office of governor for more terms than any other *Mayflower* migrant, seemed most concerned with government-to-government relations with Natives. Winslow had similar concerns but also expressed a genuine curiosity in Wampanoag language, religion, and culture—there's a reason his observations came up so frequently in previous chapters. Once they met Squanto, these two men were among his closest English friends.[12]

It wasn't until late February, just as the spate of colonial deaths was finally slowing down, that they laid eyes on Patuxet's nearest neighbors. A party of twelve Wampanoags passed near the village and absconded with some tools the English had left in the woods. The next day, two men appeared atop a hill half a mile away. They seemed to be beckoning the colonists toward them. Tisquantum easily could have been among them.

An awkward far-away pantomime began, with the English attempting to wave the Natives their way instead. Standish and Hopkins decided to head over to establish peaceful contact, but as they got closer, they heard a chorus of distant unseen voices, singing or calling, which they took for an ominous sign and turned around.[13]

Sufficiently spooked, the English immediately brought more guns ashore from the *Mayflower*. From then on, they kept their weapons close at hand. When Bradford wrote about this moment years later, he reflected on all the things the colonists did not know about their neighbors, such as how many truly loathed the English and "how farr these people were from peace." It was a miracle that the colonists survived, considering "with what danger this plantation was begune."[14]

Ousamequin, the man they called the Massasoit, was at an impasse. For more than four months, he and his neighbors had debated what to do about the families squatting at Patuxet. The few Natives who were spotted on the outskirts were probably from Nemasket (and could have included Squanto), and they seemed to be most open to engaging. The Nausets near Pamet were justifiably furious at the invaders, who had raided their food stores, disturbed their graves, and engaged them in a firefight. To the southeast, the Noepe islanders still bore a grudge against the English in general, and most recently Dermer and his men—they surely also had misgivings about his translator. Others feared the *Mayflower* was a vessel sent on behalf of the French to avenge the sailors they had killed and enslaved.

The question of whether to approach the invaders could not be separated from their concerns that the foreigners had the backing of potent, vindictive manitous. Any path of action required the help of spirits. A group of powwaws from across the shore gathered at a marsh, where for three days they prayed and danced, asking their gods to curse the newcomers, to rid the country of them.

Squanto was there and later described the ceremony to Bradford, which is how we know what happened. To his Christian ears, every detail sounded ungodly: the "horid and divellish maner" of the holy men's "cunjurations," and the mere fact they met in "a darke dismale swampe." To the monotheistic Europeans, any divine power that was not their God was merely Satan in disguise, and unproductive wetlands were associated with pests, disease, criminality, and witchcraft. Seen from the Wampanoag perspective, their location and actions could not be more holy. Marshes were, to them, refuges where their manitous protected them from enemies. Their powwaws associated evil forces and profane actions with Europeans.[15]

After so many lives had been lost, it was a desperate attempt to fight a spiritual war instead of a physical one, using every possible sacred action to rally their manitous to their side: prayers, gifts, songs, dances, and spells. Those unseen voices that frightened colonists in February were likely powwaws leading another such dance, hoping to frighten the unwelcome squatters and compel them to leave. But this was a holy battle they could not win. A decade after the fact, Natives would tell a colonist they had no choice but to "acknowledge the power of the English-mans God, as they call, him, because they could never yet have power by their conjurations to damnifie the English either in body or goods."[16]

As each attempted exorcism fizzled and the settlers did not budge, the case for practical politics grew stronger. Ousamequin heard reassuring intelligence from Squanto, who would insist that the English were not all the same: some could be trustworthy friends. He would have reminded the sachem of Dermer's civil visit a year ago. From his time in Newfoundland, he could detail the trade items that the English might offer—sharp knives, brass kettles, colorful cloth, attractive beads. Still, Tisquantum was considered suspect for his too-close friendship with Dermer, who despite his politeness when meeting with the two brothers, had fought with other Wampanoags who blamed him for starting these conflicts. The Patuxet man's word alone was not enough. But Samoset, a visitor from the north, could also make the same case. This Wabanaki from Mawooshen almost certainly ran into Squanto before, during the Patuxet man's stay at Monhegan with Dermer in April 1619. Together they both could reassure the sachem that there were benefits of friendship with the English.[17]

The leader and his council considered all this information carefully. They were in a bad place politically. To the south, their old enemies the Narragansetts were thriving; their lack of contact with their neighbors had effectively quarantined them from the epidemic's ravages. To the north, the seaborne Mi'kmaqs continued to raid villages. Narragansetts traded with the Dutch and Mi'kmaqs with the French, but Wampanoags had no such partner. In short, the Pokanoket people needed allies.

While their numbers were small and their actions were suspicious, the English had goods to trade. They also had guns, which could make them potent allies. And they had brought women and children with them, a sign of peaceful intent. Their frantic waving in the February encounter suggested they too were desperate for friends.[18]

Ousamequin chose Samoset, not Squanto, to make first contact. In late March, his designated ambassador came striding into Patuxet. He was alone and unarmed, save for two symbolic arrows, one with a head, the other without, a straightforward illustration of two paths that lay before them. The colonists were alarmed as he approached, then stunned when Samoset said, "Welcome, Englishmen." They began peppering him with questions, which he could answer reasonably well in his limited English. He told them about his experiences at Monhegan, described his home shores and named the local leaders from across the Dawnlands. He explained how Hunt's raid had created so much hostility toward the English and told them about the superior translator named Tisquantum. He explained who the Massasoit was and what his intentions were, assuring them that the locals planned to return their tools and hoped to resolve the ill will between the English and Nausets. The colonists were delighted at the prospects of making peace, even if they were, by their own admission, a little nervous around Samoset.[19]

A day later, the Wabanaki returned with five more men, who had probably been waiting nearby in Nemasket to hear how the meeting went. They advanced negotiations by returning the pilfered tools and offering a few skins to trade, readying the ground for a proper summit between leaders. The Wampanoag envoys danced and sang to celebrate the new alliance. The English, for their part, rose to the occasion, offering the most generous meal they could spare to the visitors and giving each man gifts.

Samoset lingered a couple of days longer, willfully ignoring the colonists' hints that they would rather he left with the others. When the Wampanoags did not return on the day they planned, the colonists sent Samoset to ask after them, though not before outfitting him with "a hat, a pair of stockings and shoes, a shirt, and a piece of cloth to tie about his waist." From their time spent reading accounts by Smith and others, the English were able to get the most rudimentary elements of Native diplomacy right: they made sure that ambassadors did not leave empty-handed.[20]

The Massasoit was almost ready to make his entrance. Upon hearing reports that had been relayed from Samoset, his council and kinsfolk had reached consensus that attempting an alliance was the best path forward. They decided to use Squanto as an additional translator for this next step—he spoke better English than Samoset. The former captive was probably living in or around Nemasket at the time, following the news out of Patuxet with great interest. A large group from Sowams readied themselves for the journey. Ousamequin, his brother Quadequina, and their families were accompanied by a party of leading men with their families in tow. On their two- or three-day walk to the small falls, they carried with them several skins to trade and some herring as a gift. Squanto likely joined them at Nemasket with friends and relations of his own. They arrived at Patuxet around one in the afternoon on a pleasant early spring day. It was beneath the dignity of a sachem to simply barge into the village so he sent his two interpreters ahead of him to announce his impending arrival.[21]

It was Tisquantum's first visit to the new settlement. It must have been a peculiar sight to see foreign structures rising out of such familiar ground and to witness English women and children here in the place he had been raised. He would also notice the conspicuous burial pit atop the hill and the freshly planted fields where the colonists had set their own seeds just days before. Perhaps he took pity on them: the men who greeted him looked hollow-cheeked from their grueling winter.

Their half-finished homes indicated they were still tethered to their ship, a beat-up vessel that rode at anchor in the harbor. He was quick to inform the English that Patuxet was his home and told them about his time in Spain, England, and Newfoundland. While he was obviously helpful, Tisquantum didn't make the best first impression. The colonists at first thought he could only "speak a little English" and "could not well express" his thoughts, and when Winslow made a welcoming address to the Massasoit later in the day, he complained "the interpreters did not well express it."[22]

No doubt his English had gotten a little rusty since parting with Dermer. It also didn't help that his Wampanoag-inflected pronunciation could be difficult to understand at first, and that many of the leading colonists spoke with unfamiliar accents. William Bradford hailed from Yorkshire in the north. Edward Winslow and Myles Standish came from the Midlands. Perhaps the colony's first governor, John Carver, was the easiest for him to understand as Carver had lived for a while in London and so his accent might have reminded Tisquantum of the Slanys. Even today fluent English speakers from outside Britain can have trouble understanding its regional accents, which could explain some of Squanto's early inconsistency as a translator. In short order, he would become proficient again. For the moment, he just had to work with Samoset to make sure the Massasoit's meeting with the colonists went well.

As the translators looked back from the village, they could see the sachem and his men standing on a hill to the south. It was easy to pick out Ousamequin from the crowd: he wore his customary chains of wampum and a knife hanging from his neck and he had applied cranberry-red paint on his face. His leading men stood around him, also ready for the occasion, having freshly applied oils to their hair and black, red, yellow, and white paint on their skin.

Looking back at the colonists, they would see a small gathering of men, clad in typical coat-man excess: shoes, stockings, breeches, shirts, coats, and hats. Some held armor, swords, and muskets at the ready, their helmets and barrels glinting under the bright sun. The Pokanoket delegation waited for the colonists to approach them first. Likewise, the colonists wanted the visitors to take the initial step. It was up to Tisquantum to go back and forth relaying each side's good intentions. The colonists caved and ended the stalemate. Winslow put on his armor, picked up a sword, and trudged over to greet the Sowams delegation. Careful to communicate warm intentions, he also brought along gifts of knives and jewelry for the sachems, plus a welcoming snack of brandy, biscuits, and butter. In an opening speech, he extended an offer of friendship from the settlers and King James.[23]

The Massasoit was pleased with these displays of good manners and appropriate deference. He deliberately took his time, in no rush to meet the rest of the settlers who were all looking on from half a mile away. He and his entourage paused to enjoy sips of liquor and bites of buttered biscuits. The sachem admired Winslow's armor and sword and made an offer, probably in jest, to buy them. Winslow politely declined. Finally it was time for the main event. The two sides met at the town's brook, just below the small falls. Before the Massasoit and his inner circle crossed the stream, they arranged a temporary trade of hostages for the duration of the meeting, one more act of insurance. Winslow waited with the sachem's brother while a few of the sachem's men stayed with colonists as collateral.[24]

Upon greeting the party at the brook, Standish and one of the *Mayflower*'s mates led the sachem a few yards up the bank where Plymouth's one sparse street ran parallel to the stream. In the center stood the near-completed house of Stephen Hopkins. They filed in the door to see a cramped room, the hearth glowing, with spring sunshine coming in through the windows. Tisquantum and Samoset were already there, waiting to do their job. Hopkins had laid out a green rug and a few sitting cushions.

Governor Carver came through the door with a fanfare of trumpet and drum, greeting the sachem warmly, bowing and kissing his hand. The Massasoit did the same. The pillows were reserved for the leaders, and perhaps the two translators if there were any to spare. The rest of the Native men in attendance would have sat in the distinct knees-drawn position they felt most comfortable in. The governor offered some fresh meat and more brandy, which the sachem drank a little too fast. He started to sweat and tremble a little, as he was visibly anxious and a bit overcome by the unfamiliar effects of brandy.[25]

The two leaders began to negotiate a mutual pact, going back and forth listening to Tisquantum's translations. Samoset might have weighed in with additional clarifications. The result was a brief six-point treaty that the colonists titled "The agreements of peace between us and Massasoit":

1. That neither he nor any of his should injure or do hurt to any of our people.
2. And if any of his did hurt to any of ours, he should send the offender, that we might punish him.
3. That if any of our tools were taken away when our people were at work, he should cause them to be restored, and if ours did any harm to any of his, we would do the like to them.
4. If any did unjustly war against him, we would aid him; if any did war against us, he should aid us.
5. He should send to his neighbor confederates, to certify them of this, that they might not wrong us, but might be likewise comprised in the conditions of peace.
6. That when their men came to us, they should leave their bows and arrows behind them, as we should do our pieces when we came to them.

The English concluded by once again invoking their monarch, telling the Massasoit that "King James would esteem of him as his friend and ally." With this being done, the mood in the room relaxed a bit. The Wampanoag delegation applauded the final agreement. Ousamequin fished his pipe out of his bag, filled it with pungent tobacco, "drank" a few draws, then passed it to the colonists, who did the same. As they were readying to go, the sachem asked to inspect their trumpet, and some of his men took turns trying to blow it.[26]

It was mid-afternoon when the group emerged from Hopkins's house and walked a few yards down to the brook, where the governor and the sachem embraced. But to the colonists' surprise, the proceedings were not over. The Massasoit's brother Quadequina, a sachem in his own right with his own councilors, also wanted to meet with Carver before they would release Winslow back to the English. Soon Quadequina's party crossed the stream and came into town. Another round of greeting, eating, toasting, and smoking followed, with all conversation still being relayed through Squanto and Samoset. The Plymouth men were starting to get impatient. They were eager to settle matters and see their guests off. The

Julian new year was a couple of days away and they had business of their own to resolve.[27]

Even with the second round of treating over, the men who came with Quadequina seemed to enjoy hanging around this funny little row of blocky houses and gawking at the English women and children—a novel sight as they had only seen visiting sailors, all of them men. Surely the colonial families gawked right back at them. A couple of these men were still lingering around at dusk and "would have stayed all night," had the English not firmly insisted that they leave. Only Samoset and Tisquantum were allowed to stay in town. Tellingly, a group of Englishmen stayed up on watch all night, still not entirely trusting either the visitors or translators. Perhaps the Massasoit's delegation had the same concern, and some also spent a sleepless night on the opposite side of the brook with a vigilant eye on the colonists.[28]

Soon after the sun rose, members of the Sowams delegation started streaming into the village, expecting the customary meals offered to visitors and also wishing to inspect the foreign settlement. This was probably when the colonists got their first look at Indigenous women and children, as the families of the sachem's council felt comfortable coming closer now that a treaty was in place. The women from Pokanoket might be most intrigued by the two women still nursing their seven-month-old and four-month-old sons, who had been born aboard the *Mayflower;* perhaps those mothers would marvel at the Pokanoket babies bound in their cradle-boards. The bigger children might peer at each other from behind their parents' legs. Shortly before noon, Ousamequin and Carver swapped parting gifts—tobacco and groundnuts from the sachem; a kettle's worth of beans from the governor.[29]

Finally the visiting party set off along the path to Nemasket. Samoset would stick around for another couple of weeks. Tisquantum also remained. For the first time since the day Hunt's crew shoved him below decks, he would make his home in Patuxet.

Although he was crucial to the actual word-by-word composition of the treaty, Squanto first appeared as a mere supporting character in the English accounts of their summit with the Wampanoag delegation. This reflected the reality that his political standing was minor compared to that of the Massasoit and his brother. The fact that Samoset preceded him as an ambassador hinted that the sachems still had concerns about the Patuxet man. Whatever priorities Tisquantum had should have come second to those of the Pokanoket leadership, and assuming he was based around Nemasket, he'd also be expected to defer to that local sachem, a figure who was never named in English sources. Squanto's proper station was his previous rank as an atoskauwou from Patuxet, which would have allowed him to participate in the Pokanoket council's deliberations as they prepared for their trip to his old home. While the Massasoit's search for stable allies was the primary mission behind their overtures to the colonists, there was a secondary agenda that Tisquantum surely played a role in crafting.

Ousamequin made a promise the day he made the treaty with the English. He told them that his people "would come and set corn on the other side of the brook, and dwell there all summer, which is hard by us." The colonists did not realize it, but this was why the sachem, his delegation, and his translators showed up almost exactly at the vernal equinox.[30]

April began the spawning season for shad and herring, anadromous fish who lay their eggs in shallow coastal ponds that drained into the sea. Their appearance swimming up the town brook was the traditional sign from manitous to start planting, a key moment in the annual cycles of death and rebirth in Wampanoag cosmology, where expired fish could help summon life out of beans and kernels. Few parts of their calendar were as mythically dense as the beginning of planting, which recalled the figures of Kiehtan the creator, overseer of the land of the dead and giver of corn, his messenger the Crow, and probably the Three Sisters as well.

The initiative to resume Wampanoag planting at the small falls (as opposed to just permitting English farming) did not just fall on Tisquantum's shoulders: it likely was his idea. His connection to that place was obviously stronger than that of any of the Pokanoket leaders'—not just because it was where he was born but also because it was where his relations and ancestors rested. Moreover, this marked the first time Wampanoags raised corn in a place that had been abandoned during the plague. The ghost villages near Sowams and elsewhere remained untouched, skeletons and all, for years to come. Colonists reported that Natives kept their distance from those sites, surely believing that coming too close risked the wrath of malevolent manitous.[31]

Somehow Patuxet became an exception, though the reasons why

were unclear. Perhaps the arrival of colonists broke the taboo and convinced them it was safe. Or perhaps Tisquantum himself played a role in the spiritual cleansing of the site—raising the question of what happened to his ancestors' bodies. Their exact location is a mystery, though they may have been intermingled within a mass grave found in Plymouth's central hill centuries later, which was traditionally assumed to hold the remains of the colonists and sailors who died in the first winter.[32]

The boneyard Dermer found in 1619 was seemingly cleared by the time the *Mayflower* settlers arrived, as he alluded to finding the villagers' remains and they did not. It's possible that Dermer's small crew buried them while he and his guide headed to Nemasket, or that Tisquantum himself, with the help of the other Patuxet survivors, had laid them to rest at some point in the interim. No matter who did the clearing, the land itself was holy to him and the decision to plant there was a bold and sacred act.[33]

Summing up Squanto's actions that coming spring and summer, Bradford declared the Patuxet man was "a speciall instrument sent of God." Their new guide might agree with that general sentiment, but it wasn't necessarily their god that brought him back to the small falls.[34]

TWELVE

Patuxet Reborn

TISQUANTUM'S RELATIONSHIP WITH HIS new friends got off to a strong start. Sure, he was struggling a little with their English, but he was critical to the successful treaty negotiations that left all participants in an optimistic mood. Soon after the sachem and his people left, he disappeared to a well-remembered fishing spot in a nearby river and came back with an armful of eels. He tenderized them by walking over them, and the English roasted them for dinner, recalling with relish that "they were sweet and fat."[1]

It was a small gesture but an impressive one—especially since he'd captured the fish with his bare hands, a feat that astonished the English but was just one of many skills he had mastered long ago in his coming-of-age training. Over the coming months, Tisquantum continued to show them where to find fish, shellfish, waterfowl, deer, nuts, and berries, familiarizing them with the immediate shoreline, wetlands, and forests. They were more than relieved by the sudden appearance of a man who had a local's knowledge, could share it in their language, *and* seemed eager to do it.

A careful read of the colonists' accounts reveals a telling pattern. They described Squanto's helpful counsel as though he were acting alone, yet at the same time they made constant references to other Wampanoags at the small falls just as Squanto began assisting them. These locals "came very often, and very many together" to the small falls, "bringing for the most part their wives and children." Some came dependably at the new and full moon when the tide went out the farthest, making it easier to gather abundant lobsters from the harbor. These farmers and shellfishers identified themselves as Namascheucks, meaning they came from Nemasket—the inland town that was one of the Massasoit's allied villages and the home to Tisquantum's kin. When the English finally visited Nemasket, they were surprised to learn how far it was from Patuxet because the villagers "flocked so thick amongst us."[2]

When we remember that the former captive was accompanied by "very many" fellow Natives, it seems all the more likely that some feats attributed to Squanto were actually a communal effort. It would be especially true for that famed moment of the first planting, which fell under the domain of women's knowledge and work. When the colonists credited their guide with "showing them both the maner how to set it, and after how to dress and tend it," perhaps the actual demonstration was performed by Wampanoag women with Tisquantum explaining their methods and passing along their wisdom.[3]

The fact that the texts were not explicit about this process of show-and-tell would be consistent with the general invisibility of women—whether English or Native—in the writings of male colonists. This theory of female-led farming lessons is also consistent with the most elemental facts we know about traditional Wampanoag gender roles. There was a social aspect to this work that explained why the Massasoit specifically connected the act of farming to the new alliance he was initiating with the English. An English writer described planting as an act of "friendly joyning," when women—and their better-behaved husbands—flocked by the dozens to help neighboring villages sow their fields, in "a very loving sociable speedy way." Later colonists observed that Native men were free to opt out of planting; a man only pitched in "out of love to his Wife, or care for his Children, or being an old man." A Dutch colonist who observed the same dynamic among the nearby Lenape people noted that when men aided in the planting season, they worked "under the direction of the women."[4]

No matter whether women were at his side when he led the planting and harvesting lessons, the colonists gathered to hear him repeat their wisdom. By positioning himself as teacher, Tisquantum was in a way re-enacting the myth of the Crow. He was inaugurating binding relationships, forming the new bonds between him, the Patuxet survivors, the nearby Nemasket villagers, and the colonists. He also may have seen himself as creating spiritual ties between the colonists, Kiehtan, the sisterly crop spirits, and the land itself. There was one more crucial part of the instructions he relayed from the women: Tisquantum (and probably several other Natives) helped them build a weir in the stream, allowing them to take herring and shad "with great ease," to use as fertilizer.[5]

The colonists recalled that these renewed fields had to "be watched by night to keep the Wolves from the fish," until they completely rotted into the earth. The men sat up for two weeks, keeping an eye over the acres of aromatic mounds. The "wolves" they were guarding against had a secret though. An environmental historian has recently pointed out that Indigenous peoples' pet *Canis lupus familiaris* (who physically resembled wolves more than European dogs) far outnumbered the wild population of *Canis lupus* in the Dawnlands. The Great Dying left most of the former animals masterless. In the coming years, colonists would write about encounters with "wolves" who smiled, barked, and even seemed to play with them, all characteristic behavior of domesticated dogs, not wild wolves. Those canines who came rooting for fish dinners at night were probably packs of feral survivors who had adapted to a drastically changed landscape. No English source noted how exactly Indigenous people understood those dogs in wolves' clothing. Unlike colonists, they could surely recognize that these animals were once pets, but just as they stayed clear of the villages of the dead, they might be reluctant to re-domesticate them.[6]

Just as some of the "wolves" the colonists saw were not wolves, some of the people they characterized as guests at the small falls were in fact from that very place. Those "scarce" Patuxet survivors had to be among those Namascheucks; that's how the colonists knew that they existed. They mentioned a distinct group that kept popping up whenever Squanto was by their side. When the colonists Winslow and Hopkins passed near that river with their translator later that June, they ran into "some ten or twelve men, women, and children" whom they recognized from their appearance at the fortnightly spring tide, staying so long they "had pestered us till we were weary of them." But that little familiar group surely did not intend to "pester" the English; they were most likely engaged in a conversation with their friend or relation Tisquantum.[7]

The English settlers had not spent enough time on these shores to realize that what they saw as an itinerant community was instead a normal Indigenous village during the summer months: once fields were fully seeded and starting to flower, some groups would break away to fish, hunt, and gather. The number of wetus could expand and contract as people came and went. Most days that spring and summer, settlers stepped out of their doors and saw a cluster of wetus or open-air camps on the opposite side of the stream. The colonial descriptions of the mirror village stressed its impressive size—their neighbors "flock[ed] so thick," "very often," and "very many together"—indicating that during their first summer, there were often more Indigenous people living at Patuxet than the fifty-odd English settlers.[8]

There was one aspect of the Native presence that made the colonists uneasy: the fact that these people repeatedly showed up at their doors expecting to share their meals. It was especially bothersome in the early weeks before any crops had been harvested and when the English were subsisting on the last of their victuals from the *Mayflower* and whatever they could hunt or catch. The colonists were still worried about feeding themselves and saw these drop-ins as an imposition. The newcomers did not realize how an ethos of reciprocal visiting and entertaining supported the mobile patterns of Indigenous life. All Dawnlanders regularly stopped in each other's homes when hunting or moving between seasonal camps. Mutual hospitality was a core value. At first the English did not fully grasp how important it was for them to offer meals if they wanted their neighbors to trust them. Soon enough, though, they came to appreciate the practice when they started calling on Native friends.

Sharing a "common pot," which all ate from, was both an everyday practice at mealtimes and an ancient way of describing the shared use of lands and representing alliances between nations that Dawnlanders continued to evoke in their speeches and writings for centuries to come. All the work Squanto did teaching them to feed themselves was adding to the Patuxets' common pot, which would nourish people on both sides of the small falls, serving the needs of all.[9]

There were also literal pots being carried back and forth over the brook. A recent archaeological dig in Plymouth unearthed a trash pit from right outside the English homes. The majority of bones and artifacts clearly belonged to the colonists, but mixed in with the remains of livestock and sherds of European ceramics were dozens of pieces of Native-made pottery. Those exact fragments cannot be dated to 1621, but they illustrate the ongoing practice of shared meals between Wampanoags and colonists.[10]

This simple domestic detail might feel familiar to anyone who has ever come across a mismatched piece of tupperware or an unfamiliar serving dish in their own kitchen cupboard. It's a material reminder of a pot-luck offering from a friend who was close enough to be welcomed in your home. These archaeologists also uncovered traces of a contemporaneous

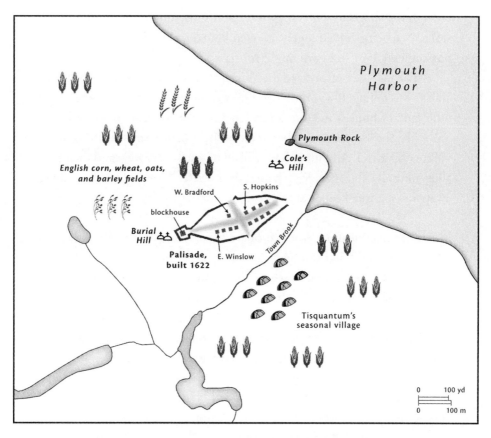

English corn, wheat, oats, and barley fields

Plymouth Harbor

Plymouth Rock

Cole's Hill

W. Bradford

S. Hopkins

blockhouse

Burial Hill

Palisade, built 1622

E. Winslow

Town Brook

Tisquantum's seasonal village

0   100 yd

0   100 m

Patuxet and Plymouth, 1621–1622. Erin Greb Cartography.

Wampanoag camp just outside the English town, further confirming the colonial reports of their cheek-to-jowl proximity.[11]

Like most next-door neighbors, the English, in spite of their out-wardly congenial manners, started to accumulate resentments. Even as they were eating from the same pots and dishes, they had yet to compre-hend the deeper "common pot" ethos, which was grounded in the logic of relational obligations that underlay so many local practices. As they started planning a follow-up visit to the Massasoit, the colonists included among their concerns their anxieties about the ebbing-and-flowing Native population across the way, thinking the sachem could "prevent abuses in their disorderly coming unto us." The Namascheucks who stayed across the brook "were welcome," the colonists wrote, and they "desired still to" entertain them generously. They were simply worried if there would be enough for all to eat when they were still subsisting on imported provisions, "we being but strangers as yet at Patuxet, alias New Plymouth, and not knowing how our corn might prosper."[12]

The fact they prioritized the Wampanoag place-name over their own "alias" was telling. It was the closest they came to admitting that their half-built lane of houses was not an isolated settlement that summer; it was more like the English neighborhood in the recently revived Indigenous village of Patuxet. And though they liked to say their colony and their new allies were all subjects of King James, the born leader who lived forty miles away was the true keeper of the peace.

Much of the education Squanto offered the colonists was a highly condensed and simplified summary of things he learned as a boy and young man living in the exact spot where they now perched. As with any such rushed cram session, a lot of the finer points were skipped over, and some pupils proved more apt than others. Along with showing them how to provide for themselves, he introduced them to some basic Wampanoag values. Soon he moved from parenting them to briefing them as fellow politicians. They would learn how to maintain relationships with other villages, how to participate in diplomatic meetings, and how to offer condolences and apologize for trespasses to avoid an escalation to bloodshed.

His star students included Bradford, Winslow, and Hopkins—the latter was the veteran of the Virginia and Bermuda colonies. John Carver, the governor who made the initial treaty, died suddenly during the planting season, and the colonists had elected Bradford to replace him. The new governor decided to remain at the small falls while Winslow and Hopkins acted as envoys. When they headed down the narrow paths to Sowams in the late spring, Squanto made sure they carried gifts: English trade beads for anyone hosting them along the way and, for the sachem, a fine copper chain, "a suite of cloaths" and "a horseman's coat of red cotton, and laced with a slight lace." Joining them on the way to Nemasket was the group of regular visitors who might have been Tisquantum's closest friends. Once they arrived at the river town, Winslow and Hopkins were warmly greeted by Namascheucks eager to return the hospitality the English had shown them. The travelers were grateful for the offer of freshly cooked shad, cornbread, and acorns—even if they did not care for the "musty" taste of the nuts. Locals started approaching Tisquantum with favors to ask of the two visitors, most pressingly to shoot at and scare off a murder of crows that would not stop pecking at their corn.[13]

As they crossed into Pokanoket country, they saw the devastation of the Great Dying all around them. Tisquantum told them that thousands had lived here a few years before. It was the first time they had come across the scattered skeletons of the epidemic; Patuxet had apparently been cleared of the bones of the dead before they arrived, perhaps by Tisquantum himself. Yet they could not help but wonder if those acres upon acres of cornfields, overgrown with head-high grasses, might become theirs for the taking. They kept coming upon and surprising small fishing parties.

Each time Squanto spoke up quickly, which calmed things down. Once they understood that the two Englishmen were the new friends from Patuxet, the locals were quick to share whatever they had just caught. Hopkins and Winslow needed those extra calories, as they were fatigued and ravenous from all the trekking. Their guide expected them to keep a brisk pace of twenty miles a day for two days in a row. Their heavier clothing made their hike especially taxing. It was obvious how impractical their kit was for woodland travel, especially when the two had to peel off their woolen breeches and wade through a river in just their long linen shirts, naked from the waist down.[14]

The sachem was not home when they finally trudged into Sowams. Upon his return, their second meeting with the Massasoit and his council started well. He was genuinely delighted by the gifts of handsome clothing, and upon listening to their concerns, the sachem was happy to address each of them. He promised that any disorderly "pestering" would cease—perhaps tasking Squanto with monitoring the behavior of those Patuxet-Nemasket villagers. He also agreed to send them seed corn for a second planting, and he pledged to help them with their request that men from his allied villages trade their skins with them. For the colonists, getting access to this trade was key to repaying Weston and the other investors who supported their colony. In affirming the plan, the Massasoit went through a customary repetitive, anaphoric call-and-response affirming that each nearby partner sachem would promise pelts. He too had obligations and debts he had to honor.[15]

Although they tried to maintain a polite facade as the assembled body went through this back-and-forth thirty times, Winslow and Hopkins confessed in their own account that they found the ceremonies "tedious." It was not the only culture shock the pair experienced on their trip. When the Massasoit honored them with lodging in his house, letting them share his sleeping platform alongside his wife and two councilors, the Englishmen barely slept. They didn't care for their cramped sleeping arrangements, they didn't like the songs the villagers sang at bed time, and they suffered without the skin treatments that Indigenous people used to keep insects away.

Adding to their discomfort, the sachem did not have abundant food to offer, as it was the lean part of spring before the first crops were harvested, when last year's stores were all but gone. The following day, when nearby sachems came calling and the Sowams men engaged them in friendly games, the two colonists felt all the more exhausted and underfed. They set out before dawn the next morning, eager to make it back to the comfort and security of Plymouth.[16]

Ousamequin was upset that the English found his hospitality wanting—perhaps he wished they and Squanto had offered the same courtesy he had done them and sent ahead messengers, which would have given him some time to prepare. Nonetheless, he and his people had fared well in their negotiations. The gift that Squanto encouraged them to bring was well-chosen and respectful. Everything the colonists asked of him served his interests as much as theirs: by making him their main point of contact for any dealings with their neighbors, they reinforced his position as the head sachem of the region. He was happy to grant their requests for seeds and pelts as another demonstration of his goodwill for the English, assuming they understood that now they were reciprocally bound to support him in any future moment of need. And in carrying out his side of the agreement by calling sachems to Sowams, he reminded each of his allies that their connection to the English trade goods ran through him.

In his conversation with Winslow and Hopkins, the sachem made it clear that he envisioned their friendship first and foremost as an alliance between birthright sovereigns—between himself and King James. He hoped the English would deter the French from trading with the enemy Narragansetts, "for it was King James his country, and he was also King James his man." To the man known as He Who Is Great, the Patuxet settlers were mere proxies for the only Englishman who equaled him in status, His Majesty. But even this man was a mystery to him—this was when he expressed his astonishment that the widowed king was still single.[17]

The Massasoit's due respect for the Stuart monarch stemmed from a conveniently loose translation that aided both sides. It's likely that Tisquantum used the word "sachem" for "king" when speaking about James I in Wampanoag. Elsewhere in the Dawnlands, colonists noticed that Natives used the title "sachem" loosely for any man "that they see have a command of men." Seeing as colonists repeatedly used the title "king" for Massasoit, it's almost certainly the word their translator attached to the great sachem. Though sachems and kings were fundamentally different in so many ways, the superficial likeness made the foreign familiar for both English and Wampanoags. The metaphor of royalty was a comforting one, it helped the Pokanoket leader envision an English sachem sitting in Westminster while allowing the colonists to make sense of the Massasoit as "their greatest king" and his allies as the "many other kings which are under him."[18]

The sachem did see one aspect of their relationship that needed fixing: Tisquantum. The fact that all parties depended on one translator was a problem. The leadership circle at Sowams was not sure of the Patuxet man's loyalties. He seemed to prioritize his relationships with his Nemasket-Patuxet allies and the English above his responsibilities to Pokanoket. Before Winslow and Hopkins departed, the Massasoit appointed them a new guide, named Tokamahamon, to aid them in their passage home and ideally serve as a secondary interpreter. Tokamahamon was hardly alone in aspiring to master the foreigners' tongue. A later colonist noted that Natives could be "not a little proud that they can speake the English tongue, using it as much as their owne, when they meet with such as can understand it." They especially appreciated when the English made an effort to speak Wampanoag: the same colonist observed that "they love any man that can utter his minde in their words."[19]

A few weeks later, another guide, Hobbamock, appeared in Patuxet. This "special and trusty man of Massasoit" was an impressive figure. He was "a proper lustie [healthy, vigorous] man," well-regarded among Natives for his valor and abilities. In time he would learn enough English to become an able go-between in his own right, but one of his first tasks seemed to be keeping a watchful eye on the Patuxet man: something about the way the former captive allied himself with the English concerned the Massasoit. At the very least, the headman at Sowams wanted to make sure that he had more than one envoy to call upon.[20]

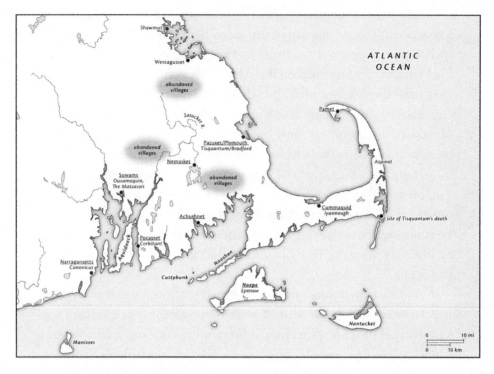

The southern Dawnlands, 1621–1622, showing sites of major communities with the name of the local sachem or governor. Erin Greb Cartography.

When the colonists headed home with Tokamahamon, Tisquantum had a new assignment: trekking "from place to place" encouraging the sachem's allies to trade with Plymouth. While Tisquantum looked to educate the colonists, the sachem also had a lesson to teach him. Giving him this task was a clear reminder that while he could continue to help the colonists, he should never forget that he served the Massasoit first and that he aided the English only at the sachem's pleasure. Still, the sachem also demonstrated his respect for the former captive's skills as a diplomat; this assignment was an important one for binding the Wampanoag towns together into a firm alliance with the English.

A new political world was dawning in the aftermath of the Great Dying and the colonists' arrival. The sachem at Sowans wanted to make sure that the Patuxet man knew his place in it.

The English still had two important wrongs to right: their theft of corn and their desecration of graves in Nauset territory. Squanto must have relayed their sincere regret when he came to call on these villages on behalf of the Massasoit to encourage them to trade with the colonists. But when an English boy named John Billington got lost in the woods and ended up in the hands of Nausets, the job of collecting him became a chance for the settlers to offer their apologies and condolences in person.

They met two welcoming sachems, Iyannough and Aspinet, on the far side of Cape Cod Bay. The former was a sachem at Cummaquid; the latter was the headman for Monomoit and Pamet. Both were willing to join the new circle of allies that the Massasoit was forming, with Tisquantum as one of his key agents. They offered the visiting party the same kind hospitality they had given the Billington boy, and they graciously accepted the Englishmen's sincere apologies for their trespasses the previous fall.[21]

Other wounds inflicted by Englishmen had not healed. On this trip the colonists encountered the woman who had lost three of her "sons" in Hunt's raid. Given that she appeared quite elderly—colonists claimed she was "no less than a hundred years old"—both she and Tisquantum were likely using the term "sons" in the elastic sense meaning grandsons or even great-grandsons, as the men who went aboard Hunt's vessel were unlikely to be old enough to have such an aged mother. The matriarch was still deeply grieving her boys; the sight of the English caused her to burst into tears.[22]

Speaking through Tisquantum, the colonists tried to offer consolation by denouncing Hunt and offering her some beads in a gesture of condolence. But even they had to admit that she seemed only "somewhat" comforted by their words of remorse. This run-in demonstrated that colonists could not depend solely on their dealings with sachems to maintain harmony with their neighbors. Given the magnitude of the offenses committed by other Europeans (to say nothing of their own transgressions), they had a long way to go before the general population would trust them.

Perhaps the English felt *too* reassured by the forgiveness they found in Nauset country. There was a touch of wishful thinking in their declaration that "their peace and aquaintance was pretty well established with the natives aboute them."[23]

THIRTEEN

Downfall

THE ENGLISH COULD NOT BELIEVE the news: Squanto was dead. It was late in the summer of 1621, and they had just seen him and Hobbamock off to Nemasket. Barely a day had passed when Hobbamock came running up the bank of the brook into the colony's single lane of houses, drenched in sweat. Squanto had been murdered, he breathlessly told Governor Bradford. Or so he thought. Or so it appeared. Even if he weren't dead, their translator's life was in grave danger. The trouble started as soon as the two men arrived in Nemasket, where they had been confronted by a disgruntled sachem. His name was Corbitant, and he was the sachem of Pocasset, the bayside land just east of Pokanoket and Narragansett territories. He was a charismatic leader—colonists who later met him vouched for his excellent sense of humor—and also a shrewd one.[1]

Corbitant faced a difficult choice. Like most Natives across the area, he viewed colonists with well-deserved suspicion. Who could say this new batch of foreigners would truly be good partners? What would his standing be in this new coalition that Ousamequin was building with Tisquantum's help? Meanwhile, rumors spread that the Narragansett sachem Canonicus had been courting Corbitant to join his side. The Pocasset leader seemed to be weighing his options as tensions heated up between the rival sachems. According to secondhand reports, the Narragansetts had captured the Massasoit and held him prisoner, presumably to warn him of the consequences of extending his alliances any further.

Their fears that the great sachem had been captured was why Tisquantum and Hobbamock went to Nemasket in the first place. They were trying to find out what happened to him. Corbitant caught wind that two of the Massasoit's top agents were staying in the river town and decided to surprise them, something he did not dare do when they were at Patuxet. According to Hobbamock, Corbitant's men surrounded a house with the two men inside. The attackers seized Tisquantum first, then got their hands on Hobbamock. The Pocasset sachem "held a knife at his breast," but he broke free and ran back to Patuxet.[2]

Once they heard the whole story of Corbitant's ambush, the colonists knew they had to act. They raised a group of ten to follow Hobbamock back to Nemasket, heading out the following day. Not only did they hope to avenge Tisquantum, they also wanted to show that they too could play this dangerous game of hostage taking. Their plan was to hold Corbitant ransom to secure Tisquantum's and the Massasoit's safe return or else to execute the hostage if their allies were already slain. They were attempting to honor article 4 of their agreement: "If any did unjustly war against him, we would aid him."[3]

The colonists stormed the village before dawn, with Captain Standish leading the way. They burst into the large wetu where Hobbamock had left Tisquantum with Corbitant. Neither the rogue sachem nor the translator was inside, just a shocked family. Some of the Namascheucks were speechless with fear. A "hurly-burly" of shouting and screaming began, the colonists trying to hold everyone in the house as temporary hostages. They attempted to state their business through Hobbamock, who could not quite keep up translating their demands. Corbitant was not here, the locals tried to tell the colonists. Whatever alarming reports they heard were overstated: the sachem had managed to resolve his dispute and left peacefully.

In the confused melee, the Englishmen fired off their guns. Three fleeing people injured themselves when they tried to climb out of a hole torn in the wetu's wall. Some women cowered behind Hobbamock. It was then that a group of boys shouted "Neen squaes"—literally "we are women," though a fuller translation might read "don't hurt us, we are like women who will not fight." Hobbamock gave up trying to mediate. He quickly scaled the roof of the wetu and shouted for Tisquantum and Tokamahamon. Somewhere in the midst of the lanes of wooden houses, they heard him and came running with friends in tow.[4]

Once the additional translators arrived, everyone began to calm down. Their translator was alive; that relieved the colonists. He could assure the locals that they meant no harm. And he reassured the English that Corbitant had left with his council. The villagers the English had just been holding hostage "came trembling," offering tobacco and food to appease them. Although they'd thoroughly terrified the whole village, the colonists were not quick to back down. They spoke through Squanto to the gathering of Nemasket villagers. The English affirmed that they would swiftly punish anyone who even threatened them or anyone loyal to them and the Massasoit. But they also tried to take some responsibility for the mess they made, apologizing to those who had been injured in the hub-bub. They invited the trio of wounded Namascheucks to come with them back to Plymouth to have "their wounds drest and cured."[5]

The moment of his supposed death marked a turning point of sorts in Squanto's relationship with the English. There could be no doubt of how much they needed him and how far they would go to protect him. His friends' bullying appearance in Nemasket also uncovered how much fear lay just beneath the surface in the everyday encounters between Natives and newcomers.

The Patuxet man correctly saw the scared reaction of these villagers as a potent force, which underscored the power he had been granted by his bond with the foreigners. When the English stayed in the village, his Namascheuck kin took responsibility for hosting them. This was when unnamed women fed them breakfast at "the house of Squanto." A group of Tisquantum's family and allies returned to Patuxet with the English, who indicated they had seen these individuals before, calling them "many other known friends accompanying us," who seemed eager to assist them on their trip home. Though the colonists had called for a halt to all threats, they had also demonstrated how effective the specter of violence could be.

The English also remembered the incident in Nemasket as a trans-formative one in their relationships with their Indigenous neighbors. Bradford noted that soon after they came seeking vengeance on behalf of Tisquantum and the Massasoit, the remaining holdout Wampanoag sa-chems paid visits to the small falls, which made for a "much firmer peace." In a subsequent visit to a Massachusett village, one local could only ap-proach the English "shaking and trembling for fear." Tisquantum encour-aged them to be rough and take whatever skins the Massachusett people did not immediately offer. The colonists, however, wanted to emphasize their peaceful intentions. They ignored their interpreter's advice. Their preferred combination of harsh warnings followed by kinder words seemed to work, for the moment at least. By that September, nine sachems had each come to Patuxet and made their marks on a page that read:

September 13. Anno Dom. 1621.

KNOW all men by these Presents, That we whose Names are under written do acknowledge our selves to be the Loyal Subjects of King James, King of Great Britain, France and Ireland, Defender of the Faith, &c. In Witness whereof, and as a Testimonial of the same, we have Subscribed our Names or Marks, as followeth.

Ohquamehud. Cawnacome. Obbatinnua. Nattawahunt. Caunbatant. Chikkatabak. Quadaquina. Hattamoiden. Apannow.

The nine men did not come on the same day, and a couple may have sent a messenger in their stead. The final signatory was none other than Epenow. He or his proxy came all the way from Noepe to make his peace, at long last, with the English. Even Corbitant had caved. Though he did not deign to appear in person at Patuxet, he requested that the Massasoit relay his willingness to join the alliance.[6]

The document itself was unlike the six-point agreement drawn up five months earlier. The English did not list their obligations to their new partners. They asked for all the sachems to declare themselves "subjects," a concept that Tisquantum could not quite translate, as it was one of those points where the king-as-sachem metaphor broke down. The English liked to believe that the headmen who signed were permanently submitting to their authority, but the sachems tended to see such arrangements as a mutual agreement of alliance and protection. All would agree, however, that the tiny village had undergone an enormous reversal of fortune in just a few months. The colonists were isolated, dying, and hungry before Samoset splashed through the brook to greet them, which made it all the more impressive that they now had the allegiance of every sachem around them, including the weightiest one at Sowams.[7]

At approximately the same time those nine sachems signaled their allegiance to the English, the Massasoit and his supporters decided to pay another visit to the small falls. The sources do not explain who or what precisely prompted him to do so. Still, the man at Sowams had good cause to make face-to-face contact with Bradford and Standish after the troubling incidents at Nemasket weeks earlier. That entire affair could have ended far worse than it did, and Ousamequin was a big believer in refreshing his

alliances with warm gestures and conversations. His party set out during
the harvest moon on a single-file march along a network of narrow paths.
It was near the height of autumn color: the forest canopy would be speck-
led with shades of yellow, gold, and red. When the great sachem last visited in March, he had encountered a dismal-looking settlement made up
of a couple of half-finished buildings, populated by a few dozen pale and
gaunt villagers. He could have been forgiven for thinking this struggling
village where the dead outnumbered the living might not last the year.[8]

As he and his ninety companions emerged from the woods outside
Patuxet, the Massasoit saw for himself that the foreign outpost had grown
considerably. Seven complete houses stood on the main hill, several more
were in progress, more brush had been cleared, and more trees had been
felled. Twenty-six acres of old planting grounds had been reseeded, the
settlers had harvested a fine crop of maize, and they had just returned from
a hunt with freshly slain waterfowl. There might have been a few wetus still
standing across the brook from the colonists, though most of the Nemasket folks had probably returned to the harvest in their own cornfields.

Coming up to greet him were the town's leading men, looking health-
ier. The sachem would be glad to see Winslow and Hopkins, the pair who
had given him the red horseman's coat. In a gesture of politeness, he was
almost certainly wearing the coat on that autumn day. Also there to welcome him was the colony's respective civilian and military leaders, Governor Bradford and Captain Standish. The Massasoit and his entourage almost tripled the population of the village. Soon after he arrived, he ordered
a few of his men to hunt some deer for a feast.[9]

What followed is the event now known as the "First Thanksgiving."
It stretched for three days, and it was a bit more fun than the prayerful
feast imagined in national myth. When the Massasoit's men returned with
five deer, the carcasses were butchered for roasting. The settlers shared
their harvested corn and beans, with plentiful "fowl"—which meant ducks,
geese, and perhaps turkey as well—and ample shellfish. The meal, as it
were, was hardly a formal banquet. Colonists had few dishes or cutlery, to
say nothing of the long dining table that is somehow magically present in
later paintings of this day. It was an outdoor cookout-style feast, as the
attendees sat on stools or the ground with simple wooden dishes of cornmeal stew set on small tables or resting in their laps, and they gnawed at
handheld spits of cooked venison and fish. Standish kicked off the revelry

by summoning his men to fire off their muskets and fowling pieces in noisy volleys. The one surviving account of the feast spoke of "other recreations," which likely included dancing and singing, and target-shooting contests with arrows and guns, something the English had proposed when they were in Sowams a couple of months earlier.[10]

Over this days-long feast, Tisquantum was indispensable. Not only was he there to translate discussions between elite men, he also helped smooth over any minor disputes or misunderstandings. Winslow was so impressed by the gathering's success that he included the only account of the feast in a letter sent to encourage further colonists to come to Plymouth. He seemed to be referring to the shared harvest with Natives when he boasted: "We entertain them familiarly in our houses, and they as friendly bestowing their venison on us."[11]

None present that day could imagine that this event, of all things, would be what later generations remembered most of the colonists' first year at Patuxet and their friendship with the Massasoit. No new political history was made on that day; they were honoring their previous agreements. Aside from Winslow's letter, there's not much evidence that either colonists or Wampanoags gave the feast much thought afterwards. It did, however, mark a moment of relative optimism and innocence among the settlers. Winslow summed up their political position in his letter when he wrote, "It hath pleased God so to possess the Indians with a fear of us, and love unto us."[12]

Tisquantum was not at the small falls when a messenger arrived that November. The envoy had come all the way from Narragansett country, crossing seventy miles of bare forest. He declared he was bearing a message to Patuxet as he crossed into enemy territory near Sowams. The great sachem appointed his trusted envoy Tokamahamon to be his minder. Upon arriving in Patuxet, the Narragansett man asked for Tisquantum but appeared visibly relieved that the translator was out of town. He was not eager to see the message "read" in front of him. It was a bundle of brand-new arrows wrapped in the skin of a rattlesnake.[13]

Upon placing it in the colonists' hands, the messenger immediately tried to leave, but Captain Standish would not let him. Drawing on his years spent at war in the Low Countries, Standish determined that they had to debrief the foreign agent, and he drafted Winslow to help him, since he was close with Tokamahamon from earlier journeys. In his typical over-aggressive fashion, Standish managed to waste several hours of everyone's time, terrifying the poor messenger and exhausting the escort, whose translation skills were not up to the task. All they could figure out was that the Narragansett had long been suspicious of them and that the message was a kind of warning or threat. Soon after they released the Narragansett man, Squanto arrived home. He confirmed the obvious: the bundle was indeed a symbol of "enmity" and could be read as "a challenge." The rattlesnake was one of the principal earthly forms of the manitou named Hobbamock, the healing protector of fighting men. The Narragansetts were not just displaying their weapons as a material threat, they were demonstrating that a powerful god was on their side.[14]

Upon consultation with his interpreter, Governor Bradford filled the snakeskin with powder and shot. A display of their literal firepower served as a clear answer. The messenger who bore it to the Narragansetts reported that they refused to touch it. The colonists were pleased with their tough retort, but they also took the original message to heart. No matter how many allies they had, they were few in number and the Narragansetts were many. A surprise attack could easily wipe their village off the map. They all agreed that the settlement needed better defenses. Standish got to work. He assigned all the adult men to four "squadrons," appointing lieutenants to lead each company, and started leading regular muster days where he drilled the men on how to defend the town. He also led their newest building project: raising a palisade to encircle the entire village and its immediate gardens. Standish was concerned that their houses could be lit ablaze in an attack, turning their fortifications into a deathtrap. He decided to bury their surplus casks of gunpowder in the earth beneath their storehouse to keep it safe during an attack.[15]

Tisquantum observed all this preparation and perhaps even lent a hand in erecting the pale around the town. For him, the colonists' spiking anxiety presented a moment of opportunity for an emerging political project of his own. It had been taking shape for months, maybe even since he first brought them that armful of eels.

Colonists described his plotting as a grab for status and influence, claiming his "ends were only to make himself great in the eyes of his Country-men, by means of his nearness and favour with us." Tisquantum probably did not begin with such naked ambition. He started to play "his own game" the previous spring when he appointed himself as the colonists' most useful friend and all those Namascheucks came flocking to Patuxet. In those weeks when he regularly crossed the stream between colonial houses and Native ones he could see the advantages of his position. On one side, he had the grateful support of the colonists, who still were afraid of their neighbors, and, on the other, he had the backing of a group that included members of an extended family, who feared the foreigners even more. It was in those months that he discovered a translator could easily omit or add details to a conversation with neither side being the wiser. He could shape how each saw the other.[16]

Bradford would later cast his plot as a selfish one, claiming that he started "drawing gifts from [Natives] to enrich him selfe." Winslow was a little more precise when he claimed that Tisquantum instead sought "gifts to himself to work their peace." Collecting gifts was something sachems did, but they also redistributed them back to their supporters. Squanto's desires were indeed more political than material: receiving those offerings was an act of self-aggrandizement and it worked. Clearly it offended the sensibilities of those who told on him to the settlers.

Still, it is a mistake to frame him as just a top-down, self-serving leader even if he wasn't a legitimate or honest one. It is yet another moment in the historical record where the English commentary on Native motives doesn't quite match their observations of Native actions and contradicts our larger contextual understanding of the Wampanoag political world. Those throngs of families who came to Patuxet did so because they saw Tisquantum as *their* ambassador to the English. When sharing their dishes and advice with the colonists, they were siding with his strategy over the Massasoit's. His opponents saw his intimations of violence as bullying threats, but his supporters would have seen them as evidence of his powers, as vows to keep them safe. Localized politics surely informed how his allies near Patuxet saw him; there isn't much evidence to suggest their relationship with Ousamequin was a deep one.

Squanto mourned the very same people they did and had reunited with them through mutual condolences. Moreover, the authority of sachems was never absolute—their rule could always be constrained by the people they claimed to lead. Not only could their council veto their plans for war but the public opinion of the entire community was the ultimate decider of whether their reign could continue. Later documents from the colonial period recorded multiple incidents of followers disowning their sachem and allying with a new one—classic examples of "voting with their feet."[17]

That exact dynamic was stirring in the seasonal village on the opposite side of the small falls. Ousamequin knew something was afoot and tried to monitor it, which is why he dispatched Tokamahamon and Hobbamock as his spies in Patuxet. Many Natives from nearby Nemasket, Manomet, and Massachusett villages gravitated toward the Patuxet man. Colonists reported they held "him in greater esteem than many of their Sachims." Some allies of the Massasoit "began to leave him, and seek after Tisquantum." His goal was to become much *like* a sachem, though he knew he could never completely become one. He lacked the born legitimacy and he had no corps of his own warriors and councilors behind him. But what he did have was a couple dozen Englishmen with guns who willingly followed him anywhere he led them, much like the train of men who accompanied a Native headman. And he could also cite the support of that great unseen sachem, King James I.[18]

His impersonation was never entirely convincing. Sachems could not invent themselves out of thin air. Their sovereign authority stemmed from generations of tradition, from annual ceremonies in which they shared their wealth, from their just decisions and carefully cultivated mystique, and most of all, from their family ties that bound them to their ancestors, their mortal followers, the lands they governed, and the manitous that watched over them all.

The Patuxet man had none of that. Near as we can tell, his core circle of supporters was just a handful of refugees who moved back and forth between Nemasket and Patuxet. He could hold secretive meetings only in the woods; genuine sachems held public meetings in plain view. He was not even that physically imposing or personally graceful—the English never wrote a word describing his looks or bearing but repeatedly remarked on the impressive stature and manners of Ousamequin, Hobbamock, Epenow, and other Native men. When they wrote the story of Corbitant's brief capture of Tisquantum, they noted that Hobbamock was strong enough to escape, an implicit hint that the Patuxet man was not.

In his attempts to keep climbing beyond his birth, Tisquantum resorted to open threats of violence. In the short term, it served his ends, but in a longer view, this appeal to brute force undermined his power. He boasted "he could lead" the colonists "to peace or war at his pleasure." If anyone doubted him, he sent "them word in a private manner, we were intended shortly to kill them." Soon, to keep the settlers on his side, he would become completely reckless with his accusations, "not caring who fell so he stood."[19]

When the colonists charged into Nemasket with guns ablaze the previous summer, they proved him right: they would indeed kill on his behalf. The rumors of Tisquantum's sway over the colonists and his favor with their manitou spread across the southern Dawnlands. The colonists noted that a parade of nine sachems came to ally with them after the Nemasket incident; surely they were also there to show due respect to their guide as well, lest he turn the English upon them. The jittery messenger who came with the arrows in November explicitly asked for Tisquantum first and seemed glad that he would not have to encounter the Patuxet man face-to-face. The symbolic missive from the Narragansetts, it seems, was addressed to both the quasi-sachem of Patuxet and the governor of Plymouth, who did not quite realize he had a Native counterpart.[20]

That winter, as the wall of tree trunks went up around Plymouth and Standish drilled his men night and day, Squanto started making the scariest claim of all. He and the colonists could control the plague itself, he said. Hobbamock, among others, was skeptical. But he could simply lead his doubters to view the dug-up floor of the colonists' storehouse where they had placed the casks of gunpowder. That was where they kept the plague, he told them. The English sources point out that the rest of the Natives probably did not know it was gunpowder specifically beneath the earth. But it would not be a huge stretch for any of them, including Tisquantum, to imagine that the explosive powder could also manifest disease. The colonists' ballistic weapons represented one of those mysterious advantages that the English had and Natives lacked. So too was the plague. It was possible that both these lethal powers could emanate from a single substance: the mightiest manitous took many forms.[21]

The forethought of a real sachem exposed the fake one. Before he knew the scope of Squanto's ambitions, the Massasoit could see the inherent problem posed by the only truly bilingual man in the southern Dawnlands. His wise decision to appoint Hobbamock as his man *in* Patuxet ultimately brought about the fall of the man *from* Patuxet. By March 1622, as the colonists finished impaling their village, Hobbamock began to air his "jealousies," meaning his misgivings, toward Tisquantum. He too could use rumors to his own ends. It was early April when he cautioned the colonists that their Massachusett neighbors had entered into an alliance with the Pocassets, the Narragansetts, and their immediate neighbors, the oft-visiting band that seemed to gravitate to Patuxet. Tisquantum himself was going to lead them into an ambush, Hobbamock warned. The colonists dismissed these warnings as alarmist; they could tell the two had a personal dislike for each other, and furthermore, they felt confident enough to go check with the Massachusett people themselves.[22]

Squanto's months-long plan was unraveling fast. Since "he could not make good these large promises" that he was mightier than the Massasoit, he became desperate. If the English and Massachusett people were able to speak to each other without him as interpreter, both parties would learn the extent of his lies. Realizing that he was running out of time, Squanto conferred with his closest allies, his own kin. They came up with an audacious last-ditch scheme. Just as the English were leaving the harbor to check in with the Massachusett people, "an Indian of Tisquantums family" came rushing up to wave them back to shore. He had dramatically slashed his own face, "the blood still fresh." He bore terrifying news. Ousamequin, Corbitant, and the hated Narragansetts had all banded together at Nemasket. They were coming to lay waste to Patuxet. Squanto's kinsman laid it on a bit thick, "oft looking behind him, as if some others had him in chase."[23]

The colonists fled inside their walls and started readying their heavy guns, when their other interpreter calmly approached them: "Hobbamock said flatly it was false." He was a member of the Massasoit's inner circle, he reminded them, he would know; the sachem alone could not start a war without the approval of Hobbamock and the rest of his council. The only threat to their safety was Tisquantum. The staged appearance of his self-wounded relative was a provocation. The Patuxet man hoped that "whilst things were hot in the heat of blood" the English would fight the Massasoit. With the Sowams leader gone, there would be no one "between him and honour; which he loved as his life, and preferred before his peace." The colonists could not quite believe what they were hearing. Bradford decided they needed direct confirmation from the man at Sowams. Hobbamock volunteered his wife to act as messenger. When she arrived in Pokanoket, she found the great sachem going about his business, unaware of all the drama unfolding at the small falls. He confirmed that he was still a friend to the English and "he was much offended" by the translator's behavior.[24]

With the truth exposed, the Plymouth colonists were furious at Tisquantum. Bradford "sharply reproved him" but hesitated before banishing him or punishing him too harshly. "He was so necessary and profitable an instrument," the governor had to confess. The English set about trying to clear the air with everyone their translator had misled, including Hobbamock, who still wanted to know if they really had the plague hidden beneath the soil, asking "whether we had such command of it." No, the English replied, "but the God of the English had it in store, and could send it at his pleasure to the destruction of his and our enemies." Squanto was wrong about what was buried in the ground, but he was speaking to a larger truth that both Natives and newcomers believed. And while the colonists did not want their neighbors to be needlessly afraid of them on the basis of lies, they *did* want them to fear the same God.

The colonists were willing to forgive Tisquantum and move on, but the Massasoit was not. He cited the first article in the agreement he made with the colonists: "if any of his did hurt to any of ours, he should send the offender, that we might punish him." Why would the English not grant him the same right? Through most of April and May, he repeatedly asked them to honor their pact and send the Patuxet man to be executed. The English agreed that by every reasonable standard, Squanto deserved death. But who would translate for them? Their defense was an admission that neither Hobbamock nor Tokamahamon were truly fluent yet.

Ousamequin persisted. He offered a generous bounty of beaver pelts if they carried out the execution. He even took the long knife off his neck and sent it to Plymouth so they could carry out the sentence. When his men arrived bearing the skins and knife, the English felt they were running out of options. They summoned Squanto to answer for his crimes. He threw himself at the mercy of Governor Bradford, but not before he angrily "accused Hobbamock as the author and worker of his overthrow." He did have a point: Hobbamock had also lied when he alleged that Squanto had allied with the Narragansetts and others to lead the colonists to their deaths. There was no basis for that rumor and the colonists clearly didn't believe it; if they had, they wouldn't have reconciled with their guide. Still, the Patuxet man's threats and falsehoods were far worse. The English declared they were unwilling to take the pelts in exchange for Squanto's life, but they conceded that they had lost the argument. The Massasoit's men stood ready to carry him back to Sowams and his doom.

They were almost "ready to deliver him into the hands of his Executioners," when a boat appeared off the coast. The colonists became distracted: Was this a French vessel? Who was this and what were their intentions? They asked the sachem's men to wait, promising to hand over the captive as soon as they resolved the situation with the approaching watercraft. The Pokanoket visitors became "mad with rage." The settlers seemed to have a bottomless reserve of excuses for this man. It was not even a ship drawing near, just a small boat. (It turned out to be some English fur traders coming from Mawooshen.) How was this more serious than honoring the literal first point of their agreement with the great sachem? "Impatient at delay," Ousamequin's agents "departed in great heat."[25]

Wily Tisquantum, that man of twists and turns, had once again cheated death.

FOURTEEN

Death

THERE WAS NO "SECOND THANKSGIVING" in the autumn of 1622. The husks, shells, and bones from the last feast lay rotting deep in the trash heap outside the English palisades, and the settlers huddled within were in a gloomy mood. With winter coming on, they worried their harvest was too meager. They'd wasted time building up their fort that summer and had neglected tending to their fields. Adding to their troubles, their backer Thomas Weston had sent along a rowdy group of new colonists in ships called the *Charitie* and *Swan* that spring. The newcomers were there to start a settlement at Wessagusset to the north of the small falls, but while they were lodging in Patuxet, they greedily depleted the colonists' stores of corn and other victuals. Before returning to England, the *Charitie* deposited supplies that would sustain the Wessagusset colony through the winter, but that still left the Plymouth settlement with thin margins. The original settlers grumbled about their poor treatment by their sponsor and fretted over their provisions as the days grew shorter.[1]

Squanto had not strayed far from the small falls since his life had been spared the previous spring. His friends reported that Ousamequin's fury and their defense of him "caused him to stick close to the English, and never durst goe from them till he dyed." It is not clear if the Nemasket-based groups once again spent the summer across the brook—though no mention of close-by Natives, other than Tisquantum and Hobbamock, appears in the sources. The whole fiasco chilled relations between the settlers and the Wampanoags at Pokanoket. Ever since the newcomers had ignored the terms of their treaty, the great sachem and his council had held the colonists at arm's length. The "Massassowat seemed to frown on us," Winslow wrote, noting he "neither came or sent to us"—hence why there was no sequel to the previous harvest feast. In time, the Pokanoket leadership resigned themselves to the fact that the colonists would never give up their interpreter. At some point that summer, a peace "was wrought" between the Patuxet man and the great sachem.[2]

Hobbamock must have been the go-between who made that reconciliation possible. The strapping man stayed on as a permanent neighbor alongside his rival, no doubt with the assignment of monitoring Tisquantum. To the English, the "emulation" or mirroring of these two figures was a positive. Bradford believed that both men were now acting "more squarely," or truthfully—an acknowledgment that Hobbamock had also spread false rumors in the midst of the unfolding plot. The governor encouraged Squanto to share news with him while Standish grew closer to Hobbamock. Two informants were better than one, offering "better intelligence." That same summer they heard news of a shockingly violent war that had broken out between the Powhatans and settlers in Virginia, which made them all the more attuned to the whispers and actions of their immediate neighbors.[3]

True to his reputation, Tisquantum had a plan that would help both his new friends and other Wampanoags. He had long been encouraging Native villagers to the south to plant surplus corn and beans to sell to the English, and he promised the colonists he could pilot their vessels to new harbors. Although Weston had severely disappointed the Plymouth settlers, his agents had left them with a fresh supply of trade goods and use of the *Swan* to accomplish the task.[4]

The expedition had several false starts. Just as the English loaded up the ship with goods to trade for crops, the *Swan*'s master Richard Greene died unexpectedly. Undaunted, Captain Standish took his place soon after they laid Greene to rest. Standish's title came from military service, not seafaring, so when the *Swan* crossed into heavy gales soon after leaving Plymouth, he wisely decided to turn the vessel around and wait out the weather. But just hours into his second attempt to head south, Standish was stricken with a "violent fever" and once again had to return to harbor. Finally William Bradford, Plymouth Colony's governor, reluctantly took command of the expedition.[5]

Squanto was confident—maybe too confident—that he could guide them through the forbidding sandbars on the Cape's far side, as he'd passed that way with Dermer and his French captives when they came back to Wampanoag country in the spring of 1620. Once on the water, though, he could not find a safe passage around the dangerous sandflats in the choppy, white-capped November seas. He piloted the *Swan* gingerly up a narrow tidal strait into the harbor at Monomoit so they could consider their next move. As evening fell he went ashore with the governor and a few others. The locals there had not met the colonists face-to-face and hid for a while, afraid to approach. Tisquantum gradually convinced them of the colonists' kind intentions, and soon enough the Monomoit locals welcomed the English warmly with venison and other dishes. The next day, the colonists traded for enough dried corn and beans to fill eight hefty hogshead casks to the brim. After this encouraging bit of business, the Patuxet man was game to try a second passage through the shoals.[6]

It was not meant to be. Before the *Swan* was even ready to leave, Squanto came down with a fever. Bradford offered the only detailed account of his last days:

> In this place Squanto fell sick of an Indean feavor, bleeding much at the nose (which the Indeans take for a simptome of death), and within a few days dyed ther; desiring the Gov[eno]r to pray for him, that he might goe to the Englishmens God in heaven, and bequeathed sundrie of his things to sundry of his English freinds, as remembrances of his love; of whom they had a great loss.

This single sentence leaves so many unanswered questions. It's the most explicit evidence we have of a dramatic rupture in Squanto's life after his political conspiracy was uncovered. While he had long allied himself with the English, they had never claimed he desired to be at one with them. His scheming had revealed a man more concerned with the opinions of his fellow Wampanoags than his relationship with the newcomers. The colonists consistently framed his threats, his boasts, his rumors, and his collection of tributes as a plot "to make himself great in the eyes of his Country-men."[7]

The revelations of the spring changed that. Ousamequin's furious rebukes surely caused the Patuxet man's supporters to scatter—especially those with no previous connection to him who only took his side out of fear. In the briefly mentioned reconciliation between Ousamequin and Tisquantum, one of the terms would surely be that Squanto was forbidden to make any overtures to his neighbors. No doubt Hobbamock had the job of making sure he obeyed.

But what became of his closest kith and kin? What happened to those "known friends" who appeared on the path between Patuxet and Nemasket, and could regularly be found in the harbor by the small falls collecting lobsters? What happened to his kinswomen who served his English companions breakfast at "the house of Squanto" in Nemasket? What about his relative who was so loyal to Tisquantum that he slashed his own face for him? Did he mention them at all in his last wishes?

The simplest reading of the text would be that Tisquantum's family and friends abandoned him. This lined up with Bradford's account of Squanto sticking "close to the English," never to "goe from them till he dyed." It also accorded with the report that he gave away his possessions to his colonial friends. If those were his only bequests, that act implied he no longer felt close with any other Indigenous people. His verbal will could even be read as his desire to be buried without the tools that Wampanoags expected to carry with them into the next life.[8]

In that case, his hope to spend his afterlife with the English was an admission that there was no going back to those who left him behind. Perhaps by order of the Massasoit, or perhaps because they felt betrayed by his dishonest ruthlessness, they shunned him. If true, this interpretation of the source meant Tisquantum was not so lucky six months earlier. It meant he died a social death before his physical one. It meant that he had spent the last six months of his life living in his own birthplace but alienated from his birth society.

Bradford's brief passage on Squanto's final wishes has shaped a lot of previous writing about him: it's the moment where he *does* come across as an unmarried sole survivor who had no family, no friends, and no gods to call his own. And at the time of his death, that may have been true. The one sentence doesn't contradict the evidence that he had reconnected with a small number of kinfolk upon his return; it only adds to the pathos of a man of many sorrows.

In this interpretation, his ties with his own people were not cut in 1614 when he was taken or because the epidemic took most of them away. Instead, his final loss came in the spring of 1622. And it wasn't because of a greedy Englishman or a malignant spirit, it was his own doing.

The tragic narrative above is one way to read Bradford's sentence, but it's not the only way. We can't be sure Squanto was at odds with his family or fellow Patuxet survivors for the same reason we don't know much about them other than the fact of their existence. The English weren't really interested in documenting the inner lives of Squanto or any other Wampanoag they met; they tended to write about how Natives' decisions and actions pertained to *them.*

The same sources that describe Tisquantum's death attest that at the moment he arrived in Monomoit, the local Nausets were reassured by his presence and treated him as an honest broker. If they were willing to forgive his trespasses against their ally the Massasoit and consider him trustworthy, why wouldn't his own kin? Is it possible that Bradford left out his interpreter's final requests on behalf of his family simply because those matters didn't concern the colonists?

A critical reader might even question whether Squanto's deathbed conversion happened at all. Winslow's account of his passing published in 1624 made no mention of any last words. Bradford was the only witness to record his requests in a narrative he composed decades after the fact. Yet Bradford certainly did not believe he would run into Squanto in heaven. Puritans, let's remember, thought most of their countrymen were damned because their ministers wore vestments and led their parishioners in prayers that weren't in the Bible. A Native who was guilty of dangerous deceit and who then expressed a vague interest in their God in his final hours could hardly be considered saved. There was, from Bradford's theological perspective, no obvious reason to invent or exaggerate the story, because it did not validate the influence of his own faith.

Another reason to believe the account was true was the snippet of Squanto's dying words that sounded like a verbatim quote, the mention of "the Englishmens God." That phrase was consistent with all we know about the spiritual world that he grew up in, in which different gods favored different peoples. No Wampanoag would deny that the settlers had a manitou of their own who worked on their behalf; they just thought it was odd that the English worshipped only one. The very nature of an animistic, polytheistic worldview was inclusive, not exclusive: new spirits simply joined the old ones, they didn't replace them. It's not even clear if Squanto's dying vision of "heaven" would be exclusive to the English— there's too much left unsaid in Bradford's account.[9]

The Patuxet man's exact beliefs about Christianity might well be the most enduring mystery about him. Though details are scarce, it is certain that multiple Europeans attempted to introduce him to their faith. It's possible that Juan Bautista Reales or another cleric attempted to baptize him in Málaga, and the Slanys surely tried as well when he was in England. It is also a given that he witnessed daily prayers and Sunday services on his various shipboard passages and when in London, Cupers, Jamestown, and Patuxet.

How much exactly did he participate or engage? That's hard to say. Catholics and Anglicans set a lower bar for conversion than Calvinist puritans did; they'd be more likely to baptize him and offer him communion if he'd gone through some basic instruction. Despite whatever exposure he had to his captors' faith in his time away, his later friends, Dermer and the colonists, did not seem to notice whether he had ever adopted any Christian beliefs or had a continued interest in the colonists' faith.

There is one missing piece of information that could explain everything: the fate of the Patuxet villagers who died in the epidemic. We don't know who buried them or where their remains rested. What if Dermer helped Squanto collect their bones and prayed for them while they filled in the grave? Wampanoags did sometimes inter their dead together in ossuaries. Or what if the people of Patuxet were laid to rest in the same place where the English later buried their dead, in that mass grave in the town's central hill? Either of those actions, combined with the English conviction that their potent manitou had long planned to place them at the small falls, could have convinced Tisquantum that most of his community had preceded him to "the Englishmens God in heaven" years ago. He might have linked his survival and the rebirth of Patuxet to evidence that the manitou who favored the settlers was also on his side. In this case, his claim that the plague lay buried in that very earth and that the English could summon it might not have been a fabrication but rather his genuine belief in the power of their prayers—and his.[10]

Though we can never know the truth of the Patuxet man's faith, we can compare him to the hundreds of Wampanoags and their neighbors who became Christians over the seventeenth century. Later New England missionaries found that those who were willing to join their "praying towns" tended to be survivors of communities that had been ravaged by epidemics who then banded together under the protection of English ministers. In some of the earliest recorded conversion narratives of Dawnlanders, the converts repented for their excesses of anger and pride. These new Christians spoke with deep regret for their previous wickedness, viewing transgressions against their own loved ones as their most sinful acts. In other words, Indigenous puritans tended to define sin in a way consistent with their value system based on kinship, reciprocity, and communal obligations. Another common motivation was a brush with death, something roughly a third of Native converts cited as a reason for their openness to Christian missionizing. Were he so inclined, Tisquantum certainly had many reasons to atone. But one problem with this theory of a repentant Squanto is that no colonist mentioned trying to convert him.[11]

Perhaps the paths that led Squanto to his dying wish were like the paths many more Natives followed in decades to come. In this reading of his motives, no one in Spain, England, Newfoundland, or the Plymouth colony swayed him to follow Christ: it was some combination of the Great Dying, his own regret for his crimes against his community, and his several brushes with death—either physical, social, or both—that made him seek out salvation from the Englishmen's god.

One mystery around Tisquantum's passing is a little easier to solve than the others. The poisoning hypothesis—the theory that someone at Monomoit performed a remote assassination for the Massasoit—is baseless. The colonists confirmed that Ousamequin had lifted his death sentence and that he and the interpreter made amends. Going against that agreement was exactly the kind of underhanded behavior that Ousamequin hated. It would violate his moral code and make him no better than Squanto at his worst. Not only was the motive unlikely, but the means are even harder to imagine. Lacing food to kill one person would be near impossible for the simple reason that "the common pot" was not just a metaphor. The women at Monomoit who fed Tisquantum, Bradford, and the other colonists dinner served themselves, their husbands, and their children from the same clay vessel.

We can therefore say with confidence that Squanto died of natural causes. Although the pathogen will never be known, he likely came down with a foreign infection, one of those that Europeans could survive but were often lethal to Natives. We can even attempt some basic contact tracing to consider who gave it to him. His illness could have been the "violent fever" that struck Captain Standish not long before the *Swan* left and was likely circulating among the colonists. Since Standish recovered, the col-

onists did not seem to think there was a link between his illness and Tisquantum. Having no inkling of germ theory or modern epidemiology, they
did not realize that the same pathogen might manifest differently in people
with different antibodies. Soon after burying their translator, the English
"found a great sickness to be amongst the Indians, not unlike the plague,
if not the same."[12]

It was one of many waves of introduced diseases that continued to
bring death and grief to Dawnland communities for decades to come. In
this one aspect of his story, there was sadly nothing unique about Tisquantum's fate.

Ultimately, it was the Patuxet man's way with words—both in Wampanoag
and English—that defined his character. He possessed a true gift for talking people into things and talking his way out of things. He may not have
been as tall or strong as Hobbamock or Epenow, but he did not lack self-
confidence. When tested again and again overseas, he proved to be a quick
study, picking up a new language and convincing his captors of his usefulness to secure his way home. Once returned, he brazenly brought a hated
Englishman with him and vouched for the foreigner. Months later, he lev-
eraged his linguistic abilities to become an indispensable envoy to that small
village of English settlers, and at the same time he used his facilities with
fiction to amass a following of old and new Native allies. Right up to his
last days on earth he remained a bold persuader, assuring Bradford and the
other English sailors that he would find a way through difficult seas.

The figure who appears in the colonial records sometimes lived up
to the lofty ideals of being an atoskauwou. On many occasions, he turned
fearful confrontations into civil conversations with his words alone. He
saved his friend Dermer's life twice. He helped ransom two Frenchmen
from their captivity. He brought together Wampanoags and English around
the small falls for at least one summer. But as he attempted to master the
ways of two worlds, he discovered a new advantage over Natives and newcomers alike, power that could go unchecked as long as all conversation
passed through him. As one biographer of politicians reminds us, "although the cliché says that power always corrupts, what is seldom said,
but is equally true, is that power always *reveals.*"[13]

Tisquantum's self-assured, silver-tongued, and risk-taking personality served him well among strangers, but when he came home, the darker

facets of these traits surfaced. His success in gathering together a new circle of friends, relations, and colonial allies led him to overestimate his abilities. He came to believe he would make a better Massasoit than the actual one. It was then that he revealed his arrogant, conniving, and reckless side.

His failed bid to become the pretend sachem of the reborn Patuxet was his gravest error. The flaw in his attempt to seize power was not just that he lacked the right bloodlines. When he made his wild claims that he could control disease and start a war, he betrayed the code of honor that bound leading men together. He put himself first, "not caring who fell as long as he stood." Winslow characterized Squanto's conspiracy as a self-destructive quest for "honour" that made him disregard the risks to his own life and the very peace he worked to achieve. Both his rise and his fall were tied to his prideful identity as a daring, fearless figure, but in his rush toward glory, he abandoned the principles that mattered the most. After he was discovered as a conspirator and charlatan who had been deceiving all sides, his reputation collapsed. But even then his forwardness saved him: he had made himself so indispensable to the English that they risked their treaty to keep the sachem's knife off his neck.[14]

Tisquantum had not grasped that the true source of Ousamequin's power did not come from his parentage, his generosity, or even his threats of violence. It came from his rare talents in leadership. Ousamequin was hardly a flawless politician—his coalition was often shaky and many partners would later complain that he sought to benefit his people over his allies—but, unlike Tisquantum, he was remarkably consistent in his words and deeds. The man from Sowams had abundant charisma, which outsiders could plainly see, and a talent for reading people. His suspicion of the Patuxet man and his confidence in Hobbamock were both clairvoyant insights. Most of all, he grasped that in the wake of the Great Dying, peace and alliance were the only way forward. The fact that he managed to convince so many others of this was a remarkable achievement.

Oddly enough, it was Squanto's rival Hobbamock, "the author and worker of his overthrow," who guarded his legacy. A year after the Patuxet man died, Hobbamock once again proved his trustworthiness to the colonists by defending them against another nearby conspirator. Within a few years, the settlers granted him a designated plot of land in their town. Hobbamock and his family lived alongside the colonists for another twenty years as their primary interpreter and guide. In some ways, he managed to live the life the Patuxet man seemingly wanted: he remained connected to his family and his people but benefited by remaining bound in friendship with the colonists. But Hobbamock could never bring about the larger elusive vision imagined by Ousamequin and his descendants, that dream of maintaining a continuous reciprocal relationship between their people and the English with each respecting the other as sovereign political equals. The goal was never realized for the simple reason that it was never what the colonists wanted.

FIFTEEN

Afterlives

TODAY PLYMOUTH, MASSACHUSETTS, looks like a lot of other middle-class New England towns, save for the attractions at the heart of its waterfront. Near the replica ship *Mayflower II* tourists enter a stone pavilion and peer over the viewing rail to see an unimpressive chunk of granite not much bigger than an ottoman footrest with the date "1620" chiseled into it. Originally known as Forefathers' Rock, it is the primary icon of the *Mayflower* myth, that larger collection of hokey and half-true stories around the Plymouth founders and Thanksgiving that serve as most Americans' introduction to Squanto.

Over the past four hundred years, as Tisquantum became an enduring literary character, he was seldom associated with this landmark—he wasn't there, after all, when the passengers disembarked. However, as a symbol, Plymouth Rock serves as both Plymouth's cornerstone and Patuxet's tombstone. The historian Jean M. O'Brien describes the link in meaning between the rock and Squanto as a process of "firsting and lasting." In her study of local histories of New England towns, she found that antiquarian authors commonly used a literary trick to erase Indigenous people from the landscape. Colonial acts were typically depicted as the "first," as in the first timber-framed house, the first white child born, the first church, and so forth, whereas at the same time, these writers took note of the death or departure of "the last living Indian" in a given town.[1]

The idea was not to portray the continent as a blank slate but rather one conveniently wiped clean. Scholars also call this trope "the elimination of the native" or a "replacement narrative." Plymouth Rock is a prime example of "firsting," in that it marks settlers' steps as a beginning point of a town, a colony, and a nation. Tisquantum's death is presented as a moment of Native "lasting." When depicted as the only surviving Native from Patuxet, he was, in O'Brien's words: "the first last Indian." According to the logic of "first" colonists replacing the "last" indigenes, his pass-ing ensured the demise of Patuxet as well.[2]

The actual boulder, dropped near this spot by a retreating glacier more than ten thousand years ago, was never mentioned in early colonial writings. Its legend as a landing point came from a single family's oral tra-dition written down a century after the *Mayflower* arrived—an account that could have been true but is impossible to verify. The original granite mass was much larger than the current one. It has since been cracked into many fragments that have been scattered across the United States, and the remaining bulk has been moved multiple times before returning to its orig-inal location. Hardly an eternal natural marker, it's an artificial symbol that would be unrecognizable to Tisquantum and the families it claims to memorialize.[3]

When the Massachusetts State Park interpreters stationed at the pa-vilion explain the rock's constructed and contested past, their audiences seldom seem surprised. Skepticism, not reverence, lures over a million visitors every year to this Boston suburb. Contemporary tourists' prevail-ing attitude of disbelief marks a departure from the rock's emergence as a national icon in the early nineteenth century, when writers and politicians invoked it as a serious symbol of America's foundations. For well over a century, pranksters and satirists have taken aim at the rock. Activists and vandals have chipped off pieces, scrawled the words "FAKE" and "LIES" on it, painted a swastika on its surface, covered it in sand, and splashed it with red, black, and blue paint.[4]

Even as a metaphor and not a physical object, the rock remains a ripe target. It has long featured in Native and Black activists' objections to the exclusionary claim that the United States is "a nation of immigrants." Poet Henry Wadsworth Longfellow's description of it as "a door-step / Into a world unknown,—the corner-stone of a nation!" is obscure these days, and far more know the Black nationalist Malcolm X's quip: "We didn't land on Plymouth Rock, the rock was landed on us!" Political cartoonists reliably use Plymouth imagery to point out hypocrisy in anti-immigration rhetoric by non-Indigenous people. Though it's so often the butt of jokes, somehow this granite hunk retains its cultural potency. There's a reason why it is still a magnet for graffiti and why Malcolm X imbued the rather small boulder with such a crushing weight.[5]

Over the centuries, as generations of colonial descendants crafted their tales of settler beginnings and Indigenous endings, Wampanoag historians were telling and writing their own narratives—narratives that sometimes purposefully minimized Tisquantum's role. We will get to those histories in a moment, but first we need to take a brief look at the creation of the dominant storyline. Like any story told again and again over four hundred years, the *Mayflower* myth has many authors, many editions, many revisions, and many critics. It began in the very sources that are the skeleton of this book.

William Bradford, Edward Winslow, the preacher Robert Cushman, and other colonists compiled their journals, letters, and notes from their first year of settlement into a multi-authored narrative that they sent to London in 1622. The manuscript fell into the hands of the puritan printer John Bellamie, who ran a printshop in Cornhill, a few doors down from the Slany house. John Slany was still living there when the type was being set, though now as a widower—Elizabeth died in 1618.[6]

Published as *A Relation or Iournal of the Beginning and Proceedings of the English Plantation Settled at Plymouth in New England,* the book established Squanto as a prominent character in the colony's first year. Winslow, who wrote the lion's share of the first book, authored a follow-up volume published two years later with a catchier title: *Good Nevves from Nevv-England.* This sequel included the first account of Tisquantum's plot, his downfall, and his death. Bellamie peddled copies of both books from his shop, a place the Patuxet man had walked by countless times. It was apparently a brisk seller. Bellamie released a second edition when Winslow sent in some edits and addenda.[7]

Bradford looked to improve upon these accounts in 1630, when he began composing a manuscript history of the colony's founding, titled *Of Plimoth Plantation.* It would become a twenty-year project that he never finished. Though his text was incomplete, the governor created a fluid and cohesive narrative that centered on the Scrooby congregation, following them from Lincolnshire to Holland to the Dawnlands. Bradford made himself a character while assuming the perspective of an omniscient narrator. It was the first source to encompass Squanto's entire story from capture to death, although other writers like Ferdinando Gorges and John Smith also mentioned Tisquantum's capture and his aid to the colonists in their histories of early English colonization.[8]

The governor's narrative remained unpublished for two centuries, yet it was a valued primary source for other chroniclers of the colonial past. When his nephew Nathaniel Morton consulted Bradford's text for a book on the early New England settlements published in 1669, he copied down much of the first nine chapters, up to the *Mayflower*'s arrival in America. Over the next century, Bradford's descendants lent out the manuscript to preachers and gentlemen historians in the region who relied on it as a major source when writing their accounts of New England's founding and the subsequent wars with Wampanoags and other Dawnlanders. These accounts made only passing remarks about Squanto as a providential figure who helped the settlers, and a couple didn't mention him at all. Two other early puritan chroniclers, Thomas Morton and Edward Johnson, did not have access to either Bradford's or Winslow's accounts, leading them to invent the long tradition of conflating Squanto with Samoset, by erasing the latter man and crediting Tisquantum with his chipper salutation: "Much welcome, Englishmen!"[9]

After decades being passed around the desks of elite New Englanders, among them Cotton Mather, Samuel Sewall, and Thomas Hutchinson, Bradford's handwritten manuscript and a collection of his correspondence came to rest in the tower library of Boston's Old South Church. In the 1770s as the conflict between colonists and their mother country escalated, British forces used the building as a garrison. When the Crown ordered its regiments to evacuate the city in 1776, some unknown member of His Majesty's troops who had been poking around the library decided to carry off Bradford's papers with him. Some of the governor's collected letters surfaced in a grocery store in Halifax, Nova Scotia, in 1793, and his narrative ended up on the far side of the Atlantic in the library of the bishop of London.[10]

Once American historians discovered it in England in 1855, they rushed to read it, transcribe it, and publish it. Its narrative of an intrepid godly community entranced stateside readers, helping spark more interest in the colony's early days. Bradford's version of the founding became the dominant one. One of his offhand biblical references, "but they knew they were pilgrims," originated the customary name for his band of exiles, replacing the term "forefathers." The governor's account was particularly influential in shaping the popular image of the Patuxet man—he had the most lavish praise for the translator, he favored the name Squanto over

Tisquantum, and he made that one tantalizing mention of his dying words.[11]

Meanwhile, in Plymouth, local historians had been cultivating a romanticized mystique around their community's founding. These antiquarians liked to obsess over their town's early years in part because what followed wasn't exactly a tale of triumph. Not long after Squanto died, the colony at Patuxet was eclipsed by rival English ventures. Founded in 1628, the neighboring Massachusetts Bay Colony was better funded and better planned. A flotilla of eleven ships carrying over seven hundred colonists arrived to found Boston in 1630, and a thousand or more colonists migrated to the colony in each year of the following decade. The older colony, which claimed all Wampanoag lands as its jurisdiction, was growing too but never at the same rate. During the seventeenth century, leaders in Boston encouraged rapid and aggressive colonial expansion, joining the new Connecticut colony in launching a genocidal war against the Pequot people in 1637.[12]

Plymouth sat out that conquest. The leadership supported their fellow puritans' actions but never actually joined their ranks. Soon enough they would take the lead in an even worse conflict. In the five decades following 1621, Wampanoags had worked tirelessly to preserve the terms of the treaty made at Patuxet. Ousamequin and, later, his son Metacom stayed in close contact with the following generations of Plymouth settlers. By the 1670s, though, many people of the dawn no longer saw the merits of the Massasoit's strategy. With each wave of disease, their numbers dwindled, and colonists continued to intrude on their land and ensnare many into debt peonage, all the while dismissing their complaints of unjust treatment. After a series of provoking incidents, Metacom and his council decided to fight back. A massive Native-colonial war broke out across the southern Dawnlands. It became known as "King Philip's War," after the English nickname for Metacom.[13]

The war raged for more than a year. It's rightfully remembered as one of the most horrific conflicts fought between Natives and colonists. Metacom and his allies laid siege to dozens of English towns, burning them to the ground and carrying off captives to torture and ransom. The colonists rounded up and imprisoned Natives indiscriminately and led aggressive campaigns against the Wampanoag-led coalition that culminated in wholesale massacres. Hundreds of settlers and thousands of Wampanoags and their allies died in the fighting. Colonists executed or enslaved many of their prisoners of war, sending ships filled with captives off to Atlantic sugar colonies and anywhere else slaves could be sold. Among the enslaved were more than a hundred men, women, and children who came to Plymouth to surrender peacefully. Unlike the first wave of men who were taken away by explorers, nearly every one of those who were shipped off never came home.[14]

The surviving people of the dawn lived in small communities that were mere islands in the sea of their original territory. Without their traditional hunting and fishing grounds, they had little choice but to farm in a manner more like their neighbors, or else to work for wages from colonial employers. Although often suffering from economic predation and exploitation at the hands of their white neighbors, Wampanoags proved resilient in the years after the war. In spite of constant colonial attempts to break them apart, the bonds of kinship remained the elemental links that kept their communities whole, and they continued to govern themselves with sachems and councils. The same could not be said for Plymouth Colony. In 1691, in the midst of a transatlantic power struggle over colonial self-rule, it was folded into the Massachusetts Bay Colony.[15]

Although they now had to answer to a governor in Boston, Plymouth residents retained their fierce local pride. By the mid-1700s, a few well-off residents owned copies of the New England histories by Morton, Mather, Sewall, and others that drew from Bradford and Winslow. They started to develop a kind of civic cult around the town founders, whom they called "Old Comers" or "Forefathers." In 1742, an elderly man whose father came to the colony in the 1620s caused a stir when he identified a shoreside rock as the place where the *Mayflower* passengers first set foot. As the imperial crisis over taxation and representation roiled the mainland British colonies, the original settlement at Plymouth suddenly came back into the minds and rhetoric of Revolutionary-era preachers and pamphleteers. The exiles' founding document of self-governance, dubbed the Mayflower Compact, made them particularly attractive to writers and preachers across New England. Together, the Compact and the Rock served as textual evidence and a material symbol of New England's independent spirit and its special destiny.[16]

In the years after the Revolution, white Yankees became more enchanted with their colonial past and the settlement at the small falls in particular. Towns across the Dawnlands established libraries and museums to celebrate their early days. By 1820, the bicentennial of the *Mayflower* landing, the legend of the "Pilgrim Fathers" was no longer just local lore. New England publishers and writers were in the midst of a literary campaign to establish that their region was the true incubator of the finest American values. Their certainty in their righteousness intensified as tensions grew between south and north, and they often invoked Plymouth Rock as a symbol of the "free" origins of Anglo-American society. The release of Bradford's account in 1856 helped cement the Plymouth myth in the national consciousness.[17]

Yankee nationalists strove to embed their rituals into the national calendar. Since the seventeenth century, puritan-led colonies had held days of "thanksgiving," prayerful holidays meant to express gratitude for God's salvation. A tradition began, probably originating in the Connecticut colony, of celebrating the harvest with an annual day of thanksgiving; it soon spread across the region. For many, the holiday began with a visit to church, followed by the big meal. By the nineteenth century, it was common for preachers to allude to local colonial beginnings and patriotic themes in their Thanksgiving sermons, but it was mostly Massachusetts ministers near Plymouth who put a particular emphasis on the *Mayflower*.[18]

White New Englanders who moved west after the Revolution brought the annual tradition to other states and territories. The New Hampshire-born writer Sarah Josepha Hale, editor of the nation's most popular magazine, *Godey's Lady's Book,* led a passionate campaign to turn the regional practice into a national one. Hale regularly wrote letters to state governors encouraging them to turn Thanksgiving into a legal holiday; by the 1850s, thirty states had set aside a day of Thanksgiving. She achieved her goal in 1863, when President Abraham Lincoln signed a Thanksgiving Proclamation that made the fourth Thursday in November a federal holiday. Lincoln, who was up for reelection in 1864, needed positive gestures to renew public faith in the grueling Civil War. The Protestant ritual, with its unifying feast and hints of divine favor, struck just the right tone.[19]

Neither Lincoln nor Hale associated the November holiday with Plymouth; that chapter was added to the *Mayflower* mythology in the late nineteenth century. Multiple writers noted that Winslow's account of the 1621 harvest feast when Ousamequin came to visit vaguely resembled a

Thanksgiving celebration, and they dubbed it the "First Thanksgiving." There was a long tradition, dating to before the Revolution, of white Americans celebrating Native people from the past at the same time living Natives were being expelled from their lands. In the nineteenth century, many white authors wrote elegiac novels, poems, and plays that lamented the tragic fate of "Indians" and "the Red Man," part of the larger trend of "firsting and lasting."[20]

Many Native peoples were indeed living under an existential threat. Ever since the War of Independence, the U.S. Army led a series of destructive campaigns against Indigenous nations, culminating with the Plains Wars that concluded in the late 1870s. Even before the shooting stopped, white-led vaudeville troops, which sometimes hired Native actors, began touring the country in circus-like Wild West shows that reenacted the conquest of the trans-Mississippi West through plays, stunts, and daredevil shows featuring large animals. Of course, this genre of theater was an old one, familiar to both Epenow and Shakespeare. At the same time that Buffalo Bill Cody and his imitators were setting up tents across the nation, tales of the Wild West quickly became a dominant genre in the popular cheap paperbacks known as "dime novels."[21]

This westward-facing vision was often imposed onto images of the First Thanksgiving. From the Gilded Age onward, Wampanoags were often depicted in Plains-style war bonnets and living in tipis made of buffalo hides. This Indigenous iconography often functioned as a metaphor for challenges faced by America's white majority. The story of vastly different people breaking bread was appealing to authors, illustrators, and advertisers in the Gilded Age and Progressive Era, especially those who fretted about the cultural assimilation of foreign-born Americans. The imagery of the feast was in keeping with the idea that America's westward expansion would heal its sectional and ethnic divisions.[22]

The addition of the Thanksgiving chapter to the *Mayflower* mythology was part of a gradual evolution of the undeniably Protestant holiday into a more secularized, nationalistic one. The crowded dining table was less a comment on real Native people and more an illustration that the American principle of tolerance extended to those who had no ancestral link to colonists. As the story of the shared November table became part of national lore, it was embraced by retailers like Gimbels in Philadelphia and Macy's in New York, which sponsored annual parades on Thanksgiving, often featuring white actors slathered in greasepaint and wearing feathered headdresses.[23]

This kitschy, commercialized version of the holiday had a firm hold in American collective memory by the early twentieth century. As their past became folded into a national origin story, Wampanoags and other Dawnlanders were put in a strange position: their ancestors were being celebrated while their own existence was either forgotten or barely acknowledged. The simplified story lost whatever sense of gravity it held to the originators of the *Mayflower* myth. The Rock and the Compact, hokey as they were, were actually serious political symbols in the late eighteenth and early nineteenth centuries, invoked in political debates, especially by parties and politicians grounded in the Northeast. When claimed by mass culture, Wampanoags and Pilgrims became popular corporate mascots, cartoon characters, and costumes worn in primary school plays.

Squanto's role was never that complicated in the modern Thanksgiving narrative. For those looking to shape an affirmative narrative of America's grand destiny, the image of a willing, advice-filled indigene eager to welcome settlers on his land was irresistible. The most popular tellings omitted his conspiracy, and many also erased his years as a captive. His character became an archetypal "good Indian" who, in his actions and words, signaled divine approval of the Pilgrims' first step on shore and every step westward that followed. The imaginary Squanto grew ever more distant from the real man. By the postwar period, children's authors revisited the Mayflower myth by imagining a new version of the Patuxet man: Squanto the peace-loving anti-segregationist. He became the hero of at least a dozen children's books published from the 1950s to the 2010s.[24] He even befriended the *Peanuts* gang in a 1988 cartoon special.

The books present the same plot. Squanto is typically portrayed as a young man or as a teenage boy. In most versions, he is taken by a bad Englishman (sometimes named Thomas Hunt, sometimes anonymous), then rescued by a good Englishman (Thomas Dermer) and repatriated in time to convince his fellow Wampanoags to befriend the newly arrived Pilgrims. Some include episodes in Spain, London, and Newfoundland; the majority of books mention the epidemic; and several make Epenow a key character as well. Without exception, the resolution of each book comes after Squanto offers his planting lessons, leading to the Thanksgiving feast. The Pilgrims greet the regal figure of the Massasoit under glorious fall colors while Squanto looks on with a satisfied smile. It's always a happy ending.

In highlighting the non-white man who set the Thanksgiving table, these authors extended the holiday's metaphoric meaning beyond healing ethnic and sectional divides, making it explicitly about the ideal of transcending America's color lines. The message was that racial harmony meant that others were best tolerated when they gladly assisted whites. One explicitly Christian text, Eric Metaxas's *Squanto and the Miracle of Thanksgiving,* put a particular emphasis on Squanto's time among Catholics in Spain and concluded with the Patuxet man offering prayers to the Christian god. The subtext is right there in the title of Clyde Robert Bulla's 1954 book *Squanto: Friend of the White Man.* Published by Scholastic Books, a publisher that markets directly to schoolchildren through book fairs, Bulla's book has remained in print continuously since its first printing. In 1982, Scholastic made a small edit to the subtitle: the Patuxet man is now billed as *Friend of the Pilgrims.* The text of the book remained the same. Similarly, Feenie Ziner's 1965 young adult book *Dark Pilgrim: The Story of Squanto* was rereleased in 1988 with the one-word title *Squanto.*[25]

The screenplay for the 1994 Disney version of Tisquantum's life, *Squanto: A Warrior's Tale,* followed the standard picture book. In it, Squanto is a young man starting a family when he is enslaved at the behest of a foppish villain, Ferdinando Gorges. When the Patuxet man is taken overseas, the holy men who save him from slavery are English, not Spanish. They teach him that some Englishmen can be kind; he teaches them how to make popcorn. Squanto's friend Epenow is also taken with him and remains embittered toward the English even after they are both repatriated. When the Pilgrims arrive at the end of the movie, Squanto softens Epenow's heart with a speech celebrating peace and kindness. Soon the turkey is served and the credits roll.[26]

Starring the Anishinaabe actor Adam Beach in the lead role and featuring Mandy Patinkin as a warm-hearted monk, the movie recouped only $3.3 million of its $19.2 million budget. Its flop at the box office was due mostly to its dopey script and clunky direction, not because of many Wampanoags' objections to its misleading portrayal of their culture and history. The studio's animated feature *Pocahontas,* which had similar inaccuracies but was a bit more capably made, was released the following year to greater success.

» » « «

Wampanoag historians have never settled on a single version of Plymouth's founding—just like the storytellers from the nation that surrounds
theirs. In different accounts over the centuries since the early 1620s, there
are consistent themes that Dawnlanders' chronicles emphasize: reciprocity, obligations, persistence, and mourning. One component that was often
missing, though, was Tisquantum. This tradition was an old one: he did
not appear in recitations of the past given at a time when some Wampanoags who knew him were still living. Metacom, the son of Ousamequin,
retold his peoples' perspective on their relations with the Plymouth Colony in a 1675 diplomatic meeting with colonial leaders:

> thay saied thay had bine the first in doing good to the English, and
> the English the first in doing rong, saied when the English first
> Came their kings father [Ousamequin] was as a great man and the
> English as a litell Child, he Constraened other indians from rong-
> ing the English and gave them Coren and shewed them how to
> plant and was free to do them ani good and had let them have a 100
> times more land, then now the king [Metacom] had for his own
> peopell.

Metacom's history was likely relayed through an English translator, then
condensed into this short summary, but there was a clear Native voice
in this account. There was a customary anaphoric couplet ("first in doing
good," "first in doing rong") and a familial simile (Ousamequin "was as a
great man" caring for "a litell Child").[27]

In this interpretation, Metacom credited his father and his people
with showing the Plymouth settlers "how to plant." In his elders' memories of those early years, the Massasoit was the central actor, and the very
act that Bradford attributed to Tisquantum was recalled as a collective
effort. It's a clue that all Wampanoags who were there in Patuxet that first
summer saw themselves as responsible for the successful harvest; they saw
the translator as merely their mouthpiece and not the sole teacher. In the
more detailed versions told among his people and not to outsiders, perhaps the former captive did appear, but only in the absentative state—in
words that could be translated as "our late friend," "the late man from
Patuxet"—as part of the practice of never speaking the name of the dead.

Metacom actually demonstrated that linguistic convention in his speech, in which Ousamequin appeared as "their kings father" but never by his personal or honorific title.

The figures of a "great man" and "litell Child" spoke to the tutoring and acts of kindness offered by the Massasoit and his many agents, including Squanto but also many more. The image of a powerful elder offering gifts and acts of kindness to a small child was a metaphor for bonds of obligation between generations, as each expected the next to uphold their responsibilities. When Metacom spoke these words to his English neighbors, he was accusing them of betrayal. In his eyes, the "child" had grown into an ungrateful adult who insulted the Massasoit's descendants, shunned the education he had given them, and never reciprocated his generosity. This passage came from a much longer oration, in which he listed the many grievances that would lead to all-out war just weeks after he gave this speech.[28]

A century and a half later, a historian from the nearby Pequot nation gave a more detailed interpretation that drew both on colonial sources and on discussions with his many Wampanoag friends. William Apess was a preacher, scholar, and political activist who became a prominent figure among his fellow Dawnlanders in the 1820s and 30s. Growing up in post-Revolutionary America, Apess was well aware of the evolving *Mayflower* myth and took particular exception to the common narratives of Native erasure and replacement, especially those deployed by President Andrew Jackson, who was in the midst of uprooting tens of thousands of southern Natives in the forced expulsion known as "the Trail of Tears."[29]

The Pequot preacher's most famous work was a eulogy for the very man who spoke of the "great man" and "child": Metacom, also known as King Philip. Apess penned the tribute a century and a half after the sachem died in the war that bears his name. His main source on early Plymouth was the work of the historian Samuel Gardner Drake, who published an overview of Native history in 1833; at this time Bradford's manuscript was still hidden away in a London archive. Apess included much of Squanto's story in his eulogy, but he never put the Patuxet man front and center.

He described both Samoset and Squanto as "young chiefs" or "gentlemen chiefs" who helped the colonists survive, only to receive "the applause of being savages." He took note of the uncovering of Tisquantum's plot, but his main concern in that episode was the way the Plymouth leaders violated their treaty so soon after agreeing to it. Apess made no secret of the fury he felt when reading about colonial dealings with his ancestors and all other Native peoples. While enumerating the Plymouth colonists' various trespasses against their Wampanoag neighbors, he was unsparing in his judgment, writing, "Now let us see who the greatest savages were."[30]

Apess was one of many Dawnlanders who shared the literary inclinations of their white neighbors and started publishing newspapers, sermons, hymns, histories, memoirs, poetry, and fiction in the nineteenth century, though he was seemingly alone among these writers in taking an interest in Tisquantum. The political concerns of many Indigenous authors at the time were firmly rooted in the present. Many Native communities were in a bind; they were not counted as citizens, yet they faced ongoing assault from state governments seeking to revoke what few legal protections they had secured for local autonomy and boundaries in the colonial era. The literature that these writers produced were testimonies to their enduring presence, their living cultures, and their wish to remain in the lands of their ancestors.[31]

By the time of the *Mayflower* tricentennial in 1920, the thousands of Wampanoags still in Massachusetts had been "detribalized" but were still living in communities tied to ancestral lands, which they had never ceded. Some even appeared at the official celebration at Patuxet to represent their people, but more showed up for a 1928 powwow in which they reaffirmed their existence as a political body. These actions helped lay the groundwork for later state and federal recognition of Wampanoag nations.[32]

In the decades after World War II, just as Squanto was being reimagined in children's literature, there was a new resurgence of Native activism. The Red Power movement of the 1960s and '70s began among nations from the Midwest and West, but it soon found adherents in the Northeast. As the 350th anniversary of the *Mayflower* landing approached, some Massachusetts politicians hoped to make an inclusive gesture by inviting a Wampanoag speaker to the official celebration. Their chosen speaker was the Wampanoag veteran Frank James, who also took the title of Wamsutta, Ousamequin's son. When he submitted his remarks on the three and a half centuries of injustice that his people faced, his hosts got nervous and disinvited him from giving the address. Determined not to be silenced, Wamsutta led a protest at Plymouth on November 26, 1970, a cool, dreary Thanksgiving Day. Over two hundred Indigenous activists interrupted the

annual celebration on the waterfront. In his impassioned speech to his
fellow protestors and gathered spectators, Wamsutta aired the feelings
shared by many of his fellow Dawnlanders about their painful history and
their present-day desire to have their survival and their sovereignty acknowledged. Although he never explicitly mentioned Tisquantum, Wamsutta
described the Massasoit's choice to make an alliance with the colonists as
his peoples' "greatest mistake."[33]

The event made the national news. It began a tradition: Wamsutta
called on his fellow Wampanoags and all other Indigenous Americans to
commemorate the fourth Thursday in November as a national day of
mourning. The tradition recalled a declaration made by Apess over a century earlier. Writing in 1836, well before Thanksgiving was associated with
either Pilgrims or Natives, the Pequot minister singled out the Fourth of
July and "Forefathers' Day," the holiday commemorating the *Mayflower*
arrival, as "days of mourning and not of joy." Each year since 1970, on each
Thanksgiving, a contingent of tribal members and their neighbors have
held a somber gathering on Cole's Hill, the spot where Wamsutta made
his remarks.[34]

Wamsutta's protest also prodded the nearby Plimoth Plantation
museum to reconsider how it approached the Indigenous side of its story.
Begun in 1945 as an institution to celebrate "Pilgrim heritage," the museum
had grown into one of the nation's largest living history museums by the
late 1960s. Its main attraction was an open-air life-size replica of the original village as it looked in 1627, built on a farm three miles south of the real
small falls. In the aftermath of Wamsutta's declaration, the Wampanoag
educator Everett "Tall Oak" Weeden began working with the museum
to create a Native-led program to interpret the Indigenous past in Patuxet
before and during the English arrival.[35]

When the Wampanoag historian Nanepashemet was working at the
museum in the 1980s, he wrote a young adult book on Tisquantum. Although his manuscript remains unpublished, the museum ran several
lengthy excerpts in *Plimoth Plantation Almanack,* then the museum's
official magazine. Nanepashemet began his narrative by noting that the
Patuxet man was considered an "anti-hero" among many of his fellow
people of the dawn. Some disliked the interpreter for plotting against the
Massasoit; others objected more to the popular myth that framed him as a
distasteful symbol of "collaboration between some natives and colonizers

which brought about hard times and the near destruction of the Native people and their way of life." Nanepashemet's fair-minded narrative drew from the latest scholarship and presented the Patuxet man as a lone survivor who fell victim to his hubris and died an outcast from his people. The author closed with a plea that his readers—Wampanoag and non-Wampanoag alike—remember the troubled yet talented man in his whole humanity, rejecting the many caricatures.[36]

In the decades since its founding in 1971, the museum's division now known as the Wampanoag Indigenous Program has faced ups and downs. The first generation of educators were eager to center an accurate, respectful version of their ancestors' story, but they were often frustrated by the marginal position they held within the museum. Visitors to the small cluster of wetus and its cornfield often greeted the Native interpreters with war whoops and crude jokes, and worst of all, open skepticism that the people staffing the site were "real Indians."[37]

On the eve of the 2020 quadricentennial of the *Mayflower*'s arrival, the museum announced it was changing its name from Plimoth Plantation to Plimoth Patuxet. Meant to emphasize the bicultural character of both the historic settlement and the museum itself, the name change came at a fraught moment. Over the previous decade, some former Indigneous staff began airing their grievances with the museum's management. They raised concerns that the Native homesite has been underfunded and they objected to some of the institution's collection practices. The COVID-19 pandemic drastically cut the museum's revenue, putting planned improvements to the Wampanoag homesite temporarily on hold. In 2022, a group of Wampanoag educators and leaders announced they were cutting ties with Plimoth Patuxet and encouraged a boycott, though a few Wampanoag tribal members still work at the museum and support its mission. In a public statement, the museum objected to claims of neglect and signaled its openness to address the concerns of its critics. Only adding to the tensions, in December 2022 the tribal chairman of the Mashpee Wampanoag Tribe faced criminal charges for his alleged involvement in a nighttime burglary at the museum, during which thieves carried off woven bullrush mats and bearskin rugs valued at $10,000 from the Wampanoag homesite.[38]

As of this writing, the two sides remain at an impasse. Though Plimoth Patuxet remains a major attraction for tourists seeking to learn the story of the colony and its neighbors, it never could be—and never attempted to be—the place that best captured the range of Native perspectives on the early colonial past. Today, many people of the dawn focus their energy on their own tribally run museums, the Mashpee Wampanoag Museum on Cape Cod (also founded in 1970) and the Aquinnah Cultural Center (founded in 2005) on Martha's Vineyard. These teachers dedicate themselves to educating their own people in community events, community schools, and pan-tribal powwows. Wampanoag historians continue to design museum exhibits; to publish poetry, essays, and op-eds; to write books for children and adult readers; to give talks across the nation and globe; and to collaborate with documentary and feature filmmakers.

Tisquantum is just one character in one small chapter of their epic tribal story. His descendants and fellow educators know that an interpreter's work is never done.

Epilogue

AROUND THE TIME OF THE American Revolution, Cape Cod was shrinking. The sandy edges of the Massachusetts peninsula had been dissolving into the sea for ages, but the pace of land loss picked up markedly in the eighteenth century. Generations of colonists had cut down mature hardwood trees that served as a natural soil retainer and windbreak. They let their cattle graze on dunes, ripping out the root systems that held the sand in place. Officials forbid grazing in sensitive lands as early as 1730, but many farmers ignored these laws, much to their own detriment. Sand and salt spray continued to drift onto their fields, stunting their crops for decades to come, and each passing tropical system or winter nor'easter washed more land away. Weakened dunes could no longer filter rainwater or fend off the rushing tides; chunks of clay cliffs came crashing down like icebergs calving off glaciers.[1]

In 1780, just four years after Massachusetts declared its independence, this ongoing erosion reopened a mystery from the state's colonial beginnings. After a torrential storm, Paul Crowell, a sixtyish widower and retired deacon living in the town of Chatham, made a grim discovery. At a spot where his land sloped toward a saltwater inlet, the rains had carved a gully in the hillside, revealing a male skeleton. The dead man's frame lay "at the depth of three feet from the surface of the earth," resting in a bed of rotting seaweed and surrounded by wooden planks in the shape of a "crib or box." Briny groundwater had preserved some of the wood and algae, though no flesh was left on the bones. Because the site "had never been used as a burying place since the English settled here," the deacon and his neighbors reasoned, "the person buried must have been a native."[2]

The body had been interred according to traditional Native practice, with tools for the afterlife. Alongside the remains were an axe, a stone pipe, and a pipe cleaner made of fishbone. The skeleton was a large one; the man must have stood about six feet tall. Taking into account the condition of the decaying organic matter, Chatham townsfolk reckoned "that this person must have been buried [for] more than a century and an half."[3]

Warren Sears Nickerson, a Cape Cod historian who came across the account of the grave in the 1950s, saw a contradiction of sorts. There was little doubt the man was Indigenous, but the "crib or box" caught his attention: aboriginal gravesites tended to be oval in shape with the dead resting in a fetal position and surrounded by woven mats. The remains, he decided, belonged to a Native man, but one who was buried "not in the usual Indian fashion." So who was this unknown indigene who lived in the seventeenth century and seemed to rest in a colonial coffin?[4]

To Nickerson, the answer was obvious: Squanto. His role in the Thanksgiving saga was so thoroughly mythologized by the mid-twentieth century that a plausible discovery of the real man's bones was a bit like finding the fossilized stump of George Washington's cherry tree. The grave that yawned open in 1780 is the most commonly cited location for his grave, but Chatham residents have proposed at least four other sites as Tisquantum's final resting place. Nickerson had previously speculated that his was one of two skeletons unearthed when a golf course was built along the shore in the 1920s. Although he later abandoned that theory in favor of Crowell's discovery, the country club didn't get wind of this recantation; it still claims on its website that the Pilgrims' friend lies beneath its links.[5]

In the 1950s, a road gang working in the Cape Cod town claimed to have dug up a headstone with the name "Squanto" etched on it, a claim no one could later verify. Around the same time, the Chatham Historical Society commissioned a memorial stone, affixed with a plaque claiming that the Thanksgiving hero was "buried somewhere within gunshot of this stone," and placed it at the Atwood House Museum in Chatham. Years later, the Nickerson Family Association had it relocated to their grounds, on the other side of town and closer to the 1780 Crowell site. As recently as 2011, the discovery of a new set of Indigenous remains on the north side of town led to renewed speculation that *this* was the true resting place of Tisquantum.[6]

Though Nickerson made the most credible-sounding claim, he was too hasty in his conclusions. Bradford was clear that Squanto gave away most of his possessions before dying. The axe, pipe, pipe cleaner, and the seaweed lining found in the 1780 grave don't quite align with the evidence. The coffin also did not fully support Nickerson's case. Dawnlanders did sometimes bury their dead within wooden frames exactly like the "crib or box" that held the six-foot-tall man. The Plymouth colonists discovered one such grave where the dead were boxed in with boards. Another Englishman described how Massachusett mourners buried people of higher status: they "put a planck" on the floor of the grave "for the corps to be layed upon, and on each side a plancke, and a plancke on the top in forme of a chest, before they cover the place with earth."[7]

The fact is, tens of thousands of Native people have lived and died in this part of the Cape. The burial found in 1780 had no evidence of colonial involvement and no clear link to the Patuxet man. It was just the remains of a well-regarded man lying in a bed of seaweed, entombed in wood, with tools for his life in the world beyond this one. The odds are remote that any one set of uncovered remains belonged to the best-known person to die there.

Even if Squanto's burial site were conclusively identified, its contents would not belong to the landowners. If found on public land, his remains would be placed under the care of his thousands of living Wampanoag relatives, whose inherent human right to prevent the desecration of their ancestors' bodies is currently safeguarded by the Native American Graves Protection and Repatriation Act. Passed in 1990, this federal law forbids anyone from disturbing Indigenous remains or artifacts or from keeping them as specimens without the consent of the culturally affiliated tribal communities. If he was found on private land, Massachusetts laws would compel the landowner to notify the state archaeologist, likely leading to a repatriation of his bones.[8]

Any deliberate hunt for Tisquantum's remains would be a sacrilege to his descendants. Few people are indifferent to seeing their ancestors or loved ones dug up against their wishes; for Wampanoags in particular, this kind of desecration is compounded by centuries of seeing their ancestors disinterred by looters, pothunters, and archaeologists. Seeing as the Patuxet man once instructed the colonists how to make amends for their acts of grave robbing, those Chatham residents who later boasted of finding his bones could have used his counsel.[9]

There's something fitting about the fact that Tisquantum cannot be located, since he believed that sometimes the most powerful kind of monument is the one that isn't there. The colonist Edward Winslow learned about collective memory-keeping practices from "discourses" with the Patuxet man in their journeys along Dawnlands paths. The Englishman did not explicitly name Squanto as his history teacher, but there can be no doubt it was he. Although a couple of fast learners near Plymouth could speak some English at the time of Winslow's writing, only Squanto was fluent enough to engage in a "discourse" that the colonist could understand. Winslow wrote that he and his guide occasionally came across a peculiar cavity, "a round hole in the ground about a foote deep." Squanto explained that these pits marked the location of a noteworthy place—the site of a supernatural occurrence, a battle, a diplomatic summit, or any other event that he and his fellow Wampanoags did not want to forget. Once a person heard the story that went with a specific memory pit, he was duty bound to learn the tale by heart and keep the hole clear every time he passed.[10]

Writing about this practice, Winslow marveled at how it kept "many things of great Antiquitie . . . fresh in memory." He wrote that if one "can understand his guide, his journey will be the less tedious, by reason of the many historical discourses [which] will be related to him." It's tempting to lament that Winslow never transcribed any of the Patuxet man's accounts, but that would be missing the point. These were narratives meant to be given a voice again and again, kept alive over the generations by speakers, not writers.[11]

Tisquantum, that teller of tales, avoided the false certainty of a marker like Plymouth Rock. He preferred a verbally preserved poetic nothingness over a heavy-handed granite somethingness. He knew that in time a forgotten hole would fill in on its own, so the absence of dirt represented the presence of historians. It was reminiscent of the absentative suffix in his language, that grammatical convention that let speakers recall a lost person without speaking their name. The missing name in a Wampanoag sentence, like a missing piece of earth alongside a Wampanoag path, demonstrated reverence for those who came before.

The search for Squanto's legacy will always end up at that particular place where his body cannot be found but his memory lives on. It is the place where Wampanoags congregate every November to mourn him and so many others; the place where he was raised; the place he longed to return to over his many years across the sea; that place at the small falls that holds stories in its soil.

Notes

Abbreviations

CWJS   Philip L. Barbour, ed., *The Complete Works of Captain John Smith, 1580–1631,* 3 vols., Chapel Hill: University of North Carolina Press, 1986

ENEV   David B. Quinn and Alison M. Quinn, eds., *The English New England Voyages, 1602–1608,* London: The Hakluyt Society, 1983

Bradford, *OPP*   William Bradford, *Bradford's History of Plymouth Plantation, 1606–1646,* ed. William T. Davis, New York: Scribner's, 1908 (1st ed., 1856)

RVCL   Susan Myra Kingsbury, ed., *Records of the Virginia Company of London, 1606–26,* Washington, DC: U.S. Government Printing Office, 1933

WMQ   *William and Mary Quarterly*

Introduction

1. The two accounts of Tisquantum's death are in Bradford, *OPP,* 150 ("an Indean feavor"); Edward Winslow, *Good News from New England: A Scholarly Edition,* ed. Kelly Wisecup (Amherst: University of Massachusetts Press, 2014), 71–72. My description of the healers' actions is extrapolated from Winslow's and other observers' descriptions of local practices for caring for the sick. See Winslow, *Good News,* 79–81; Roger Williams, *A Key into the Language of America; or, An Help to the Language of the Natives in That Part of America Called New-England . . .* (London, 1643; repr., Bedford, MA: Applewood Books, 1997), 198–99; William Wood, *Wood's New England's Prospect* (London, 1630; repr., New York: Burt Franklin, 1967), 92–94.

2. Bradford, *OPP,* 111 ("spetiall instrument"); although the "Pilgrims" title comes from a passage in Bradford ("but they knew they were pilgrims"), historian Michael Winship points out that they used the word only "in the generic sense that every Christian know that he or she was a pilgrim whose home was in heaven." Winship, *Hot Protestants: A History of Puritanism in England and America* (New Haven: Yale University Press, 2018), 72.

3. Chester P. Soliz, *Historical Footprints of the Mashpee Wampanoag Indians* (Sarasota, FL: Bardolf, 2011), 35 ("He who is great"); Lisa Blee and Jean M. O'Brien, *Monumental Mobility: The Memory Work of Massasoit* (Chapel Hill: University of North Carolina Press, 2019), 10 (the Massasoit).

4. Bradford, *OPP,* 128 ("They begane to see"); Winslow, *Good News,* 64 ("Thus by degrees").

5. Bradford, *OPP,* 150 ("to pray for him").

6. On the poisoning theory, see Nathaniel Philbrick, *Mayflower: A Story of Courage, Community, and War* (New York: Penguin Books, 2006), 138; Alden T. Vaughan, *Transatlantic Encounters: American Indians in Britain, 1500–1776* (Cambridge: Cambridge University Press, 2006), 74.

7. Serious treatments of Tisquantum's life to date include Charles Francis Adams, *Three Episodes of Massachusetts History: The Settlement of Boston Bay* (Boston: Houghton, Mifflin, 1892), 1:21–44; Lincoln N. Kinnicutt, "Plymouth and Tisquantum," *Proceedings of the Massachusetts Historical Society* 48 (1914): 103–18; Leonard A. Adolf, "Squanto's Role in Pilgrim Diplomacy," *Ethnohistory* 11.3 (1964): 247–61; John H. Humins, "Squanto and Massasoit: A Struggle for Power," *New England Quarterly* 60.1 (March 1987): 54–70; Neal Salisbury, "Squanto, Last of the Patuxets," in *Struggle and Survival in Colonial America,* ed. David J. Sweet and Gary B. Nash (Berkeley: University of California Press, 1988), 228–46; Nanepashemet (Anthony Pollard), "Tisquantum: The Real Story of Squanto" (unpublished manuscript, 1988), Plimoth Patuxet Museum Special Collections; Philbrick, *Mayflower,* 94–138; Vaughan, *Transatlantic Encounters,* 57–77; Daniel K. Richter, *Before the Revolution: America's Ancient Pasts* (Cambridge, MA: Belknap, 2011), 153–157; Betty Booth Donahue, *Bradford's Indian Book: Being the True Roote & Rise of American Letters as Revealed by the Native Text Embedded in* Of Plimoth Plantation (Gainesville: University of Florida Press, 2011), 105–20; Jace Weaver, *The Red Atlantic: American Indigenes and the Making of the Modern World, 1000–1927* (Chapel Hill: University of North Carolina Press, 2014), 58–62; Andrew Lipman, *The Saltwater Frontier: Indians and the Contest for the American Coast* (New Haven: Yale University Press, 2015), 99–102; Paula Peters, *Captured! 1614,* mobile exhibit in various museums, 2014 (the content of this exhibit is also summarized in Blee and O'Brien, *Monumental Mobility,* 178–79); David Silverman, *This Land Is Their Land: The Wampanoag Indians, Plymouth Colony, and the Troubled History of Thanksgiving* (New York: Bloomsbury, 2019), 61–85; Paula Peters, "Of Patuxet," in *Of Plymouth Plantation: The 400th Anniversary Edition,* ed. Kenneth P. Minkema, Francis J. Bremer, and Jeremy D. Bangs (Boston: Colonial Society of Massachusetts and New England Historic Genealogical Society, 2020), 25–47; Neal Salisbury, "Treacherous Waters: Tisquantum, the Red Atlantic, and the Beginnings of Plymouth Colony," *Early American Literature* 56.1 (2021): 51–73; Ned Blackhawk, *The Rediscovery of America: Native Peoples and the Unmaking of U.S. History* (New Haven: Yale University Press, 2023), 56–60.

8. William Wallace Tooker, *John Eliot's First Indian Teacher and Interpreter Cockenoe-de-Long Island: The Story of His Career from the Early Records* (London: Henry Stevens's Sons and Stiles, 1896); Jeffrey Mifflin, "'Closing the Circle': Native American Writings in Colonial New England, a Documentary Nexus between Acculturation and Cultural Preservation," *American Archivist* 72.2 (2009): 344–82; Julie A. Fisher, "Speaking Indian and English: The Bilinguals of Seventeenth Century New England" (PhD diss., University of Delaware, 2016). The literary critic Betty Booth Donahue has already proposed how we might consider Native epis-

temologies being "embedded" in texts like "Of Plimoth Plantation," in *Bradford's Indian Book,* though her argument was more about the sharing of rhetorical forms than the Native cultural information being dictated to colonists who create a flawed facsimile of Tisquantum's teachings; other critics to take the Indigenous influence upon these texts seriously include Cristobal Silva, who details what he calls Tisquantum's "counter-epidemiology," in *Miraculous Plagues: An Epidemiology of Early American Narrative* (New York: Oxford University Press, 2011), 50-61.

9. Jessie Little Doe Baird gives an overview of the language program's founding in an interview with J. Kēhaulani Kauanui, published in Kauanui, *Speaking of Indigenous Politics: Conversations with Activists, Scholars, and Tribal Leaders* (Minneapolis: University of Minnesota Press, 2018), 1-13.

10. On the robust traditions of Indigenous memory-keeping, see William Apess, *On Our Own Ground: The Complete Writings of William Apess, A Pequot,* ed. Barry O'Connell (Amherst: University of Massachusetts Press, 1992); Soliz, *Historical Footprints of the Mashpee Wampanoag;* Siobhan Senier, ed., *Dawnland Voices: An Anthology of Indigenous Writing from New England* (Lincoln: University of Nebraska Press, 2014); Christine DeLucia, *Memory Lands: King Philip's War and the Place of Violence in the Northeast* (New Haven: Yale University Press, 2018); Blee and O' Brien, *Monumental Mobility,* 1-30, 202-13; Silverman, *This Land Is Their Land;* Peters, "Of Patuxet." There are a wide variety of models of how non-Native and Native scholars alike can productively engage with Indigenous experts outside the academy. In the field of Early American history, specific work that has shaped and challenged my thinking and practice beyond those cited above include Melissa Fawcett [Melissa Tantaquidgeon Zobel], "The Role of Gladys Tantaquidgeon," *Papers of the Fifteenth Algonquian Conference,* ed. William Cowan (Ottawa: University of Carleton, 1984), 135-45; Daniel K. Richter, "Whose Indian History?" *WMQ* 50.2 (April 1993): 379-93; Lisa Philips Valentine, "Twenty-Five Analytic Pitfalls in Algonquian Research," *Papers of the Twenty-Seventh Algonquian Conference,* ed. David H. Pentand (Winnipeg: University of Manitoba, 1996), 324-36; Shirley Blancke and John Peters Slow Turtle, "Indigenous Peoples' Control over and Contribution to Archaeology in the U.S.A.," *Bulletin of the Massachusetts Archaeological Society* 57.2 (Fall 1996): 64-68; Patricia E. Rubertone, *Grave Undertakings: An Archaeology of Roger Williams and the Narragansett Indians* (Washington, DC: Smithsonian Institution Press, 2001); Ramona L. Peters, "Consulting with the Bone Keepers: NAGPRA Consultations and Archaeological Monitoring in the Wampanoag Territory," and Brona G. Simon, "Collaboration between Archaeologists and Native Americans in Massachusetts: Preservation, Archaeology, and Native American Concerns in Balance," in Jordan E. Kerber, ed., *Cross-Cultural Collaboration: Native Peoples and Archaeology in the Northeastern United States* (Lincoln: University of Nebraska Press, 2006), 32-43, 44-58 (Mass. Unmarked Burial Law); Alyssa Mt. Pleasant, Caroline Wigginton, and Kelly Wisecup, "Materials and Methods in Native American and Indigenous Studies: Completing the Turn," *WMQ* 75.2 (April 2018): 207-36.

11. For an overview of the need for archaeology to challenge the written record, not just confirm it, see Bert Salwen, "The Development of Contact Period Archaeology

in Southern New England and Long Island: From 'Gee Whiz!' to 'So What?'" *Northeast Historical Archaeology* 18 (1989): 1–9. On repatriations, see William S. Simmons, *Cautantowwit's House: An Indian Burial Ground on the Island of Conanicut in Narragansett Bay* (Providence: Brown University Press, 1970), 50–62; Rubertone, *Grave Undertakings,* 152–58; Peters, "Consulting with the Bone Keepers," 32–43; Christine DeLucia, "Antiquarian Collecting and the Transits of Indigenous Material Culture: Rethinking 'Indian Relics' and Tribal Histories," *Commonplace: The Journal of Early American Life* 17.2 (Spring 2017) https://commonplace.online/article/antiquarian-collecting-and-the-transits-of-indigenous -material-culture/.

12. My approach builds off examples set by historians who faced similar challenges with biographies/microhistories, especially Camilla Townsend, *Pocahontas and the Powhatan Dilemma* (New York: Hill and Wang, 2004); Jon F. Sensbach, *Rebecca's Revival: Creating Black Christianity in the Atlantic World* (Cambridge, MA: Harvard University Press, 2005); Townsend, *Malintzin's Choices: An Indian Woman in the Conquest of Mexico* (Albuquerque, University of New Mexico Press, 2006); Joshua Piker, *The Four Deaths of Acorn Whistler: Telling Stories in Colonial America* (Cambridge, MA: Harvard University Press, 2013); Anna Brickhouse, *The Unsettlement of America: Translation, Interpretation, and the Story of Don Luis de Velasco, 1560–1945* (New York: Oxford University Press, 2014); Julie A. Fisher and David J. Silverman, *Ninigret, Sachem of the Niantics and Narragansetts: Diplomacy, War, and the Balance of Power in Seventeenth-Century New England and Indian Country* (Ithaca: Cornell University Press, 2014); Tiya Miles, *All That She Carried: The Journey of Ashley's Sack, a Black Family Keepsake* (New York: Random House, 2021). I thank John Kenney for reminding me of many languages' interchangeable use of "history"/"story."

13. Martyn Whitlock, *Mayflower Lives: Pilgrims in a New World and the Early American Experience* (New York: Pegasus Books, 2019), 105 ("an outsider"); the crux of my argument expands significantly on Neal Salisbury's thesis that Squanto was the leader of a reconstituted Patuxet band in his chapter "Squanto, Last of the Patuxets," 228–46, though I also take exception to many parts of Salisbury's argument.

14. Hellenists call this theme *nostos,* meaning "the return." The word is the root of "nostalgia," a term coined as the medical diagnosis of homesickness. See Bernard Knox, "Introduction," in Homer, *The Odyssey,* trans. Robert Fagles (New York; Penguin Books, 1996), 59–64; Anna Bonifazi, "Inquiring into Nostos and Its Cognates," *American Journal of Philology* 130.4 (Winter 2009): 481–510.

15. These broader points are made on a global scale by Steven Pincus, Tiraana Bains, and Alec Zuercher Reichardt in their essay "Thinking the Empire Whole," *History Australia* 16.4 (2019): 610–37; Alison Games, *Web of Empire: English Cosmopolitans in an Age of Expansion, 1550–1660* (New York: Oxford University Press, 2008); and about Plymouth in particular by Carla Gardina Pestana in *The World of Plymouth Plantation* (Cambridge, MA: Belknap, 2020).

16. The overall structure of this book takes inspiration from Joseph Campbell's archetypal "hero's journey." Campbell, *The Hero with a Thousand Faces* (Novato, CA: New World, 2008 [1st ed., 1949]).

Chapter 1. Infancy

1. Samuel de Champlain, *Les voyages du Sieur de Champlain Xaintongeois, capitain ordinaire pour le Roy en la marine, Où, Journal très-fidele des observations faites és descouvertures de la Nouvelle France* (Paris: Jean Berjon, au Cheval Volant, 1613), 78-79.

2. Thomas Morton, *New English Canaan, or New Canaan Containing an Abstract of New England, Composed in Three Bookes* (London, 1637; repr., Boston, 1883), 137-38 (mobile settlement); Roger Williams, *A Key into the Language of America; or, An Help to the Language of the Natives in That Part of America Called New-England* . . . (London, 1643; repr., Bedford, MA.: Applewood Books, 1997), 3 (mobile settlement); Francis Higginson, *New-Englands Plantation; or, A Short and True Description of the Commodities and Discommodities of that Countrey* (London, 1630; repr., Washington, DC, 1835), 12 (mobile settlement).

3. Williams, *Key*, 163 (sachem's house); Emmanuel Altham to Sir Edward Altham, September 1623, in *Three Visitors to Early Plymouth*, ed. Sidney V. James, Jr. (Bedford, MA: Applewood Books, 1997 [1st ed., 1963]), 29 (two thousand estimate); Bert Salwen, "Indians of Southern New England and Long Island: Early Period," in *Handbook of North American Indians*, vol. 15: *Northeast*, ed. Bruce Trigger (Washington, DC: Smithsonian Institution Press, 1978), 214-15 (population estimate); Kathleen Bragdon, *Native People of Southern New England, 1500-1650* (Norman: University of Oklahoma Press, 1996), 25, 55-79 (semi-sedentary settlement, population estimate).

4. Giovanni da Verrazzano, "Translation of the Cèllere Codex," trans. Susan Tarrow in Lawrence C. Wroth, ed., *The Voyages of Giovanni da Verrazzano* (New Haven: Yale University Press, 1970), 138 (corncakes); Williams, *Key*, 11 (corncakes), 112 (cornmeal stew), 113 (whale meat), 114 (oyster/venison flavoring); William Wood, *Wood's New England's Prospect* (London, 1630; repr., New York: Burt Franklin, 1967), 43 (bear haunch), 75-76 (stews, shellfish, fish, roasted meat); Morton, *New English Canaan*, 41-42 (cornmeal, fish, chestnuts); Daniel Gookin, *Historical Collections of the Indians in New England* (orig. ms., 1674; repr., Boston: Massachusetts Historical Society, 1792), 150 (meat skewers, cornmeal stew); Adriaen van der Donck, *A Description of New Netherland*, ed. Charles T. Gehring and William Starna, trans. Diederik Goedhuys (Lincoln: University of Nebraska Press, 2008), 77 (cornmeal/bread/stew), 78 (oyster flavoring).

5. Williams, *Key*, 149 (maize mortars), 98-101 (field work), 177-78 (gaming); Wood, *New England's Prospect*, 85-86 (gaming); Joshua Abram Kercsmar, "Wolves at Heart: How Dog Evolution Shaped Whites' Perceptions of Indians in North America," *Environmental History* 21 (2016): 516-40; Strother E. Roberts, "That's Not a Wolf: English Misconceptions and the Fate of New England's Indigenous Dogs," *WMQ* 79.3 (July 2022): 357-92.

6. Edward Winslow, *Good News from New England: A Scholarly Edition*, ed. Kelly Wisecup (Amherst: University of Massachusetts Press, 2014), 86 ("merry jests & squibs"); van der Donck, *Description of New Netherland*, 95 (taciturnity, "hunting, fishing, and warfare," "the young men").

7. Williams, *Key*, 54-62 (discourse/news), 182-91 (wartime); Katherine Grand-

jean, *American Passage: The Communications Frontier in Early New England* (Cambridge, MA: Harvard University Press, 2015), 45–109 (discourse, rumor, gossip).

8. Dwight B. Heath, ed., *Mourt's Relation: A Journal of the Pilgrims at Plymouth* (New York: Corinth, 1963), 67 (nighttime singing, noises); Wood, *New England's Prospect,* 17 (seasonal burning); Morton, *New English Canaan,* 172–73 (seasonal burning).

9. William Cronon, *Changes in the Land: Indians, Colonists, and the Ecology of New England* (New York: Hill and Wang, 1983), 49–52 (fire ecology); Shepard Krech III, *The Ecological Indian: Myth and History* (New York: W. W. Norton, 1999), 101–10 (fire ecology); Glenn Motzkin and David R. Foster, "Grasslands, Heathlands and Shrublands in Coastal New England: Historical Interpretations and Approaches to Conservation," *Journal of Biogeography* 29 (October 2002): 1569–90; T. Parshall, D. R. Foster, E. Faison, D. MacDonald, B. C. S. Hansen, "Long-Term History of Vegetation and Fire in Pitch Pine-Oak Forests on Cape Cod, Massachusetts," *Ecology* 84.3 (March 2003): 736–48.

10. Morton, *New English Canaan* (women's appearance and clothing); Wood, *New England's Prospect,* 108 (women's clothing); Winslow, *Good News,* 110 (clothing, strings on legs).

11. Bragdon, *Native People,* 156–61; see also Ann Marie Plane, *Colonial Intimacies: Indian Marriage in Early New England* (Philadelphia: University of Pennsylvania Press, 2000), 96–100; Lisa Brooks, *Our Beloved Kin: A New History of King Philip's War* (New Haven: Yale University Press, 2018), 29–30, 35.

12. Colonial men's descriptions of Native women are notoriously freighted with cultural baggage. See David D. Smits, "The 'Squaw Drudge': A Prime Index of Savagism," *Ethnohistory* 29.4 (1982): 281–306; Kathleen M. Brown, *Good Wives, Nasty Wenches, and Anxious Patriarchs: Gender, Race, and Power in Colonial Virginia* (Chapel Hill: University of North Carolina Press, 1996), 42–74; Kathleen J. Bragdon, *Native People of Southern New England, 1500–1650* (Norman: University of Oklahoma Press, 1996), 175–83; Kirsten Fischer, "The Imperial Gaze: Native American, African American, and Colonial Women in European Eyes," in Nancy A. Hewitt, ed., *A Companion to American Women's History* (Oxford, UK: Wiley Blackwell, 2002), 3–10.

13. The literary critic Lisa Brooks has argued that the relative status of women to men in Algonquian societies surpassed that of English women in *Our Beloved Kin,* esp. 27–71, 253–98. Brooks makes solid points about women's landed property and the relative privileges enjoyed by female sachems, but I favor the long-standing consensus of feminist anthropologists and historians who take care to neither overstate nor dismiss the evidence of ordinary Southern New England Algonquian women's political and physical subordination. See Bragdon, *Native Peoples,* 49–52, 175–83 (gender inequality, violence); Ann Marie Plane, "Colonizing the Family: Marriage, Household and Racial Boundaries in Southeastern New England to 1730" (PhD diss., Brandeis University, 1995), esp. 288–312; Plane, *Colonial Intimacies,* 13–40 (esp. 20–22), 67, 72, 150–51 (gender inequality, violence); Ann M. Little, *Abraham in Arms: War and Gender in Colonial New England* (Philadelphia: University of Pennsylvania Press, 2006), 13–14 (gender inequality); R. Todd Romero, *Making*

War and Minting Christians: Masculinity, Religion, and Colonialism in Early New England (Amherst: University of Massachusetts Press, 2011), 64–65; Rubertone, *Grave Undertakings*, 152–58 (gender inequality); Isaack de Rasières to Samuel Blommaert, 1628, in *Three Visitors*, 72–73 (violence against women); Wood, *New England's Prospect*, 91–92 (violence against women); Williams, *Key*, 147 (violence against women); John Eliot to Thomas Shepard, September 24, 1647, in Shepard, *The Clear Sun-Shine of the Gospel Breaking Forth on the Indians in New England* (London: R. Cotes, 1648), 5–7, 21 (violence against women).

14. Plane, *Colonial Intimacies*, 129–30 (divorce); Winslow, *Good News*, 109 (courtship); Morton, *New English Canaan*, 145 (courtship); de Rasières to Blommaert, 1628, in *Three Visitors*, 108 (adultery); Williams, *Key*, 147 (adultery), 150 (divorce).

15. Williams, *Key*, 146–47 (elite polygyny); Gookin, *Historical Collections*, 149 (elite polygyny); see also Plane, *Colonial Intimacies*, 5, 22–23, 56–58; Bragdon, *Native People*, 175–83.

16. Wood, *New England's Prospect*, 105–6 (wetu structure); Morton, *New English Canaan*, 134–36 (wetu structure); Williams, *Key*, 31–33 (wetu structure), Edward Johnson, *Johnson's Wonder-Working Providence* (New York: Charles Scribners' Sons, 1910), 162 (wetu structure).

17. Higginson, *New-Englands Plantation*, 13 (wetu structure, housewares); Heath, ed., *Mourt's Relation*, 28–29 ("wooden bowls"), 67 (lice, fleas, mosquitos); Williams, *Key*, 46 (fleas, ash, cleaning, moving), 191 (smoky interiors).

18. Wood, *New England's Prospect*, 105 (shellfishing).

19. Winslow, *Good News*, 109–10, 148 (women's roles/work); Williams, *Key*, 31–32 (menstrual hut/menstrual taboo), 146–49 (women's roles/work).

20. Later evidence suggests male colonists exaggerated how readily Native women traveled with their infants. In 1671, when the Sakonnet female sachem Awashonks was slow to respond to colonial summons, she explained her delay was because she "hath a young Child that it was the Reson that shee ded not Come down to the Cort." John Almy to Thomas Prince, March 16, 1670/1, Winslow Family Papers II, Massachusetts Historical Society. On English postpartum care, see Leah Astbury, "Being Well, Looking Ill: Childbirth and the Return to Health in Seventeenth-Century England," *Social History of Medicine* 30.3 (August 2017): 500–519. For accounts of Native childbirth and postpartum activity, see Winslow, *Good News*, 105–6; John Josselyn, *An Account of Two Voyages to New England: Made during the Years 1638, 1663* (Boston: W. Veazie, 1865 [1st ed., London, 1675]), 99–100; Morton, *New English Canaan*, 145–46; Wood, *New England's Prospect*, 105–8; Williams, *Key*, 50, 149–50. On corresponding practices from a nearby cultural group, see Rebecca Kelly, "Caring for the Seven Generations: A Study of the Delaware/Lenape Traditional Child Rearing Practices" (master's thesis, Sarah Lawrence College, 1994), 15–17 (pregnancy taboos); Gladys Tantaquidgeon, *Folk Medicine of the Delaware and Related Algonkian Indians* (Harrisburg: Pennsylvania Historical and Museum Commission, 1972), 43–44, 86–87 (pregnancy taboos).

21. Morton, *New English Canaan*, 146–47 (anointing/skin color); Wood, *New England's Prospect*, 108 ("the young Infant being greased and sooted"); Williams, *Key*, 52 (anointing/skin color); Josselyn, *Two Voyages to New England*, 100 (anointing/skin color); de Rasières to Blommaert, in J. Franklin Jameson, ed., *Narratives of New*

Netherland (New York: Scribner's, 1909), 106 (gamey smell); Charles Wolley, *A Two Years' Journal in New York: And Part of Its Territories in America* (1701; digital repr., Lincoln: University of Nebraska, 2009), 15 (insulator, repellant, sunblock); Fischer, "Imperial Gaze," 7–8 (white/dyed skin theory); Joyce Chaplin, *Subject Matter: Technology, the Body, and Science on the Anglo-American Frontier, 1500–1676* (Cambridge, MA: Harvard University Press, 2001), 255–59 (white/dyed skin theory).

22. Morton, *New English Canaan,* 147 (cradleboard shape); Josselyn, *Two Voyages,* 99–100 (cradleboard shape); John Pory, *John Pory's Lost Description of Plymouth Colony in the Earliest Days of the Pilgrim Fathers* (Boston: Houghton Mifflin, 1918), 51 (cradleboard/swaddling).

23. Morton, *New English Canaan,* 147 (swaddling); Wood, *New-England's Prospect,* 108 (cradleboard/swaddling, "their children . . . are as quiet as if they had neither spleene or lungs"); Josselyn, *Two Voyages to New England,* 100 (cradleboard/swaddling); Kelly, "Caring for the Seven Generations," 23–24; James S. Chisholm, "Swaddling, Cradleboards, and the Development of Children," *Early Human Development* 2.3 (1978): 255–75.

24. Gabriel Archer, "The Relation Captain Gosnols Voyage to the North Part of Virginia . . . ," *ENEV,* 134 (" Grey-hounds vpon their heeles"); Wood, *New England's Prospect,* 106 ("it being as rare to see an *Indian"*); Morton, *New English Canaan,* 148 ("he sitteth . . . as a dogge does on his bum"); Johnson, *Wonder-Working Providence,* 162 ("legs doubled up").

25. Williams, *Key,* 118 (children's clothes); Gookin, *Historical Collections,* 152 (children's clothes).

26. William S. Simmons, *Cautantowwit's House: An Indian Burial Ground on the Island of Conanicut in Narragansett Bay* (Providence: Brown University Press, 1970), 60 (red ochre); David F. Lancy, "Why Anthropology of Childhood? A Short History of an Emerging Discipline," *AnthropoChildren* (French Studies in the Anthropology of Childhood), 1.1 (January 2012): 9–10.

27. Simmons, *Cautantowwit's House,* 151; Lancy, "Why Anthropology of Childhood?" 9–10.

28. Simmons, *Cautantowwit's House,* 45–47, 89–93, 97–101, 110–16, 134 (grave goods in childrens' graves), 81–82, 101–2, 151 (infant graves), 82–89, 154, 156 (children buried with adults); for corresponding examples, see Charles C. Willoughby, "Indian Burial Place at Winthrop, Massachusetts," *Papers of the Peabody Museum of American Archaeology and Ethnology, Harvard University* 11.1 (1924), 12 (one year old without grave goods), 13–15 (two- to three-year-old girl with beads, bowl, and toys in burial), 15–19 (boy with tobacco pipe).

29. James W. Bradley, "Taylor Hill: A Middle Woodland Mortuary Site in Wellfleet, MA," *Bulletin of the Massachusetts Archaeological Society* 69.1 (2008): 28–29 (Wellfleet woman and child burial with effigies).

30. Willoughby, "Indian Burial Place," 12–13 (mixed adult/child burial); Simmons, *Cautantowwit's House,* 82–89 (high-status burial); Heath, ed., *Mourt's Relation,* 28 ("bound strings . . . odd knacks," man and child burial), 78 (sachem's grave); Winslow, *Good News,* 103 (Kiehtan), 108 (burial practices); Wood, *New England's Prospect,* 103–4 (burial practices). For relevant studies of gravesites among the

neighboring and culturally similar Narragansett people, see Simmons, *Cautantow-wit's House,* 50–62; Rubertone, *Grave Undertakings,* 152–58.

31. Samson Occom, "Account of the Montauk Indians, on Long Island" (1761), in Joanna Brooks, ed., *The Collected Writings of Samson Occom, Mohegan: Leadership and Literature in Eighteenth-Century Native America* (New York: Oxford University Press, 2006), 50–51.

32. Winslow, *Good News,* 109.

33. Baird quoted in Kauanui, *Speaking of Indigenous Politics,* 7 (variations and mis-translations); Ives Goddard and Kathleen J. Bragdon, *Native Writings in Massachusett* (Philadelphia: American Philosophical Society, 1988), 1:3; Ives Goddard, "The Use of Pidgins and Jargons on the East Coast of North America," in *The Language Encounter in the Americas, 1492–1800: A Collection of Essays,* ed. Edward G. Gray and Norman Fiering (New York: Berghahn Books, 2000), 67. From correspondence and conversation with multiple Algonquian language experts, I found there is no clear consensus on the meanings of Tisquantum/Squanto's name. The basis for the theory that "Tisquantum" and "Squanto" was a reference to the god Squanto came from a possibly spurious etymology offered by the antiquarian linguist James Trumbull, but there is some cultural context to support the theory: other leading Native men in the area also went by the title of a known god (Tanto/Tantum, Hobbamock, the Abenaki sachem Squando). See James Hammond Trumbull, *Natick Dictionary* (Washington, DC: U.S. Bureau of Ethnology, 1903).

Chapter 2. Education

1. Wood, *New England's Prospect,* 103 ("hard to learne"); Winslow, *Good News,* 111 ("very copious").

2. Will Oxford, "Algonquian Languages," in Daniel Siddiqi, Michael Barrie, Carrie Gillon, Jason D. Haugen, and Éric Mathieu, eds., *The Routledge Handbook of North American Languages* (New York: Routledge, 2019), 504–6.

3. George F. Aubin, "Toward the Linguistic History of an Algonquian Dialect: Observations on the Wood Vocabulary," *Papers of the Ninth Algonquian Conference,* ed. William Cowan (Ottawa: Carleton University, 1978), 127–37; Ives Goddard and Kathleen Bragdon, *Native Writings in Massachusett* (Philadelphia: American Philosophical Society, 1988), 1:1–4; Francis Joseph O'Brien, Jr. (Moondancer) and Julianne Jennings (Strong Woman), *Understanding Algonquian Indian Words* (Newport, RI: Aquidneck Indian Council, 1996), 77–84; Lyle Campbell, *American Indian Languages: The Historical Linguistics of Native America* (New York: Oxford University Press, 1997), 152–54; and the website of the Wôpanâak Language Reclamation Project, http://www.wlrp.org/. Trumbull, *Natick Dictionary,* 67 (mug-wump); *OED,* s.v. "caucus," "totem."

4. Robert S. Grumet, *Manhattan to Minisink: American Indian Place Names of Greater New York and Vicinity* (Norman: University of Oklahoma Press, 2013), 2, 94–95 (mhuweyok/Mohawk, Kanyékeha:ka), 172 (Ptukwsiituw/tuxedo).

5. Jessie Little Doe Fermino [Baird], "An Introduction to Wampanoag Grammar" (master's thesis: Massachusetts Institute of Technology, 2000), 8–10 (00); Trum-

bull, *Natick Dictionary*, 66 (*moos*); David J. Costa, "The Dialectology of Southern New England Algonquian," *Papers of the Thirty-Eighth Algonquian Conference*, ed. H. C. Wolfart (Winnipeg: University of Manitoba, 2007), 93–95 (nasalized ô); John Eliot, *The Indian Grammar Begun; or, An Essay to Bring the Indian Language into Rules, for the Help of Such as Desire to Learn the Same, for the Furtherance of the Gospel among Them* (Cambridge: Marmaduke Johnson, 1666; repr., Bedford, MA: Applewood Books, 2001), 2 (00).

6. [Baird], "Wampanoag Grammar," 13 (*waskeetopâak*).

7. C. C. Uhlenbeck, *Outline for a Comparative Grammar of Some Algonquian Languages: Ojibway, Cree, Micmac, Natick [Massachusett-Wampanoag], and Blackfoot*, trans. Joshua Jacob Snider (Petoskey, MI: Mundart Press, 2013 [1st ed., 1910, Dutch]), 25–28 (animate/inanimate); [Baird], "Wampanoag Grammar," 10–13 (animate/inanimate examples).

8. Ives Goddard offers a strong caution against a "popular (or we might better say vulgarized) Neo-Whorfian view of Algonquian grammatical gender as giving a direct insight into the Algonquian mental world" in "Grammatical Gender in Algonquian," in H. C. Wolfart, ed., *Papers of the Thirty-Third Algonquian Conference* (Winnipeg: University of Manitoba, 2002): 198 (quotation); Melissa Tantaquidgeon Zobel gives an excellent explanation of how grammatical animacy/inanimacy does or does not influence Algonquian-speakers' spiritual understandings of animacy in "Algonquian Naming, Power, and Relationality in a Rare Native Love Poem," in Monica Macaulay and Margaret Noodin, eds., *Papers of the Forty-Sixth Algonquian Conference* (East Lansing: Michigan State University Press, 2017), 214–16.

9. Baird quoted in Kauanui, *Speaking of Indigenous Politics*, 10; Eliot, *Indian Grammar*, 23 ("elegancy"); Edward Sapir, *Language: An Introduction to the Study of Speech* (New York: Harcourt, Brace, 1921), 244 ("tiny imagist poems").

10. [Baird], "Wampanoag Grammar," 15–16 (locative),

11. [Baird], "Wampanoag Grammar," 13, 21 (absentative); Morton, *New English Canaan*, 52 ("a thing very offensive to them"); Williams, *Key*, 202 (postmortem naming fines and war); James Axtell "Last Rights: The Acculturation of Native Funerals in Colonial North America," in William Cowan, ed., *Papers of the Eleventh Algonquian Conference* (Ottawa: Carleton University Press, 1980), 104–5 (Metacomet threatening to execute Nantucket man for speaking his father's name, examples of absentative in colonial documents).

12. [Baird], "Wampanoag Grammar," 23–24 (*-neechan-* variations); Jonathan Edwards, *Observations on the Language of the Muhhekaneew Indians*, ed. John Pickering (Boston: Phelps and Farnham, 1823 [1st ed., 1788]), 13 ("more carefully").

13. Bragdon, *Native People*, 162–64 (kinship terms); [Baird], "Wampanoag Grammar," 21–23 (sister variations); see also Baird quoted in in Kauanui, *Speaking of Indigenous Politics*, 7.

14. Williams, *Key*, 28–29 ("their affections . . . this extreme affection"); Pory, *Lost Description*, 50 ("greate lovers of their children").

15. John Demos, *A Little Commonwealth: Family Life in Plymouth Colony* (New York: Oxford University Press, 1970 [2nd ed., 2000]), 100–106, 127–44 (English childrearing); Morton, *New English Canaan*, 149 ("always obedient"); Winslow, *Good News*, 109; John Davenport quoted in Bragdon, *Native People*, 156 ("are carefull to preserve").

16. Bragdon, *Native People*, 28-29, 135-36, 161-63.

17. Robin Wall Kimmerer, *Braiding Sweetgrass: Indigenous Wisdom, Scientific Knowledge and the Teachings of Plants* (Minneapolis: Milkweed Editions, 2015).

18. William M. Denevan, "The Pristine Myth: The Landscape of the Americas in 1492," *Annals of the Association of American Geographers* 82.3 (September 1992): 369-85. Examples of studies exploring Indigenous peoples' own self-inflicted environmental crises include Robert Brightman, "Conservation and Resource Depletion: The Case of the Boreal Forest Algonquians," in *The Question of the Commons: The Culture and Ecology of Communal Resources*, ed. Bonnie J. McCay and James M. Acheson (Tucson: University of Arizona Press, 1987), 121-41; William Woods, "Population Nucleation, Intensive Agriculture, and Environmental Degradation: The Cahokia Example," *Agriculture and Human Values* 21.2-3 (Summer/Fall 2004): 255-61; Kent Redford, "The Ecologically Noble Savage," *Cultural Survival Quarterly* 15 (1991): 46-48.

19. The relationships between Native peoples and their environments is a controversial topic that has driven academic debates for decades. One of the staunchest defenders of the idea of harmony was Vine Deloria, Jr., who generally rejected scholarship that countered Indigenous religious beliefs in his polemic *Red Earth, White Lies: Native Americans and the Myth of Scientific Fact* (New York: Scribner, 1995). Other examples include Calvin Martin's unsubstantiated apologia for Indigenous overhunting in *Keepers of the Game: Indian-Animal Relationships and the Fur Trade* (Berkeley: University of California, 1978), which was thoroughly dismantled by the essays in Shepard Krech III, ed., *Indians, Animals, and the Fur Trade: A Critique of* Keepers of the Game (Athens: University of Georgia Press, 1981); other arguments for green Native practices include Annie L. Booth and Harvey L. Jacobs, "Ties That Bind: Native American Beliefs as a Foundation for Environmental Consciousness," *Environmental Ethics* 12.1 (1990): 27-43. The most extensive debunking/challenge to the idea of inherent Indigenous ecological harmony was Krech's *The Ecological Indian*, an interpretation that was in turn critiqued productively by Paul Nadasdy in "Transcending the Debate over the Ecologically Noble Indian: Indigenous Peoples and Environmentalism," *Ethnohistory* 52.2 (2005): 291-331, and Michael E. Harkin and David Rich Lewis, eds., *Native Americans and the Environment: Perspectives on* The Ecological Indian (Lincoln: University of Nebraska Press, 2007). The anthropologist Dave Aftandilian makes the case for looking at specific groups rather than overgeneralizing, finding that Indigenous perspectives can indeed inspire conservation principles, but that it's a mistake to fetishize Native land use in excessively romantic ways in "What Other Americans Can and Cannot Learn from Native American Environmental Ethics," *Worldviews* 15.3 (2011): 219-46. Two scientists, Kimmerer and Jane Mt. Pleasant, have stressed the overlap between Indigenous epistemologies and sustainable land use and conservation in Kimmerer, *Braiding Sweetgrass*, and Mt. Pleasant, "A New Paradigm for Pre-Columbian Agriculture in North America," *Early American Studies* 13.2 (Spring 2015): 374-412.

20. On manitou, see Neal Salisbury, *Manitou and Providence: Indians, Europeans, and the Making of New England, 1500-1643* (New York: Oxford University Press, 1982), 37-39; Bragdon, *Native People*, 184-7 (manitou); [Baird], "Wampanoag Grammar," 24 (manut8/"creator/god"); David J. Silverman, *Faith and Boundaries:*

Colonists, Christianity, and Community among the Wampanoag Indians of Martha's Vineyard, 1600–1871 (Cambridge: Cambridge University Press, 2005), 26–30; Winslow, *Good News*, 103 ("divine powers"); Williams, *Key*, 103 (manitou, gods, "excellency").

21. William S. Simmons, *Spirit of the New England Tribes: Indian History and Folklore* (Hanover, NH: University Press of New England, 1986), 172–234 (cultural heroes, Maushop); Helen Manning, "From Maushop's Footsteps," in *Dawnland Voices*, 390.

22. Winslow, *Good News*, 102–6; Eliot to Shepard, September 24, 1647, in Shepard, *Clear Sun-Shine of the Gospel*, 17–29; Romero, *Making War and Minting Christians*, 31–45; Silverman, *Faith and Boundaries*, 16–48.

23. Winslow, *Good News*, 102–5 (Kiehtan/Hobbamock); Christopher Levett, "My Discouery of Diverse Riuers and Harbours, with Their Names, and Which Are Fit for Plantations, and Which Not," in *Sailors' Narratives of Voyages along the New England Coast, 1524–1624*, ed. George Parker Winship (Boston: Houghton, Mifflin, 1905), 282 ("the god they love/hate"); Higginson, *New-Englands Plantation*, 14 ("The good god"); John Josselyn, *An Account of Two Voyages to New-England* (London: Giles Windows, 1674), 132–33 (Squantum/Abbamocho).

24. Trumbull, *Natick Dictionary*, 220 (s.v. "anger"); on anger in both Native and Christian belief systems, see Daniel K. Richter, *Facing East from Indian Country: A Native History of Early America* (Cambridge, MA: Harvard University Press, 2001), 127–29.

25. Williams, *Key*, 89 (playing structures).

26. Simmons, *Cautantowwit's House*, 50–62 (southwest, reverence of crows); Bragdon, *Native Peoples*, 189–99, 233–36 (southwest); Wood, *New England's Prospect*, 104 (crow legend); Williams, *Key*, 89–90 (crow legend). The Crow remains a potent figure in modern Nipmuc and Wampanoag traditions and poetry. See Kitt Little Turtle (George Munyan), "Nipmuck Legend," Larry Spotted Crow Mann, "The Crow (in His Own Words)," Robert Peters, "Grandfather," in *Dawnland Voices*, 390, 422, 482.

27. Elizabeth Chilton, "The Origins and Spread of Maize (*Zea mays*) in New England," in John E. Staller, Robert H. Tykot, Bruce F. Benz, eds., *Histories of Maize: Multidisciplinary Approaches to the Prehistory, Linguistics, Biogeography, Domestication, and Evolution of Maize* (Burlington, MA: Academic Press, 2006), 539–48; Mt. Pleasant, "New Paradigm," 374–412.

28. David Pietersz. de Vries, "Korte Historiael Ende Journales Aenteyckninge," in J. Franklin Jameson, ed., *Narratives of New Netherland* (New York: Scribner's, 1909), 224 (singing).

29. Lynn Ceci, "Fish Fertilizer: A Native North American Practice?" *Science*, n.s. 188.4183 (1975): 26–30; Lynn Ceci, "Squanto and the Pilgrims: On Planting Corn 'in the Manner of the Indians,'" in *The Invented Indian: Cultural Fictions and Government Policies*, ed. James A. Clifton (New York: Routledge, 1990), 71–90; Nanepashemet, "It Smells Fishy to Me: An Argument Supporting the Use of Fish Fertilizer by the Native People of Southern New England," *Algonkians of New England: Past and Present*, ed. Peter Benes (Boston: Boston University Press, 1993), 42–50; Stephen A. Mrozowski, "The Discovery of a Native American Cornfield on

Cape Cod," *Archaeology of Eastern North America* 22 (Fall 1994): 47–62, 57–58 (fish fertilizer).

30. Kimmerer, *Braiding Sweetgrass,* 128–33 (corn, bean growth), 130 ("circle dance").

31. Higginson, *New-Englands Plantation,* 7 (kernel colors); Chief Pine Tree (Narragansett) quoted in Princess Red Wing, editorial, *Narragansett Dawn* (1935), in *Dawnland Voices,* 511 ("how I hated"). Regarding the last citation of Chief Pine Tree's childhood: the phrase "rows and rows" suggest that nineteenth-century Narragansett farmers were growing their corn in a way that partially resembled European farming as opposed to the interspersed hills favored before contact, and the introduction of European plants meant that the species of weeds would be different from in the seventeenth century, but corn was still their staple crop and they put children to work just as their ancestors did, which suggests a thread of cultural continuity stretching back centuries before colonists arrived.

32. Kimmerer, *Braiding Sweetgrass,* 131 (Three Sisters legends).

33. Heath, ed., *Mourt's Relation,* 75 ("Neen squaes").

34. Wood, *New England's Prospect,* 97–98 (toy bows, swim training); Morton, *New English Canaan,* 65 (canoe making); Williams, *Key,* 106–8 (canoeing/canoe making); Heath, ed., *Mourt's Relation,* 23 (powerful snare), 59 (hand-fishing for eels).

35. The only other use of the term "pniese" in a colonial-authored text is found in Phinehas Pratt's narrative, which had several direct paraphrases lifted from Winslow's *Good News.* See Phinehas Pratt, *A Declaration of the Affairs of the English People That First Inhabited New England,* ed. Richard Frothingham (Boston: T. R. Marvin and Son, 1858 [1st ed., 1662]), 18.

36. Winslow, *Good News,* 107 ("most forward and likeliest"); Ives Goddard and Kathleen J. Bragdon, *Native Writings in Massachusett* (Philadelphia: American Philosophical Society, 1988) 1:2–4, for examples of *-atoskauwoag* in context, see the Aquinnah Wampanoag sachem Muttaak's deeds from September 1675 and August 1703, *Native Writings,* 1:83, 855 (Neaane nen Mittark Sachim kah Nuttohtoskouomog kah wong missinnooog ut Gayheat [Accordingly, I Mittark, the sachem, and my chief men, and also the (common) people of Gay Head]), 1:87, 89 (Nen Yonohhumuh ahtoskou Ut Gayheat [I Yonohhumuh, a chief man at Gay Head]), 1:95, 97 (Neen Muttaak kah nuttahtohkauwom [I Muttaak and my chief men]); 2:600 ("my council or chief men").

37. Goddard and Bragdon, *Native Writings,* 2: On the dispositive evidence that Tisquantum earned the rank of "pniese"/*atoskauwou* see Salisbury, "Squanto, Last of the Patuxets," 230–31.

38. Winslow, *Good News,* 106–7 (training); de Rasières to Blommaert, in James, ed., *Three Visitors,* 77–79 (trainings); Wood, *New England's Prospect,* 72 (training), 98–99 (hunting/trapping); Morton, *New English Canaan,* 166 (identifying scat), 199–203 (hunting/trapping); Williams, *Key,* 80–84 (portents), 171–77 (hunting/trapping).

Chapter 3. Manhood

1. De Rasières to Blommaert, in James, ed., *Three Visitors,* 78 ("When there is a youth who begins to approach manhood, he is taken by his father, uncle, or nearest

friend, and is conducted blindfolded into a wilderness, in order that he may not know the way, and is left there by night or otherwise, with a bow and arrows, and a hatchet and a knife"); de Rasières's account offers the only known details of the wilderness-trial portion of the Wampanoag initiation rites, though Winslow hints that exposure and endurance was a key part of process, while offering more details of the poison-resistance training portion, in Winslow, *Good News*, 107 ("then must go forth into the cold").

2. Sam White, *A Cold Welcome: The Little Ice Age and Europe's Encounter with North America* (Cambridge, MA: Harvard University Press, 2017), 19–23. Recently a couple of scientists have advanced the thesis that the sudden dying off of Native peoples in the Americas caused a rapid reforestation of parts of the continents and the recapturing of atmospheric carbon reversed a warming trend. White provides a good overview of why the much-publicized theory of anthropogenic causes for this cooling period just isn't credible or convincing as a major factor in causing this global cooling. See White, *Cold Welcome*, 23–26.

3. Thomas Wickman, *Snowshoe Country: An Environmental and Cultural History of Winter in the Early American Northeast* (Cambridge: Cambridge University Press, 2018), 39–42 (frostfish, shellfish, groundnuts).

4. Morton, *New English Canaan*, 199–203 (hunting deer, trapping/snares); Wickman, *Snowshoe Country*, 43–48 (winter tracking and trapping).

5. Wickman, *Snowshoe Country*, 51 (winter deer hunting); Ann Marie Plane, *Dreams and the Invisible World in Colonial New England: Indians, Colonists, and the Seventeenth Century* (Philadelphia: University of Pennsylvania Press, 2014), 41–45.

6. De Rasières to Blommaert, *Three Visitors*, 78–79 (May poison rite, "the most poisonous and bitter"); Winslow, *Good News*, 107 (poison rite, sticks/thorns gauntlet, Hobbamock vision, "seem to be all blood . . . scarce stand on their legs"); John Josselyn identified the plant used in this rite as "white hellbore," a European species commonly confused with the American species *V. viride*, writing, "the Indians, who steeping of it, in water sometime, give it to young lads gathered together a purpose to drink, if it come up they force them to drink again their vomit (which they save in a Birchen-dish) till it stays with them, he that gets the victory of it is made Captain of the other lads that year," in John Josselyn, *An Account of Two Voyages to New England: Made during the Years 1638, 1663* (Boston: W. Veazie, 1865 [1st ed., London, 1675]), 50.

7. De Rasières to Blommaert, *Three Visitors*, 79 ("if he has been able to stand it all well, and if he is fat and sleek").

8. De Rasières to Blommaert, in *Three Visitors*, 79 ("a wife is given to him"). Though Rasières claimed that young men were "given" a wife for excelling in the manhood rites, there's no other source implying that Indigenous marriages in this region were ever thus arranged. With the exception of some strategic marriages between sachem's lines, marriages appeared to be completely consensual and initiated by both women and men. On marriage and women's hairstyles see Winslow, *Good News*, 109; Morton, *New English Canaan*, 145 ("a redd cap made of lether").

9. John Brereton, "A Briefe and True Relation of the Discoverie of the North Part of Virginia" (London, 1602), *ENEV*, 157–58 (hairstyles, facial hair); Wood, *New En-*

gland's Prospect, 64 (facial hair grooming), 72 (boys' and men's hairstyles), 74 (tattoos and brandings).

10. Williams, *Key,* 179 (football matches, wampumpeak); Wood, *New England's Prospect,* 96–97 (football matches).

11. For an extensive and insightful analysis of Native sporting and gaming, see Romero, *Making War and Minting Christians,* 46–50; Wood, *New England's Prospect,* 83 ("the goale being wonne"); "Niantick Indiens Petition October 1667: to ye Genll Assembly," Samuel Wyllys Papers, John Hay Library, box 2, folder 1, ms. 453 ("contrary to our laws").

12. Winslow, *Good News,* 103–5, 107 (Hobbamock's powers and forms).

13. Heath, ed., *Mourt's Relation,* 53 (mountain lion skin); Altham to Altham, *Three Visitors,* 30 (wampum belt, black wolfskin); Heath, ed., *Mourt's Relation,* 72 (beaded jewelry); Williams, *Key,* 1 (social distinctions), 118–22 (clothing, turkey coats), 146–47 (elite polygamy); Wood, *New England's Prospect* (sachem wearing earrings and "a good store of Wamponpeage begirting his loynes"), 91 (elite polygamy), 108 (turkey coats); Daniel Gookin, *Historical Collections of the Indians in New England* (orig. mss. 1674; repr., Boston: Massachusetts Historical Society, 1792), 9 (elite polygamy); Matthew Mayhew, "A Brief Narrative of the Success Which the Gospel Had among the Indians of Martha's Vineyard," *Collections of the Massachusetts Historical Society,* 2d ser., ed. Charles Hudson et al. (Boston: William White, 1853–54), 119:8–9 (social distinctions).

14. Morton, *New English Canaan,* 150–51 (sachems as powwaws); Williams, *Key,* 185 (sachems' entourages).

15. Heath, ed., *Mourt's Relation,* 65–66 (rhetorical questions, call and response); Williams, *Key,* 56–59 (political discourse), 58 (anaphora), 132 (metaphor); Wood, *New England's Prospect,* 103 (political discourse); *Mourt's Relation,* 66 (political discourse, anaphora); Winslow, *Good News,* 80 (anaphora); Phinehas Pratt, *A Declaration of the Affairs of the English People That First Inhabited New England,* ed. Richard Frothingham (Boston: T. R. Marvin and Son, 1858 [1st ed., 1662]), 10 (metaphor, anaphora); Eliot, *Indian Grammar,* 4 (rhyming); Ninigret's testimony to the Commissioners of the United Colonies, in Nathaniel Shurtleff and David Pulsipher, eds., *Records of the Colony of New Plymouth in New England* (Boston: William White, 1859–1861), 10:8–9 (rhetorical questions, anaphora); Josselyn, *Account of Two Voyages,* 105 (rhyming).

16. Morton, *New English Canaan,* 149 ("The younger mens opinion"); Winslow, *Good News,* 106 ("will not war").

17. Winslow, *Good News,* 106–7 ("men of great courage . . . arrows, knives hatchets"); Wood, *New England's Prospect,* 85–86 (bravery/chivalry).

18. Winslow, *Good News,* 106–8 (honesty/reputation); Williams, *Key,* 58–59 (honesty), 184–87 (reputation/insults); Morton, *New English Canaan,* 154–57 (reputation); James F. Brooks, *Captives and Cousins: Slavery, Kinship, and Community in the Southwest Borderlands* (Chapel Hill: University of North Carolina Press, 2002), 9 ("continuously reaffirmed yet . . . never secure").

19. Winslow, *Good News,* 79 ("when any [especially of note] are dangerously sick"); Morton, *New English Canaan,* 170 ("to lament and bewaile . . . dignity of the per-

son"); Wood, *New England's Prospect,* 104 (public mourning); Williams, *Key,* 201–3 (public mourning).

20. Williams, *Key,* 28–29 ("they hold"); Gookin, *Historical Collections,* 9 (condolence/ retribution).

21. Lion Gardiner, "Gardener His Relations of the Pequot Warres," *Collections of the Massachusetts Historical Society,* 3d ser., 3:154 ("bretheren," "say brother"); Bragdon, *Native People,* 162 (neemat). See also Cynthia Van Zandt, *Brothers among Nations: The Pursuit of Intercultural Alliances in Early America* (New York: Oxford University Press, 2008), esp. 65–85.

22. Morton, *New English Canaan,* 153–54; Williams, *Key,* 182–88.

23. Romero, *Making War,* 162–64; John Mason, *A Brief History of the Pequot War: Especially of the Memorable Taking of Their Fort at Mistick in Connecticut in 1637* (1736; repr., Lincoln: University of Nebraska Press, 2007), 5 (ring, speeches); Mary Rowlandson, "The Captivity and Restoration of Mrs. Mary Rowlandson," in *Journeys in the New World: Early American Women's Narratives,* ed. William L. Andrews (Madison: University of Wisconsin Press, 1990), 55–56 (ring, pounding, singing, dancing, speeches); Benjamin Church, *A Diary of King Philip's War,* ed. Alan and Mary Simpson (Little Compton, R.I.: Lockwood, 1975), 125–27 (ring, dancing, singing, torches, speeches).

24. There are sporadic mentions of coastal Southern New England Algonquians taking and releasing captives from rival tribes in the colonial record (the capture of Pequot women in particular in the Pequot War, or Ninigret's kidnapping of Wayandance's wife in the 1650s), but the best-documented examples are of Natives capturing and ransoming colonists. The general patterns show Native fighters clearly delineating between genders in treatment, taking trophies from male bodies, and using torture/execution rites among a select few male captives as a strategy of intimidation. One salient set of examples are the capture and ransom of two English girls by the Pequots in 1636 versus the dismemberments of John Oldham and John Tilley in that same conflict. A similar pattern arises in King Philip's War, where Native fighters ransomed many English captives regardless of gender but reserved torture and execution for a few adult men in front of a larger audience. While focused on Plains captive taking, Patricia C. Albers sums up the logic of captive taking in ways that also apply to Southern New England Algonquians in her essay "Symbiosis, Merger, and War: Contrasting Forms of Intertribal Relationship among Historic Plains Indians" in *The Political Economy of North American Indians,* ed. John H. Moore (Norman: University of Oklahoma Press, 1993), 94–132, 128 ("a quintessential element").

25. Wood, *New England's Prospect,* 84–85 (battle tactics); Morton, *New English Canaan,* 153–54 (battle tactics); John Underhill, *Newes from America; or, A New and Experimentall Discoverie of New England* . . . (1638; repr., Lincoln: University of Nebraska Press, 2007), 3–5 (arrow wounds); Williams, *Key,* 188–89 (battle tactics); Lion Gardiner, "Relation of the Pequot Warres," *Early American Studies* 9.2 (Spring 2011): 475–79 (arrow wounds).

26. Charles C. Willoughby, "Indian Burial Place at Winthrop, Massachusetts," *Papers of the Peabody Museum of American Archaeology and Ethnology, Harvard University* 11.1 (1924), 6–7 (embedded arrowhead); James W. Bradley, "Taylor Hill: A

Middle Woodland Mortuary Site in Wellfleet, MA," *Bulletin of the Massachusetts Archaeological Society* 69.1 (2008): 2, 34 (traumatic death, embedded arrowheads, lethal and premortem cranial fractures), 40 (traumatic death on seven bodies); Simmons, *Cautantowwit's House*, 52–55 (Burial 13, headless woman).

27. Williams, *Key*, 50–51 (trophy taking); Wood, *New England's Prospect*, 95 (trophy taking); William Hubbard, *The History of the Indian Wars in New England from the First Settlement to the Termination of the War with King Philip, in 1677*, 2 vols., ed. Samuel G. Drake (1865; repr., New York: Kaus Reprint, 1969), 1:63, 2:206 (trophy taking); James Axtell and William C. Sturtevant, "The Unkindest Cut, or Who Invented Scalping?" *WMQ* 37.3 (July 1980): 451–72; the role of trophies in wartime politics in Southern New England is explored in greater depth in Andrew Lipman, "A Meanes to Knitt Them Togeather: The Exchange of Body Parts in the Pequot War," *WMQ* 65.1 (January 2008): 3–28.

28. Underhill, *Newes from America*, 20 (torture in Pequot War); Gardiner, "Relation of the Pequot Warres," 475 (torture in Pequot War); Hubbard, *History of the Indian Wars*, 1:213, 237, 2:63–64 (torture in King Philip's War).

29. For dismissals of Native warfare compared with European warfare, see Underhill, *Newes from America*, 36; Williams, *Key*, 188–89; Wood, *New England's Prospect*, 85.

30. Winslow, *Good News*, 59–60 (arrows), 61 (council approval); Wood, *New England's Prospect*, 94–95 (war preparation, combat); Williams, *Key*, 182–91 (wampum as restitution); Heath, ed., *Mourt's Relation*, 51 (arrows); Bradford, *OPP*, 125–26 (arrows).

Chapter 4. Dawnlands

1. The most literal translation of Wampanoag/Wabanaki is "People of the White Light," but "white light" was also their term for "dawn"/"first light"/"east." Trumbull, *Natick Dictionary*, 194 (s.v. "wompag-"); Matthew R. Bahar, *Storms of the Sea: Indians and Empires in the Atlantic's Age of Sail* (New York: Oxford University Press, 2019), 52 (dawn/white light). On using "Dawnland," see Senier, ed., *Dawnland Voices;* DeLucia, *Memory Lands*, 24; Brooks, *Our Beloved Kin*, 11, 17.

2. On Wampanoags and Narragansetts, see Heath, ed., *Mourt's Relation*, 58, 73–76; Winslow, *Good News*, 58–59; Gookin, *Historical Collections*, 7–8; Increase Mather, *A Brief History of the Warre with the Indians in New-England* (Boston: John Foster, 1676), 9.

3. Lisa Brooks, "Awikhigawôgan ta Pildowi Ôjmowôgan: Mapping a New History," *WMQ* 75.2 (April 2018): 259–94 (links, paths, monuments). While I believe the overall argument of this piece is sound and insightful, recent scholarship has raised serious concerns about the parts of the article that cite modern Abenaki individuals as sources on Indigenous geographies. The sociologist Darryl Leroux has examined the genealogy of the state-recognized Abenaki bands of Vermont and concluded that some of the very individuals cited as Native authorities in this article have no Indigenous ancestors. See Darryl Leroux, "State Recognition and the Dangers of Race Shifting: The Case of Vermont," *American Indian Culture and Research Journal* 46.2 (2023): 53–84; Winslow, *Good News*, 111–12 (regional geog-

raphy); Morton, *New English Canaan,* 234–40 (regional geography); Gookin, *Historical Collections,* 16–18 (regional geography).

4. Timothy G. Baugh and Jonathon E. Ericson, eds., *Prehistoric Exchange Systems in North America* (New York: Plenum Press, 1994); Bragdon, *Native People,* 35 (mica, shells), 92 (copper, shells); Colin G. Calloway, *One Vast Winter Count: The Native American West before Lewis and Clark* (Lincoln: University of Nebraska Press, 2003), 25–115; Elizabeth A. Fenn, *Encounters at the Heart of the Continent: A History of the Mandan People* (New York: Hill and Wang, 2014), 18–21.

5. The scale of foot and canoe travel by Indigenous people before and after contact with Europeans is well illustrated in a number of continental studies. Calloway, *One Vast Winter Count;* Richter, *Before the Revolution;* Pekka Hämäläinen, *Indigenous Continent: The Epic Contest for North America* (New York: Liveright, 2022); Timothy R. Pauketat, *Gods of Thunder: How Climate Change, Travel, and Spirituality Reshaped Precolonial America* (New York: Oxford University Press, 2023); Blackhawk, *Rediscovery of America.*

6. Bradford, *OPP,* 105 ("a hidious and desolate wildernes, full of wild beasts and willd men").

7. Laurier Turgeon, "The Tale of the Kettle: Odyssey of an Intercultural Object," *Ethnohistory* 44.1 (1997): 1–29; Giovanni da Verrazzano, "Translation of the Cèllere Codex," trans. Susan Tarrow, in Lawrence C. Wroth, ed., *The Voyages of Giovanni da Verrazzano* (New Haven: Yale University Press, 1970), 137–39.

8. James A. Williamson, *The Voyages of the Cabots and the English Discovery of North America under Henry VII and Henry VIII* (London: Argonaut Press, 1929); Verrazzano, "Translation of the Cèllere Codex," 137–39; Wood, *New England's Prospect,* 87 (moving islands).

9. Brian Fagan, *Fish on Friday: Feasting, Fasting, and the Discovery of the New World* (New York: Basic Books, 2006), 3–13.

10. Harold A. Innis, *The Cod Fisheries: The History of an International Economy* (New Haven: Yale University Press, 1940), 48–50.

11. Callum Roberts, *The Ocean of Life: The Fate of Man and the Sea* (New York: Viking Books, 2012), 59–61; W. Jeffrey Bolster, *The Mortal Sea: Fishing the Atlantic in the Age of Sail* (Cambridge, MA: Harvard University Press, 2012), 20–21; Jack Bouchard, "'Gens sauvages et estranges': Amerindians and the Early Fishery in the Sixteenth-Century Gulf of St. Lawrence," in *The Greater Gulf: Essays on the Environmental History of the Gulf of St. Lawrence,* ed. Ed Macdonald, Brian Paine, and Claire Campbell (Montreal: McGill-Queens University Press, 2020), 42–44.

12. John Rut to Henry VIII, August 3, 1527, in Williamson, *Voyages of the Cabots,* 105 ("all a fishing"); Marc Lescarbot, "The Voyage of Monsieur De Monts into New France" (1605), in Charles Herbert Levermore, ed., *Forerunners and Competitors of the Pilgrims and Puritans* (Brooklyn, NY: The New England Society of Brooklyn, 1914), 1:176 ("huts like the natives"); John Downing, "The Maner of Catching and Makeing Drie Fishe in Newland," (1676) British Library, Egerton Manuscripts 2395/565; on the fishery's first century, see also Fagan, *Fish on Friday,* 73–90, 193–256; Bouchard, "'Gens sauvages et estranges,'" 46–57.

13. David Beers Quinn, "The Voyage of Etienne Bellenger to the Maritimes in 1583: A New Document," *Canadian Historical Review,* 43.4 (December 1962): 341–42,

342 ("scarlet, vermillion, red"); David B. Quinn and Alison M. Quinn, "Introduction," *ENEV*, 1–110.

14. Willoughby, "Indian Burial Place," 1–24; Bruce J. Bourque and Ruth H. White-head, "Trade and Alliances in the Contact Period," in Emerson W. Baker et al., eds., *American Beginnings: Exploration, Culture, and Cartography in the Land of Norumbega* (Lincoln: University of Nebraska Press, 1995), 131–47; Christopher L. Miller and George R. Hamill, "A New Perspective on Indian-White Contact: Cultural Symbols and Colonial Trade," *Journal of American History* 73 (1986): 321–322; Laurier Turgeon, "The Tale of the Kettle: Odyssey of an Intercultural Object," *Ethnohistory* 44.1 (1997): 1–29; James B. Petersen, Malinda Blustain, and James W. Bradley, "'Mawooshen' Revisited: Two Native American Contact Period Sites on the Central Maine Coast," *Archaeology of Eastern North America* 32 (2004): 1–71; Marcel Moussette, "A Universe Under Strain: Amerindian Nations in North-Eastern North America in the 16th Century," *Post-Medieval Archaeology* 43.1 (2009): 30–47.

15. Ruth Holmes Whitehead, "Navigation des Micmacs le long de la côte est de l'Atlantique," in Charles A. Martijn, ed., *Les Micmacs et la mer* (Montreal: Recherches amérindiennes au Québec, 1986), 225–36; Bahar, *Storm of the Sea*, 39–48. For comparative discussion of European and Native watercraft and their mutual exchanges, see Lipman, *Saltwater Frontier*, 44–84.

16. Quinn, "Voyage of Etienne Bellenger," 341; Ferdinando Gorges, "A Briefe Narration of the Originall Undertakings of the Advancement of Plantations into the Parts of America," in *Sir Ferdinando Gorges and His Province of Maine*, 3 vols., ed. James Phinney Baxter (Boston: Prince Society, 1890), 2:10 ("which they can manage").

17. Henry Juet, "The Third Voyage of Master Henry Hudson, Written by Henry Juet, of Lime-House," *Sailors' Narratives*, 182 ("two French shallops"); John Pory, "A Coppie of a Parte of Mr. Poreys Letter to the Governor of Virginia," in *John Pory's Lost Description of Plymouth Colony in the Earliest Days of the Pilgrim Fathers*, ed. Champlin Burrage (Cambridge, MA, 1918), 49 ("which they can").

18. Bahar, *Storm of the Sea*, 45 (gear, shot); Gabriel Archer, "The Relation Captain Gosnols Voyage to the North Part of Virginia," and John Brereton, "A Briefe and True Relation of the Discoverie of the North Part of Virginia," *ENEV*, 117 (captain's clothes, deerskin, sealskin), 145 (captain's clothes, "eie-browes").

19. Bahar, *Storm of the Sea*, 2–3 ("extractive . . . plundering enterprises").

20. Whitehead, "Navigation des Micmacs," 225–36; Bahar, *Storm of the Sea*, 45 (trading gear, "many other things"), 61–64 (1607 raid).

21. Colonists offered the most detailed reports of Mi'kmaq raids south of Mawooshen in the 1620s and 1630s, and they noted that these predatory attacks had been going on for decades prior. Historians Ruth Holmes Whitehead and Matthew Bahar offer multiple examples of their presence in the early 1600s along the southern Dawnlands coast. See Whitehead, "Navigation des Micmacs," and Bahar, *Storm of the Sea*, 39–65; Bradford, *OPP*, 130 ("The people were much affraid of the Tarentins, a people to the eastward which used to come in harvest time and take away their corne, and many times kill their persons."); Wood, *New England's Prospect*, 57 ("scumme of the country," "cruell bloody people"), 60 ("deadly enemies"); Gorges, "Briefe Narration," 2:76 ("war-like"); Johnson, *Wonder-Working Provi-*

dence, 78 ("came quaking"); Winthrop, *History of New England,* 1:59 (Mi'kmaq visits).

22. Trumbull, *Natick Dictionary,* 265 (watâhk8nog).

23. Verrazzano, "Cèllere Codex," 137–39; Wood, *New England's Prospect,* 87 (moving islands); Simmons, *Spirit of the New England Tribes,* 65–72; Richter, *Facing East,* 11–40; Annette Kolodny, *In Search of First Contact: The Vikings of Vinland, the Peoples of the Dawnland, and the Anglo-American Anxiety of Discovery* (Durham: Duke University Press, 2012), 280–326.

24. The date offered in the text for their first entry into Cape Cod Bay is May 14/24, 1602. Archer, "Relation of Captain Gosnols Voyage," and Brereton, "Briefe and True Relation," *ENEV,* 112–36, 139–203 (quotations: 120, 147).

25. Archer, "Relation of Captain Gosnols Voyage," *ENEV,* 124.

26. Quinn and Quinn, "Introduction," Sir Walter Ralegh to Sir Robert Cecil, August 21, 1602, *ENEV,* 32–33 (Gosnold bio). Gosnold's height comes from the discovery of his grave by the Jamestown Rediscovery Project in 2002. For a summary of their findings, see https://historicjamestowne.org/history/captain-bartholomew-gosnold -gosnoll/.

27. Archer, "Relation of Captain Gosnols Voyage," and Brereton, "A Briefe and True Relation," *ENEV,* 136 (house), 150–51 (plantings), 159–60 (house); John Charles Huden, *Indian Placenames of New England* (New York: Museum of the American Indian, Heye Foundation, 1962), 62 (Poocadahunkanow).

28. Martin Pring, "A Voyage Set Out from the Citie of Bristoll at the Charge of the Chiefest Merchants and Inhabitants of the Said Citie with a Small Ship and a Barke for the Discouerie of the North Part of Virginia, in the Year 1603," *ENEV,* 220.

29. Pring, "Voyage Set Out," *ENEV,* 225 (sassafras, "French Poxe").

30. Pring, "Voyage Set Out," *ENEV,* 221 ("When we would be ride"), 224 (plantings), 225 (sassafras, "French Poxe"), 227 (burning).

31. Samuel de Champlain, *Les voyages du Sieur de Champlain Xaintongeois, capitain ordinaire pour le Roy en la marine, Où, Journal très-fidele des observations faites és descouvertures de la Nouvelle France* (Paris: Jean Berjon, au Cheval Volant, 1613), 78 ("qua[n]tité de cabannes & iardinages"), 79 (18. out 20 savages . . . se mirent à danser . . . quelques bagatelles, dont ils surent fort contens").

32. Champlain, *Les voyages du Sieur de Champlain,* 82–88, 88 ("Il se faut donner garde de ces peuples, & vivre en misfiance avec eux, toutefois sans leur faire apperçevoir").

Chapter 5. Sassacomoit and Epenow

1. John Smith, "Description of New-England," in *CWJS,* 1:339 ("high craggy . . . than delight"). "Mawooshen" is a political place-name that described a then-existing realm of the sachems known by the title Bashabas, not a geographically based one. I use it here because it was the term Sassacomoit and his fellow captives used consistently to name their home. There's also some debate about whether the Wabanaki people found here at this time, whom the English referred to as Etchimen, were ancestors of the later Penobscot or Maliseet-Passamaquoddy peoples. See Dean R. Snow, "The Ethnohistoric Baseline of the Eastern Abenaki," *Ethno-*

history 23.3 (Summer 1976): 291–306; James Dennis Wherry, "Abnaki, Etchemin, and Malecite," *Papers of the Tenth Algonquian Conference,* ed. William Cowan (Ottawa: University of Carleton, 1979), 181–90; Petersen, Blustein, and Bradley, "'Mawooshen' Revisited."

2. James Rosier, "A True Relation of the Most Prosperous Voyage Made This Present Yeere 1605, by Captaine George Waymouth, in the Discouery of the Land of Virginia Where He Discouered 60 Miles vp a Most Excellent Riuer; Together with a Most Fertile Land," *ENEV,* 309 ("servant"); Ferdinando Gorges described Sassacomoit and his fellow Etchimen captives as "all of one-Nation, but of severall parts, and severall Families," which neither fully supports nor disproves the theory that Sassacomoit was a captive of the Etchemin. Ferdinando Gorges, "Description of New-England," in Baxter, ed., *Sir Ferdinando Gorges,* 2:8.

3. Rosier, "True Relation," 284 ("shewed . . . heads"); Champlain, *Les voyages du Sieur de Champlain,* 94.

4. Rosier, "True Relation," 309 ("gentlemen").

5. David B. Quinn and Alison M. Quinn, "Preludes to the Waymouth Voyage, 1605," *ENEV,* 231–47 (Weymouth background); James Rosier, "The Description of the Countrey of Mawooshen, 2 Discouered by the English, in the Yeere 1602. 3. 5. 6. 7. 8. and 9," *ENEV,* 470–80.

6. In an account written decades after the fact, Sir Fernando Gorges wrote that the Patuxet man was taken along with Sassacomoit in 1605. His claim made no sense, seeing as Squanto lived two hundred miles south of Mawooshen and did not appear in the original source on the voyage by James Rosier. Since the nineteenth century, historians have debated whether to take Gorges's claims at face value. James Phinney Baxter voiced his skepticism in his annotations of Gorges's text, and Charles Francis Adams also called attention to the problem. Gorges, "Description of New-England," 2:8 (Weymouth taking Squanto), 8n2 (Baxter's commentary); Adams, *Three Episodes of Massachusetts History: The Settlement of Boston Bay* (Boston: Houghton, Mifflin, 1892), 1:21–22n2; Neal Salisbury does an expert job parsing the origins of these conflations in his article "Treacherous Waters: Tisquantum, the Red Atlantic, and the Beginnings of Plymouth Colony," *Early American Literature* 56.1 (2021); 67n1, 68n2. Recent accounts that got tripped up by the complex details of Squanto's life include Russell M. Lawson, *The Sea Mark: Captain John Smith's Voyage to New England* (Hanover, NH: University Press of New England, 2015), 25–26, 196n4; Donahue, *Bradford's Indian Book,* 105–20; Weaver, *Red Atlantic,* 58–62.

7. Alan Gallay, *The Indian Slave Trade: The Rise of the English Empire in the American South, 1670–1717* (New Haven: Yale University Press, 2002); Mark Santiago, *The Jar of Severed Hands: Spanish Deportation of Apache Prisoners of War, 1770–1810* (Norman: University of Oklahoma Press, 2011); Nancy E. Van Deusen, *Global Indios: The Indigenous Struggle for Justice in Sixteenth-Century Spain* (Durham: Duke University Press, 2014); Andrés Reséndez, *The Other Slavery: The Uncovered Story of Indian Enslavement in America* (New York: Houghton Mifflin, 2016); Paul Conrad, *The Apache Diaspora: Four Centuries of Displacement and Survival* (Philadelphia: University of Pennsylvania Press, 2021).

8. The finest overviews of transatlantic Indigenous captives' trials overseas and their

resentments include Vaughan, *Transatlantic Encounters;* Brickhouse, *Unsettlement of America;* Coll Thrush, *Indigenous London: Native Travelers at the Heart of Empire* (New Haven: Yale University Press, 2016); Caroline Dodds Pennock, *On Savage Shores: How Indigenous Americans Discovered Europe* (New York: Alfred A. Knopf, 2023).

9. Rosier, "True Relation," *ENEV,* 284 ("After perceiving . . . understanding").

10. A 1643 image of the approach to Plymouth harbor is found in Baxter, ed., *Sir Ferdinando Gorges,* 2:ii; William George Hoskins, *The Making of the English Landscape* (London: Hodder and Stoughton, 1955), 137–63; Ian Mortimer, *The Time Traveler's Guide to Elizabethan England* (New York: Penguin Books, 2013), 1–24.

11. Martha L. Finch, "'Fashions of Worldly Dames': Separatist Discourses of Dress in Early Modern London, Amsterdam, and Plymouth Colony," *Church History* 74.3 (September 2005): 494–533; Emilie M. Brinkman, "Sex, Culture, and the Politics of Fashion in Stuart England" (PhD diss., Purdue University, 2008), 61–67 (cosmetics); Mortimer, *Time Traveler's Guide,* 138–62 (cosmetics, men's and women's clothing); Danae Tankard, *Clothing in 17th-Century Provincial England* (London: Bloomsbury Academic, 2020), 73–180 (cosmetics, hair, swords, men's and women's clothing).

12. Quinn and Quinn, "Introduction," *ENEV,* 71–72.

13. Quinn and Quinn, "Introduction," *ENEV,* 72.

14. David B. Quinn, "James I and the Beginnings of Empire in America," *Journal of Imperial and Commonwealth History* 2.2 (1974): 135–52; Quinn and Quinn, "Introduction," *ENEV,* 64–77.

15. A summary of their descriptions were later compiled by Rosier, almost certainly working with Sassacomoit's help, in 1609 as "The Description the Countrey of Mawooshen," *ENEV,* 470–76.

16. Quinn and Quinn, "James I and the Beginnings of Empire in America," 135–52; Karen Kupperman, *The Jamestown Project* (Cambridge, MA: Harvard University Press, 2009), 183–209.

17. Kupperman, *Jamestown Project,* 210–64, 238 ("gilded durt").

18. Quinn and Quinn, "The First Expedition to North Virginia under the 1606 Charter: The Fate of the *Richard,* Henry Challons Captain," deposition of Nicholas Hind, master of the *Richard,* February 16, 1607 (British National Archives HCA 14/38), and narrative of John Stoneman, pilot of the *Richard,* December 1607, *ENEV,* 355–56, 357–59.

19. Tessa Murphy, *The Creole Archipelago: Race and Borders in the Colonial Caribbean* (Philadelphia: University of Pennsylvania Press, 2021), 1, 30–31; Hind and Stoneman, *ENEV,* 357–58, 364–68.

20. Hind and Stoneman, *ENEV,* 357–59, 364–70 (quotations).

21. Gorges, "Briefe Narration," 2:15–17 (fire in fort, "all our former . . . over cold"); Ferdinando Gorges, "A Briefe Relation of the Discovery and Plantation of New England," in Baxter, ed., *Sir Ferdinando Gorges,* 1:206–7 (fire in fort, "a wonderfull discouragement"); Gorges to Robert Cecil, February 7, 1607/8, in Baxter, ed., *Sir Ferdinando Gorges,* 3:161 (captives' opposition); Quinn and Quinn, "Introduction," in *ENEV,* 9–11; Alfred A. Cave, "Why Was the Sagadahoc Colony Aban-

doned? An Evaluation of the Evidence," *New England Quarterly* 68.4 (December 1995): 625–40; Peter H. Morrison, "Architecture of Popham Colony, 1607/8: An Archaeological Portrait of English Building Practice at the Moment of Settlement" (master's thesis, University of Maine, Orono, 2002), esp. 66–67 (evidence of fire in fort); Christopher J. Bilodeau, "The Paradox of Sagadahoc: The Popham Colony, 1607–1608," *Early American Studies* 12.1 (Winter 2014): 1–35; Anya Zilberstein, *A Temperate Empire: Making Climate Change in Early America* (New York: Oxford University Press, 2016), 27–28; White, *Cold Welcome,* 142–49; Wickman, *Snowshoe Country,* 57–58.

22. Gorges, "Description of New-England," 2:25.

23. Gorges, "Briefe Narration," 2:20–22; Smith, "The Generall Historie of Virginia, the Somer Iles, and New England . . . ," *CWJS,* 2:399 (betrayal, Pamet, Nantucket).

24. Smith, "Generall Historie," 2:399 ("After many yeeres in England . . . warres of Bohemia").

25. Smith, "Generall Historie," 2:399 ("of so great a stature," "up and down London"); Gorges, "Briefe Narration," 2:20–21 ("a goodly man of brave aspect," "welcome, welcome").

26. William Shakespeare, *The New Oxford Shakespeare, The Complete Works: Critical Reference Edition,* ed. Gary Taylor, John Jowett, Terri Bourus, and Gabriel Egan (Oxford: Oxford University Press, 2017), 2:1553–54 (*The Tempest,* 2.2.28–29, "will not give"), 2:2825 (*Henry VIII,* 5.3.30 "some strange Indian," 5.3.50, "youths that thunder").

27. Alden T. Vaughan, "Trinculo's Indian: American Natives in Shakespeare's England," in Peter Hulme and William H. Sherman, eds., *The Tempest and Its Travels* (Philadelphia: University of Pennsylvania Press, 2000), 49–59; Thrush, *Indigenous London,* 44–47; Gorges, "Briefe Narration," 2:21 ("growne out of the peoples wonder").

28. Gorges, "Briefe Narration," 2:21.

29. Gorges, "Briefe Narration," 2:21.

30. Gorges, "Briefe Narration," 2:23–24 (voyage, escape); letter from Dermer, in Bradford, *OPP,* 112–13.

31. Gorges, "Briefe Relation," 1:204n255 (Epenow and Manamet), 210 (death of Manamet); Gorges, "Briefe Narration," 2:23 (Epenow, Sassacomoit, and Wanape); Smith, "Description of New-England," *CWJS,* 1:353 ("returned as shee went"); Council for New England, *A Briefe Relation of the Discouery and Plantation of Nevv England and of Sundry Accidents Therein Occurring, from the Yeere of our Lord M.DC.VII. to This Present M.DC.XXII. Together with the State Thereof as Now It Standeth; the Generall Forme of Gouernment Intended; and the Diuision of the Whole Territorie into Counties, Baronries, &c.,* hereafter cited as *Discovery and Plantation* (London: John Haviland and William Bladen, 1622), 6 (Manamet); letter from Dermer, in Bradford, *OPP,* 122 (the Massasoit's account of an attack by an English ship); Thomas Dermer to Samuel Purchas, 1619, in *Sailors' Narratives of Voyages along the New England Coast, 1524–1624,* ed. George Parker Winship (Boston: Houghton Mifflin, 1905), 255 (Epenow's version).

32. Orlando Patterson, *Slavery and Social Death: A Comparative Study* (Cambridge, MA: Harvard University Press, 1982), 5 ("slavery was a substitute for death"), 5–14,

35–76. Many expansions upon and critiques of Patterson come from the field of African/Atlantic slavery. Saidiya Hartman, *Lose Your Mother: A Journey along the Atlantic Slave Route* (New York: Farrar, Straus and Giroux, 2006); Stephanie Smallwood, *Saltwater Slavery: A Middle Passage from Africa to American Diaspora* (Cambridge, MA: Harvard University Press, 2007); Vincent Brown, "Social Death and Political Life in the Study of Slavery," *American Historical Review* 114.5 (December 2009): 1231–49; Terri L. Snyder, *The Power to Die: Slavery and Suicide in British North America* (Chicago: University of Chicago Press, 2015).

33. Demos, *Little Commonwealth,* 49–50, 134–36; Pestana, *World of Plymouth Plantation,* 142–44.

34. Aspects of the English view of their Native captives aligns with Patterson's theory of "liminal incorporation" of the enslaved. *Slavery and Social Death,* 45–51.

35. Dermer to Purchas, 255 ("laughed at").

Chapter 6. Capture

1. Philip L. Barbour, *The Three Worlds of Captain John Smith* (Boston: Houghton Mifflin, 1964), 305–7.

2. Barbour, *Three Worlds;* Lawson, *Sea Mark,* xi–xviii, 5–10.

3. Barbour, *Three Worlds,* 305–7; Lawson, *Sea Mark,* 5–10; Frederic W. Gleach, "Pocahontas and John Smith Revisited," *Papers of the Twenty-Fifth Algonquian Conference,* ed. William Cowan (Ottawa: University of Carleton, 1994), 167–86; Kupperman, *Jamestown Project,* 52–60, 228–30.

4. Smith, "Description of New-England," and "New Englands Trials," *CWJS,* 1:323 ("Mynes of Gold"), 1:433 (on Hunt's raid coinciding with Epenow's return).

5. David B. and Alison M. Quinn, Philip Barbour, and Russell M. Lawson have speculated that Tantum was Tisquantum. Barbour, *Three Worlds,* 471; Lawson, *Sea Mark,* 25–26, 196n4; variations of "Patuxet" and "Accomack" are common place-names in Eastern Algonquian languages—echoed in places like Pawtucket, Rhode Island, and Accomack County, Virginia. See John Charles Huden, *Indian Place-names of New England* (New York: Museum of the American Indian, Heye Foundation, 1962), 16–17 (Accomack), 172, 176 (Patuxet).

6. Smith, "Description of New-England," *CWJS,* 1:323 ("Mynes of Gold"); Lawson, *Sea Mark,* 25–26, 196n4.

7. Smith's account noted that Hunt's crew produced "dry fish," which referred to a technique for processing codfish with salt. This specialized process had been pioneered in the Newfoundland fishery, an indicator that Hunt had previously led vessels to the Grand Banks. Making "dry fish" that was well preserved and could thus fetch the highest price was a complex enough process that fishermen guarded their methods. Smith, "Description of New-England," *CWJS,* 1:323; John Downing, "The Maner of Catching and Makeing Drie Fishe in Newland," (1676) British Library, Egerton Manuscripts 2395/565; Harold A. Innis, *The Cod Fisheries: The History of an International Economy* (New Haven: Yale University Press, 1940), 48–50; Fagan, *Fish on Friday,* 73–90, 193–256; will of Thomas Hunt, British National Archives, PROB/11/134/418; Nick Bunker, *Making Haste from Babylon: The Mayflower Pilgrims and Their World* (New York: Vintage, 2011), 454n15.

8. Smith, "New England's Trials," *CWJS*, 1:401 ("This Virgins sister").

9. For examples of men donning face and body paint to meet visitors, see Gabriel Archer, "Relation of Captain Gosnols," and Brereton, "Briefe and True Relation," *ENEV*, 117, 144; Heath, ed., *Mourt's Relation*, 53.

10. Smith, "Description of New-England," *CWJS*, 1:339-40.

11. Smith, "Description of New-England," *CWJS*, 1:340 ("much kindnesse"); 1:433 ("West country men . . . wounded and much tormented with the savages that assaulted their ship, they did say themselves, in the first year I was there 1614").

12. Smith, "Description of New-England," *CWJS*, 1:340 ("some were hurt"), 340-41.

13. Barbour, "Introduction to Description of New-England," and Smith, "Description of New-England," *CWJS*, 1:294, 352 ("oft arguing . . . one Hunt"); *OED*, s.v. "slow."

14. Smith, "Description of New-England," *CWJS*, 1:352-53; the name of the *Isabella* comes from the deeds surrounding Hunt's transfer of his captives, Archivo Histórico Provincial de Málaga, Legajo 1004 (II), folios 542-44.

15. Heath, ed., *Mourt's Relation*, 70 ("aboard his ship"); Gorges, "Briefe Relation," 1:209 ("confidence of").

16. Smith, "Description of New-England," *CWJS*, 1:352; Council for New England, *Discovery and Plantation*, 5-6 ("under hatches").

17. Size extrapolated from William A. Baker, *The Mayflower and Other Colonial Vessels* (Annapolis: Naval Institute Press, 1983), 14 (tonnage equation/ratios), 95-100; Lawson, *Sea Mark*, 24 (ship/crew size); Smith, "Generall Historie," *CWJS*, 2:401n2 (Hunt on larger ship).

18. Marcus Rediker, *The Slave Ship: A Human History* (New York: Penguin Books, 2007), 132-56 ("floating dungeons"); Archivo Histórico Provincial de Málaga, Legajo 1004 (II), folio 544 (ship damage); J. H. Parry, *The Discovery of the Sea* (Berkeley: University of California Press, 1981), 7-13; Baker, *Mayflower*, 1-7 (heads, weather deck); Stephen R. Berry, *A Path in the Mighty Waters: Shipboard Life and Atlantic Crossings to the New World* (New Haven: Yale University Press, 2015), 57-58 (heads), 67-76 (slave ship conditions); Lawson, *Sea Mark*, 28-29.

19. Levett, "My Discouery," 284 ("they call all Masters of Shippes Sagamore, or any other man, that they see have a commaund of men"); Smith, "A Sea Grammar," *CWJS*, 3:84-86 (watches); Lawson, *Sea Mark*, 28-29 (watches, prayers).

20. Lawson, *Sea Mark*, 27-29 (crew positions); Berry, *Path in the Mighty Waters*, 90-95 (crew-passenger relations); Smith, "An Accidence for Young Sea-Men: Or, Their Pathway to Experience," and "Sea Grammar," *CWJS*, 3:15-19, 82-91 (crew positions).

21. Smith, "Accidence," and "Sea Grammar," *CWJS*, 3:19-21, 70-73 (lines and rigging), 112-13 (diet); Berry, *Path in the Mighty Waters*, 35-38 (diet), 51-54 (sea legs).

22. Berry, *Path in the Mighty Waters*, 171-96 (tedium); for other examples of sailors teaching captives English at sea, see James Rosier, "A True Relation," *ENEV*, 284; Olaudah Equiano, *The Interesting Narrative and Other Writings*, ed. Vincent Carretta (New York: Penguin Classics, 1995), 65-68.

23. Fisher, "Speaking Indian and English," 49, 49n47.

24. Heath, ed., *Mourt's Relation*, 70 ("could not behold").

25. [Baird], "Wampanoag Grammar," 13.

Chapter 7. Spain

1. My description of the Spanish coast draws from a visit to Málaga in June 2019 and the historic account of Edmund Dummer from 1687 in "A Voyage into the Mediterranean Seas, Containing (by Way of Journall) the Viewes and Descriptions of . . . Lands, Cities, Towns, and Arsenalls, Their Seuerall Planes and Fortifications, with Diuers Perspectives of Particular Buildings Which Came within the Compass of Said Voyage," (1687) British Library, Kings Manuscripts, 40, 94 (Málaga description/image), 97 (Gibraltar description); Francisco Guillen Robles, *Historia de Málaga y su Provincia* (Málaga: Imprenta de Rubio y Cano, 1874), 507–8 (cathedral construction).

2. Gillian T. Cell, *English Enterprise in Newfoundland, 1577–1660* (Toronto: University of Toronto Press, 1969), 22–24; In a general overview of the Spanish economy in 1613, England's ambassador to Spain wrote, "as for Sea-matters, thei are now in farr differing Estate, from what thei were, in the tyme of Queene Elizabeth. For then every bodye armed, and went to sea to robb. Now no man goethe to sea, but only a fewe Merchants." John Digby to James I, September 22/October 2, 1613, British National Archives, State Papers, 94/20. On Málaga and Cádiz as major depots for Newfoundland fish, see Smith, "Generall Historie," *CWJS*, 2:401–3; Gorges, "Briefe Narration," 2:26–27.

3. Reséndez, *Other Slavery,* 46–47; Van Deusen, *Global Indios,* 3–5, 198 ("contradictory and piecemeal").

4. Reséndez, *Other Slavery,* 68 (reinterpretations/euphemisms), 74–75 ("rebels," "criminals"), 127–28 (wartime exceptions); Van Deusen, *Global Indios,* 7–9, 64–72; Salisbury, "Treacherous Waters," 55–57; Stuart B. Schwartz, *All Can Be Saved: Religious Tolerance and Salvation in the Iberian Atlantic World* (New Haven: Yale University Press, 2008), 160–63 (exemptions for African enslavement).

5. Van Deusen, *Global Indios,* 12 ("multicultural ethnoscape"); Robert C. Davis, *Holy War and Human Bondage: Tales of Christian-Muslim Slavery in the Early-Modern Mediterranean* (Stuttgart, Germany: Holtzbrinck, 2009), vii–viii ("faith slavery"), 9–28; Daniel Hershenzon, *The Captive Sea: Slavery, Communication, and Commerce in Early Modern Spain and the Mediterranean* (Philadelphia: University of Pennsylvania Press, 2018), 1–9.

6. Hershenzon, *Captive Sea,* 22–30, 22 ("traumatic cacophony"); Van Deusen, *Global Indios,* 80–81; Davis, *Holy War and Human Bondage,* 39–40 (10,000 estimate).

7. The English accounts of Hunt's arrival in Málaga are found in Gorges, "Briefe Relation," 1:210; Gorges, "Briefe Narration," 2:26–27, 27n315; Heath, ed., *Mourt's Relation,* 52; Purificación Ruiz García, "Málaga, Squanto, y el día de acción de gracias," *Sociedad: Boletín de la Sociedad de Amigos de la Cultura de Vélez-Málaga* 20/21 (2022/2023): 89.

8. Archivo Histórico Provincial de Málaga, Legajo 1004 (II), folios 542–44. The two deeds are very similar documents and share a number of identical or near-identical phrasings, with slightly more detail on the legal status of the captives in the second deed. Their texts are reproduced in part (and in Spanish) in Ruiz's article "Málaga, Squanto, y el día de acción de gracias," 89–90, 93–94. My thanks to Antonio Giron for sharing his translation of the full deeds.

9. Archivo Histórico Provincial de Málaga, Legajo 1004 (II), folio 542.

10. Ruiz, "Málaga, Squanto, y el día de acción de gracias," 89, 92–93; Archivo Histórico Provincial de Málaga, Legajo 1004 (II), folios 542–44.

11. Ruiz, "Málaga, Squanto, y el día de acción de gracias," 92–93.

12. On the conversion of captives in Spain, see Schwartz, *All Can Be Saved*, 173–76; Hershenzon, *Captive Sea*, 1, 125–26; Brickhouse, *Unsettlement of America*, 52–53. For comparative examples of the interactions between Spanish missionaries and Native converts in eighteenth-century Tejas, see Julianna Barr, *Peace Came in the Form of a Woman* (Chapel Hill: University of North Carolina Press, 2007), 38–42 (Marian iconography), 128–29; 149–50 (clothing); for the same from eighteenth-century Alta California, see Steven W. Hackel, *Children of Coyote, Missionaries of St. Francis: Indian-Spanish Relations in Colonial California, 1769–1850* (Chapel Hill: University of North Carolina Press, 2005), 11 ("rich in Catholic association"), 127–66 (pre-baptismal instruction), 127 ("highly scripted"), 140 ("superficial"), 163–65 (Native/Catholic cultural cognates).

13. Ruiz, "Málaga, Squanto, y el día de acción de gracias," 93; on the fate of freed "indios" in Spain, see also Van Deusen, *Global Indios*, 151–54.

14. Smith, "Description of New-England," *CWJS*, 1:353 ("treacherie"), "Generall Historie," 2:401 ("dishonestly and inhumanely," "vilde act"); Gorges, "Briefe Relation," 1:209 ("a worthless fellow of our Nation"), 210 ("devillish"); John G. Turner notes their inconsistency in *They Knew They Were Pilgrims: Plymouth Colony and the Contest for American Liberty* (New Haven: Yale University Press, 2020), 66.

15. Some scholars have made unsubstantiated leaps about the scope and significance of Tisquantum's time in Spain. The literary scholar Anna Brickhouse describes him as "hispanophone" and "Catholic-educated," not differentiating between the first-person account Squanto gave to Bradford, in which he "got away," and Gorges's account of Hunt's captives being "instructed in the Christian faith," which did not mention Tisquantum's involvement specifically. In the brief accounts the colonists dictated directly from the Patuxet man, he said nothing about Catholics attempting to convert him in Spain. Brickhouse, *Unsettlement of America*, 37–45; Heath, ed., *Mourt's Relation*, 55 ("dwelt'); Johnson, *Wonder-Working Providence*, 43 ("two year or thereabout").

16. Archivo Histórico Provincial de Málaga, Legajo 1004 (II), folios 543–44 ("Enrique Loque" and "Joseph Toquer"). In a typically foggy recounting, an elderly Fernando Gorges recalled that upon learning of a captive Native person in Málaga, he "had him sent [to] me" in 1615, but this was a clear case of him conflating Tisquantum with Sassacomoit, who had been redeemed from Spain in 1608. In a separate account Gorges wrote that he first heard of Squanto from Dermer when they both were in Newfoundland. Gorges, "Briefe Narration," 2:26–27, 27n315.

17. Peter E. Pope, *Fish into Wine: The Newfoundland Plantation in the Seventeenth Century* (Chapel Hill: University of North Carolina Press, 2004), 91–97; Cell, *English Enterprise in Newfoundland*, 53–80; Cell, "The Newfoundland Company: A Study of Subscribers to a Colonizing Venture," *WMQ* 22.4 (1965): 612 ("one constant focus"); John Mason, *A Brief Discourse of the Nevv-found-land, with the Situation, Temperature, and Commodities Thereof, Inciting Our Nation to Goe Forward in That Hopeful Plantations Begunne* (Edinburgh: Andro Hart, 1620), [6] ("being but the half of the way to Virginia").

18. John Downing, "A Brief Narrative Concerning Newfoundland," September 24/ October 4, 1676, British Library, Egerton Manuscripts 2395/560–63; John Guy to John Slany and the Council of the Newfoundland Company, May 16/26, 1611, in David Beers Quinn, *Newfoundland from Fishery to Colony* (New York: Arno Press, 1979), 146–49.

19. Ingeborg Marshall, *A History and Ethnography of the Beothuk* (Montreal: McGill-Queen's University Press, 1996), 3–41; John Guy, "A Journall of the Voiadge of Discoverie Made in a Barke Builte in Newfoundland Called the Indeavour, Begunne the 7 [17] of October and Ended the 25th [4th] of November [December] Following," Quinn, *Newfoundland from Fishery to Colony,* 154–56; Cell, *English Enterprise,* 40–42.

20. Cell, "Newfoundland Company," 611–25; see also Kupperman, *Jamestown Project,* 12–72; Alison Games, *The Web of Empire: English Cosmopolitans in an Age of Expansion* (New York: Oxford University Press), 81–116.

21. Charter by King James I to the Newfoundland Company in Quinn, *Newfoundland from Fishery to Colony,* 133–39 (role of treasurer); Cell, "Newfoundland Company," 614–15, 615 (Cell drew the "audacious merchants" quotation from Astrid Friis, *Alderman Cockayne's Project and the Cloth Trade: The Commercial Policy of England in Its Main Aspects, 1603–1625* [London: Oxford University Press, 1927], 100); Cell, *English Enterprise,* 54 ("there was hardly"); Edmond Smith, *Merchants: The Community That Shaped England's Trade and Empire* (New Haven: Yale University Press, 2021), 145–46 (H. Slany); will of John Slany, Merchant Tailor of London, April 26/May 6, 1632, British National Archives, PROB 11/161/478; correspondence between Newfoundland merchants show that H. Slany was in constant contact with Mediterranean ports. Richard Newall to H. Slany and William Clowbury, Sr., July 8/18, 1623; Richard Newall to James Man with the rest of the owners of the *Lute of London,* July 8/18, 1623, University of Oxford, Bodleian Library, Malone Manuscripts, 2, 5; Slany's time in the Azores and contact with Englishmen in Spain is alluded to in a 1605 letter from Spain that describes him as "Londone merchante last [of] the Island of St. Mighell [Sao Miguel]," British National Archives, State Papers, 94/12.

22. Instructions from the Council to John Guy in Quinn, *Newfoundland from Fishery to Colony,* 141 ("farther discoverie of [the] Country"); William Gilbert, "Beothuk-European Contact in the 16th Century: A Re-evaluation of the Documentary Evidence," *Acadiensis* 40.1 (2011): 2 ("a safe and free commerce with").

Chapter 8. England

1. Margarette Lincoln, *London and the Seventeenth Century: The Making of the World's Greatest City* (New Haven: Yale University Press, 2021), 35–37, 76; Smith, *Merchants,* 111–14; Mortimer, *Time Traveler's Guide,* 207–8.

2. Will of John Slany; Lovell v. Slany, British National Archives, C 2/Jasl/L4/31; Finch, "'Fashions of Worldly Dames,'" 494–533; Mortimer, *Time Traveler's Guide,* 138–62.

3. Lincoln, *London,* 4–5, 10–11; will of John Slany; Alexander Brown, ed., *The Genesis of the United States* (Boston: Houghton Mifflin, 1890), 1004.

4. Lincoln, *London*, 35–37; Smith, *Merchants*, 59–79, 113–14.

5. Will of John Slany; the deaths of his two sons are not included in the St. Martin parish register but Slany's will attested that they died young and were buried in St. Martin's churchyard on Ironmonger Lane next to their mother. Joseph Lemuel Chester, ed., *The Parish Registers of St. Michael, Cornhill, London, Containing the Marriages, Baptism, and Burials from 1546 to 1754* (London: Publications of the Harleian Society, 1882), 211–22.

6. Will of John Slany; Lincoln, *London*, 10–11.

7. Lincoln, *London*, 11, 32–33; Smith, *Merchants*, 16–23.

8. Bradford, *OPP*, 112 ("entertained by," "imployed"); Thrush, *Indigenous London*, 53–58.

9. Townsend, *Pocahontas*, 135–58; Emily M. Rose, "Did Squanto Meet Pocahontas, and What Might They Have Discussed?" *The Junto: A Group Blog on Early American History*, November 21, 2017, https://earlyamericanists.com/2017/11/21/did-squanto-meet-pocahontas-and-what-might-they-have-discussed/.

10. Lincoln, *London*, 8–12, 19; William M. Cavert, *The Smoke of London: Energy and Environment in the Early Modern City* (Cambridge: Cambridge University Press, 2016), 17–31.

11. Lincoln, *London*, 5–7, 11–12.

12. Lincoln, *London*, 5–6, 8–9, 55.

13. Lipman, *Saltwater Frontier*, 44–84, 222–35.

14. David Crystal, "Introduction," in *The Oxford Dictionary of Original Shakespearean Pronunciation* (Oxford: Oxford University Press, 2016), ix–xl.

15. Crystal, "Introduction," ix–xii, xlv–vi.

16. Crystal, "Introduction," xlvi; Bradford, *OPP*, 25 ("warr," "wher"), 26 ("farr"), 31 ("ther").

17. Wood, *New England's Prospect*, 103 ("much difficulty . . . Nobstann"); Eliot, *Indian Grammar*, 2 (*l/n/r*); Williams, *Key*, 105 (*l/n/r*); Winslow, *Good News*, 81 ("Winsnow"); Crystal, *Oxford Dictionary*, xlvi–ii (Irish *t/th*).

18. Fisher, "Speaking Indian and English," 81n36 (immersion). It's possible that Squanto was still in London in March 1617/8 when Elizabeth Slany died, but given the problems verifying his presence then, I've refrained from making any speculative points about this. I thank Richard Pickering for pointing me to this event in the parish records. Chester, ed., *Parish Registers of St. Michael*, 221.

19. Although it is not completely clear when Tisquantum first arrived in Newfoundland, circumstantial evidence from accounts by Smith, Gorges, and Dermer all indicate that he must have returned to England with Dermer at the end of the 1618 fishing season, which is when Smith places Dermer back in England, so the latest he left for Newfoundland was spring 1618, though he could have left the year before. Mason, *Brief Discourse of the Nevv-found-land*, [6] (pigs and goats), [9] (iceberg season); John Downing, "The Maner of Catching and Makeing Drie Fishe in Newland," (1676) and "A Brief Narrative Concerning Newfoundland," September 24, 1676, British Library, Egerton Manuscripts, 2395/565, 2395/562.

20. Pope, *Fish into Wine*, 50–53.

21. Mason, *Brief Discourse of the Nevv-found-land*, [10] (Beothuks on northern side); Ralph Pastore, "The Collapse of the Beothuk World," *Acadiensis* 19.1 (1989): 52–71;

Ingeborg Marshall, *A History and Ethnography of the Beothuk* (Montreal: McGill-Queen's University Press, 1996), 3-41.

22. Marshall, *History and Ethnography,* 420-37; Donald H. Holly, Jr., "A Historicity of an Ahistoricity," *History and Anthropology* 14.2 (2003): 133-43 (language).

23. Donald H. Holly, Jr., "The Beothuk on the Eve of Their Extinction," *Arctic Anthropology* 37.1 (2000): 79-95; The archaeologist William Gilbert points out that "aside from humans, prior to contact there were only fourteen terrestrial mammals on the island. . . . Of these only four, the arctic hare, black bear, beaver, and caribou fit into the general definition of prey species. However, unless the Beothuk were very different from their Algonqui[a]n cousins, the muskrat, otter and martin were almost certainly hunted for food as well as for fur and even the ermine, fox, lynx and wolf were probably consumed at least occasionally." William Gilbert, "Beothuk-European Contact in the 16th Century: A Re-evaluation of the Documentary Evidence," *Acadiensis* 40.1 (2011): 28 (quotation).

24. Annette Kolodny, *In Search of First Contact: The Vikings of Vinland, the Peoples of the Dawnland, and the Anglo-American Anxiety of Discovery* (Durham: Duke University Press, 2012), 58-59, 90-92; Gilbert, "Beothuk-European Contact," 22-44.

25. Gilbert, "Beothuk-European Contact," 22-44; John Guy, "A Journall of the Voiadge of Discoverie," in Quinn, *Newfoundland from Fishery to Colony,* 154-56; Marshall, *History and Ethnography of the Beothuk,* 25-41.

26. Mason, *Brief Discourse of the Nevv-found-land,* [12-13] ("hope of trade . . . Verbum sapienti").

Chapter 9. The Angry Star

1. Letter from Dermer, in Bradford, *OPP,* 122 ("inveterate malice"), 123 (French shipwreck and attack); Phinehas Pratt recorded a Native description of the French shipwreck and aftermath told to him by a Massachusett man named Pecksuot. The preacher and historian Increase Mather subsequently published part of Pratt's account. Both appear in a later nineteenth-century edition of Pratt's narrative. I quote from Mather in the main text because Pratt used idiosyncratic spelling and a lot of shorthand whereas Mather's judicious editing generally made his meaning clearer. Pratt, *Declaration of the Affairs,* 8 (Pratt's original account of French shipwreck), 18 (Mather's version).

2. Pratt, *Declaration of the Affairs,* 8 (Pratt), 18 (Mather: "wept very much," "such meat"); Bradford, *OPP,* 123 ("sent from one Sachem"); Morton, *New English Canaan,* 23 (wood and water). Morton conflated the details of the Cape Cod wreck (in which five Frenchmen survived as captives) with the Boston Harbor attack on M. Finch's ship (in which all the Frenchmen aboard died).

3. Pratt, *Declaration of the Affairs,* 8-9; John Winthrop, *The History of New England from 1630 to 1649,* 2 vols., ed. James Savage (New York: Arno Press, 1972), 1:59 (July 30, 1631: "two pieces of French money").

4. Pecksuot/Pexworth, Pratt's Massachusett informant, claimed that the Frenchman's son was still alive in the 1620s, but the gravesite the Plymouth colonists found strongly suggests otherwise, or else the sailor had two sons and only one died with him. That same account claimed that all the captured Frenchmen died, which we

know to be incorrect. Pratt, *Declaration of the Affairs,* 8 (Pratt: "Thay [the French captives] liued but a little while. On of them Liued Longer than the Rest, for he had a good master & gaue him a wiff. He is now ded, but hath a sonn Alive"); 18 (Mather: "Only one of them having a good Master, he provided a Wife for him, by whom he had a Son, and lived longer than the rest of the French men did"); Heath, ed., *Mourt's Relation,* 27–28 ("a knife . . . some of the flesh").

5. Heath, ed., *Mourt's Relation,* 27–28.

6. Dermer to Purchas, in *Sailors' Narratives,* 252 (redemption of Frenchmen). While Dermer took credit for the ransoming, the entire negotiation had to be the work of Tisquantum.

7. Pratt, *Declaration of the Affairs,* 8 (Pratt: "On of ym had a Booke he would ofen Reed in. We Asked him 'what his Booke said.' He answered, 'It saith, ther will a people, lick French men, com into this Cuntry and driue you all a way'"), 18 (Mather: "one of them was wont to read much in a Book (some say it was the New-Testament) and that the Indians enquiring of him what his Book said, he told them it did intimate, that there was a people like French men that would come into the Country, and drive out the Indians, and that they were now afraid that the English were the people of whose coming the French man had foretold them"); Morton, *New English Canaan,* 132 ("for their bloudy deed'); Kolodny, *In Search of First Contact,* 280–83 (Indigenous storytelling tropes).

8. Gorges, "Briefe Narration," 2:18 (headache); Dermer to Purchas, in *Sailors' Narratives,* 251 (pox/spots); Gookin, *Historical Collections,* 8 (jaundice); Morton, *New English Canaan,* 130–34.

9. Sherburne F. Cook, "The significance of disease in the extinction of the New England Indians," *Human Biology* 45.3 (September 1973): 485–508; T. L. Bratton, "The Identity of the New England Indian Epidemic of 1616–19," *Bulletin of the History of Medicine* 62.3 (Fall 1988): 351–83; John S. Marr and John T. Cathey, "New Hypothesis for Cause of Epidemic among Native Americans, New England, 1616–1619," *Emerging Infectious Diseases* 16.2 (February 2010): 281–86.

10. The term "Great Dying" has been popularized by the scholar Paula Peters. See "Of Patuxet," 30–31. There have been challenges to the use of the "virgin soil" frame; these scholars caution against seeing the death rates from these epidemics as monocausal, pointing out the disruptive impact of colonists' actions in heightening death tolls, which is a sound point, though not particularly applicable in the case of the 1616 epidemic. I find these objections to be tendentious when they try to discredit the very idea of "virgin soil epidemics" on the dubious grounds that noting the genuine differences in Indigenous populations' historic disease exposures somehow creates a slippery slope toward biological racism or determinism. See Alfred W. Crosby, "Virgin Soil Epidemics as a Factor in the Aboriginal Depopulation in America," *WMQ* 33.2 (April 1976): 289–99; David S. Jones, "Virgin Soils Revisited," *WMQ* 60.4 (October 2003): 703–42; Silva, *Miraculous Plagues,* 24–50.

11. Morton, *New English Canaan,* 23–24 (scavengers, "the Plague fell," "new found Golgatha"); Bradford, *OPP,* 118 ("sad spectackle").

12. Johnson, *Wonder-Working Providence,* 40–43; Smith, "Generall Historie," *CWJS,* 2:229; Silva, *Miraculous Plagues,* 54–61.

13. Winslow, *Good News,* 106 ("more and more cold").

14. Johnson, *Wonder-Working Providence,* 39–40 ("ancient Indians," "Blazing Star").
15. Bunker, *Making Haste,* 17–21; David A. J. Seargent, *The Greatest Comets in History: Broom Stars and Celestial Scimitars* (New York: Springer, 2008), 110–12 (global sightings); Ronald Stoyan, *Atlas of Great Comets* (Cambridge: Cambridge University Press, 2014), 66–68.
16. James Doelman, "The Comet of 1618 and the British Royal Family," *Notes and Queries* 54.1 (2007): 30–35, 30 ("firebrand in her arse"); the version of James's poem quoted here is the one held in the British National Archives, State Papers, Domestic James I 14/104/16v, as republished in A. Maclean, "King James' Poem on the Great Comet of 1618," *Journal of the British Astronomical Association* 97.2 (1987): 74; Crystal, *Oxford Dictionary,* 61 (blood rhyming with good, wood, understood), 112 (conceit rhyming with bait, straight, wait).
17. Francis J. Bremer, *One Small Candle: The Plymouth Puritans and the Beginning of English New England* (New York: Oxford University Press, 2020), 1–7, 37–41; Winship, *Hot Protestants,* 1–4; Shakespeare, *New Oxford Shakespeare,* 2:2181 (*Twelfth Night* 2.3.118).
18. Bremer, *One Small Candle,* 11 ("priesthood"), 11–27; Winship, *Hot Protestants,* 18–25.
19. Bremer, *One Small Candle,* 25–38; Edmund S. Morgan, *Visible Saints: The History of a Puritan Idea* (Ithaca: Cornell University Press, 1965 [1st ed., 1963]), 1–32.
20. Bremer, *One Small Candle,* 26 ("one Doctrine . . . or else do worse"); Morgan, *Visible Saints,* 18–20.
21. Bradford, *OPP,* 23–33; Bremer, *One Small Candle,* 21–41, 27 ("thick Antichristian darkness"); Winship, *Hot Protestants,* 59–63, 63 ("a fair amount").
22. Bradford, *OPP,* 33–37; Pestana, *World of Plymouth Plantation,* 147–56; John Seelye, *Memory's Nation: The Place of Plymouth Rock* (Chapel Hill: University of North Carolina Press, 2012), 1–5.
23. Carla Pestana argues convincingly that the labels "Separatist" and "Brownist" obscure the true position of the Scrooby-Leiden congregation and grossly mischaracterize the eventual church that took shape in the colony, a point that aligns with her welcome challenge to exceptionalist narratives about Plymouth. But it's worth noting that in recent work, most historians of religion are still comfortable characterizing the colony's founding church as lower-case "separatists," placing the Scrooby-Leiden group on the more reconciliatory side of the spectrum of radical congregationalists. Pestana, *World of Plymouth Plantation,* 147–56, 151 ("walked a fine line"); Winship, *Hot Protestants,* 61–63, 71–75; Bremer, *One Small Candle,* 23–25, 42–64, 150–67; Turner, *They Were Pilgrims,* 11–13, 20–31.
24. Bradford, *OPP,* 41–49; Bremer, *One Small Candle,* 62–63; Turner, *They Were Pilgrims,* 39.
25. Bremer, *One Small Candle,* 67–76; David B. Quinn, "The First Pilgrims," *WMQ* 23.3 (July 1966): 359–90.
26. Bunker, *Making Haste,* 17–21.
27. Smith, "Generall Historie," *CWJS,* 2:441 ("understanding and industrious").
28. Smith, "Description of New-England," and "New-Englands Trials," *CWJS,* 1:350–51, 359–60, 398–99.
29. Smith, "Description of New-England," "New-Englands Trials," *CWJS,* 1:161–65, 183–84; Bradford, *OPP,* 121 (Tisquantum saving Dermer's life, "honored freind").

30. In spring 1618, around the most likely time Squanto and Dermer were in Virginia, Governor Samuel Argall approved "some persons to trade with the Indians," which was probably *not* them but nonetheless leaves open the distant possibility. *RVCL*, 3:79 ("some persons"). The only other window of time in which Tisquantum conceivably could have been to Virginia was in summer 1622, when two ships went back and forth between the southern colony and Plymouth. He had good reason to want to leave the area for a while, as the Massasoit had just called for his head. Still, the evidence still favors the received wisdom that Squanto spent that whole summer in Plymouth. Bradford commented that his falling out with the Massasoit "caused him to stick close to the English, and never durst goe from them till he dyed." That does not dispositively rule out a side trip to Virginia as he would *technically* be sticking "close to the English" if he went with some of them to another colony. But the phrasing that Tisquantum "never durst *goe from* them" strongly implies he was rooted in Plymouth in the period from his downfall to his death. Winslow indicated that Squanto told his fellow Wampanoags about his experiences in Virginia, which supports the idea that he went with Dermer around 1617 or 1618 and informed them about the Chesapeake soon after his return, as he may have been estranged from most Natives by summer 1622. Bradford, *OPP*, 121 ("to New-foundland"), 137 ("stick close to the English"), 146–50 (ships between Plymouth and Virginia); Winslow, *Good News*, 112 ("went in an English Ship thither").

31. Neal Salisbury notes the aside ("Treacherous Waters," 69n8) but discredits it as a misunderstanding on Winslow's part. Given that Winslow spent as much or more time with Squanto than any other colonist—he accompanied him on several expeditions and was the colonist most interested in getting Wampanoag lessons from him—I think his claim should carry a lot of weight.

32. James Horn, *Adapting to a New World: English Society in the Seventeenth Century Chesapeake* (Chapel Hill: University of North Carolina Press, 1994), 136 (population numbers); Smith, "Generall Historie," *CWJS*, 2:262 ("decaying . . . broken . . . in pieces . . . spoiled . . . Swine"); Governor Samuel Argall to the Virginia Company, March 10/20, 1616/17, John Rolfe to Sir Edwin Sandys, June 8, 1617, and Argall to William Cradock, February 20/March 2, 1617/8, *RVCL*, 3:68–69, 71 ("crooked"), 92 ("ruinous condicion").

33. Smith, "Generall Historie," *CWJS*, 2:262 ("the Salvages as frequent in their houses as themselves"), Argall to the Virginia Company, *RVCL*, 3:68–70; Rolfe to Sandys, June 8, 1617, *RVCL*, 3:71 ("great plenty").

34. Gorges, "Briefe Relation," 1:212 ("to worke a peace," "persuaded him").

Chapter 10. Homecoming

1. Smith, "New-Englands Trials," 1:183–84 (voyage details, £2100); Thomas Dermer to Samuel Purchas, 1619, in *Sailors' Narratives of Voyages along the New England Coast, 1524–1624*, ed. George Parker Winship (Boston: Houghton Mifflin, 1905), 251–52.

2. Dermer to Purchas, in *Sailors' Narratives*, 251.

3. Dermer to Purchas, in *Sailors' Narratives*, 251; letter from Dermer, in Bradford, *OPP*, 112.

4. Dermer to Purchas, in *Sailors' Narratives*, 251.

5. Dermer to Purchas, in *Sailors' Narratives*, 251–52; letter from Dermer in Bradford, *OPP*, 122 ("they would have kiled me").

6. Dermer to Purchas, in *Sailors' Narratives*, 251–52.

7. Heath, ed., *Mourt's Relation*, 53 (height, hair, complexion), 57–58 ("a very lustie man," Massasoit's face paint, dress, tobacco bag, beaded necklace, and knife), 61; Altham to Altham, September 1623, *Three Visitors*, 30 (black wolfskin, belt); Morton, *New English Canaan*, 79–80.

8. Altham to Altham, September 1623, *Three Visitors*, 30 ("as proper a man"); Winslow, *Good News*, 80 ("ruled by reason," "governed his men," "oft-times restrained"); Heath, ed., *Mourt's Relation*, 57 ("a very lustie man"); Jennifer Jordan, "'That Ere with Age, His Strength Is Utterly Decay'd': Understanding the Male Body in Early Modern Manhood," in Kate Fisher and Sarah Toulalan, eds., *Bodies, Sex and Desire from the Renaissance to the Present* (London: Palgrave Macmillan, 2011), 27–48.

9. It's not clear what event they were describing: it doesn't quite match any documented visit by any of the three European nations then operating in the area, the English, French, and Dutch. No doubt the story was distorted; it was early in Tisquantum's career as a translator, and he likely elided some details while relating the essence of the story, which were further abridged in Dermer's letter. Still, the account does bear a loose resemblance to the 1614 visit that brought Epenow back to Noepe: surviving secondhand accounts mention that the English fired at the Wampanoags freeing their kinsmen, though did not admit to killing any. Dermer seemed to recognize the details when he heard the story straight from Epenow's mouth weeks later, as he thought the man from Noepe "was reported to haue beene slaine, with diuers of his Countrey-men, by Saylors, which was false." Dermer was likely connecting the story the Pokanokets told him and Epenow's escape as they were mentioned in two different letters, since the previous conversation with the Massasoit was the only one in which he reported hearing about the death of other Natives. Letter from Dermer in Bradford, *OPP*, 122 (Ousamequin's version); Dermer to Purchas, in *Sailors' Narratives*, 255 (Epenow's version); Gorges, "Briefe Relation," 1:204, 210 (first English version of Epenow's return); Gorges, "Briefe Narration," 2:23 (second mention of Epenow's return).

10. Dermer to Purchas, in *Sailors' Narratives*, 252 ("desirous of noveltie").

11. A number of historians have assumed that when Dermer said he left Tisquantum at "Sawahquatooke," he meant Saco or Sagadahoc in Maine, which would be a strange place to leave a Wampanoag man in search of any living relations or allies. The confusion is understandable because Dermer's letter is a bit disorganized and scattered, but the detail about where he left Squanto is an aside, not a sequential detail, so it didn't necessarily happen right before he sailed south again from Monhegan. Not only is *Satucket* at the very least no further away phonetically from *Sawahquatooke* than either *Saco* or *Sagadahoc*, the river was close by Nemasket, where later Pilgrim sources mentioned that Tisquantum had relations. Others have proposed Dermer left Squanto at a similarly named place on Cape Cod, but Dermer was quite explicit that his translator left him before he came to the peninsula. Dermer to Purchas, *Sailors' Narratives*, 253–54.

12. Dermer to Purchas, *Sailors' Narratives*, 253–54.

13. A few scholars have suggested that Tisquantum was held as a captive by the Massasoit for part of this time; they base this claim on the account of Dermer's spring 1620 encounter with Epenow and on a marginal note in a book written eighteen years later by Thomas Morton. The report itself was garbled, almost to the point of incoherence. Morton did not name Squanto directly; he mentioned "a Salvage" who was a composite of Squanto and Samoset and who was held as a captive by an unnamed sachem. That figure seems to be a conflation of Ousamequin and Epenow; the latter sachem *did* briefly hold Squanto hostage before the colonists arrived. He then segued into a convoluted account of the translator's political plot that wildly contradicted the versions written by those who witnessed it firsthand. Salisbury, "Squanto, Last of the Patuxets," 37–38; Morton, *New English Canaan*, 104–5.

14. Bradford, *OPP*, 128 ("sought his owne ends").

15. This pattern is also identified in Salisbury, "Squanto, Last of the Patuxets," 242–43; Dermer to Purchas, in *Sailors' Narratives*, 251 ("a remnant remaines"); Bradford, *OPP*, 110 ("a native of this place").

16. Robert Cushman, *Sermon Preached at Plimmoth in New-England* (London: John Bellamie, 1622), 4 ("Wee found the place").

17. Bradford, *OPP*, 110 ("He was a native"), 127 ("an Indean belonging"); Heath, ed., *Mourt's Relation*, 75 ("house of Squanto"). On women serving food, see Winslow, who was a little more explicit in recalling a later stop in the village of Mattapoisett, near Sowams, where "the *squasachim*, for so they call the sachim's wife, gave us friendly entertainment." *Good News*, 33.

18. Pestana, *World of Plymouth Plantation*, 15–27, 22 ("were either absent").

19. Neal Salisbury, "Treacherous Waters," 65 ("Tisquantum of Patuxet was unmarried [probably widowed]"); Donahue, *Bradford's Indian Book*, 109 ("as far as we know, Tisquantum was not married"). Donahue downplays Squanto's will to power by citing his supposed bachelordom, writing, "Had Tisquantum really been seeking political primacy, he must first have married. Had he been unable to find a wife, he would then have asked a large family dominated by women to adopt him" (110). I agree with these points, but I differ from Donahue in reading the sources as indicating rather unambiguously that Squanto intended to wield power in his own right, which makes it all the more likely that he remarried upon return.

20. On optional cohabitation, see Plane, *Colonial Intimacies*, 21–23.

21. Bradford, *OPP*, 113; Dermer to Purchas, in *Sailors' Narratives*, 253–54, 254 ("besides hope," "I take it was").

22. Bradford, *OPP*, 113–14; Dermer to Purchas, in *Sailors' Narratives*, 254–55.

23. Bradford, *OPP*, 113; Dermer to Purchas, in *Sailors' Narratives*, 256–57.

24. Letter from Dermer in Bradford, *OPP*, 112; Smith, "Generall Historie," *CWJS*, 2:246 (November 1619 "one Master Dirmer sent out by some of the Plimoth for New-England, arrived in a Barke of five tunnes, and returned the next Spring [1620]").

25. Letter from Dermer in Bradford, *OPP*, 112–13.

26. Robert Cushman to Leiden congregation, May 8/18, 1619, Bradford, *OPP*, 59–60, 59 ("packed togeather"), 60 ("heavie news"), 61 ("a good . . . blessing").

27. Bradford, *OPP*, 78–79n2 (*Mayflower* name).

28. Bradford, *OPP*, 63–87.

29. Bremer, *One Small Candle*, 67–68; Smith, "Description of New-England" and "The True Travels," *CWJS*, 1:330 ("of all the foure parts"), 3:221 ("my books and maps").

30. Lawson, *The Sea Mark*, 21–22; Bradford, *OPP*, 54 ("well weaned").

Chapter 11. The Treaty

1. Bradford, *OPP*, 87–94, 99 ("leakie as a seive"); Heath, ed., *Mourt's Relation*,15–17, 15 ("boysterous stormes").

2. Bradford, *OPP*, 87–94, 103 ("periles . . . troubles"); Heath, ed., *Mourt's Relation*, 15–17; Pestana, *World of Plymouth Plantation*, 18.

3. Bradford, *OPP*, 95–99.

4. Bradford, *OPP*, 95–100, 104 ("they had now"); Heath, ed., *Mourt's Relation*, 15–25, 20 ("tore our very armor").

5. Bradford, *OPP*, 97–100; Heath, ed., *Mourt's Relation*, 20–30, 28 ("the prettiest things").

6. Bradford, *OPP*, 101–3, 102 ("extraordinary shrike"); Heath, ed., *Mourt's Relation*, 35–37, 36 ("Woach woach").

7. Bradford, *OPP*, 99–101; Heath, ed., *Mourt's Relation*, 35–37, 37 ("we could not").

8. Bradford, *OPP*, 106–7; Heath, ed., *Mourt's Relation*, 38–39 ("a goodly . . . hopeful place").

9. Bradford, *OPP*, 108–10; Bremer, *One Small Candle*, 1–2.

10. Heath, ed., *Mourt's Relation*, 42–48.

11. Jonathan Mack, *A Stranger among Saints: Stephen Hopkins, the Man Who Survived Jamestown and Saved Plymouth* (Chicago: Chicago Review Press, 2020); Alden T. Vaughan, "Namontack's Itinerant Life and Mysterious Death," *Virginia Magazine of History and Biography* 126.2 (2018): 179–92.

12. Turner, *They Were Pilgrims*, 52–54; Pestana, *World of Plymouth Plantation*.

13. Heath, ed., *Mourt's Relation*, 49–50.

14. Bradford, *OPP*, 114 ("how farr . . . was begune").

15. Bradford, *OPP*, 114 ("horid and divellish . . . dismale swampe").

16. Wood, *New England's Prospect*, 94 ("acknowledge the power").

17. Bradford, *OPP*, 110–11; Salisbury, "Treacherous Waters," 61–63; Phinehas Pratt later reported that Tisquantum made an explicit case for the English as allies: he "tould Masasoit what wonders he had seen in Eingland & yt if he Could make Einglish his ffreinds then Enemies yt weare to strong for him would be Constrained to bowe to him." Pratt, *Declaration of the Affairs*, 14. There is a long tradition of writers connecting Samoset to a Wabanaki sagamore (sachem) known as John Somerset, but as the antiquarian scholar Albert Matthews argued, the connection is a weak one. Matthews, "Note on the Indian Sagamore Samoset," *Publications of the Colonial Society of Massachusetts* (Boston: Colonial Society of Massachusetts, 1904), 6:59–70.

18. Heath, ed., *Mourt's Relation*, 50–51, 58–59.

19. Heath, ed., *Mourt's Relation*, 50–53; Bradford, *OPP*, 110.

20. Heath, ed., *Mourt's Relation,* 53–55, 54 ("a hat, a pair of stockings"); Bradford, *OPP,* 110.

21. Heath, ed., *Mourt's Relation,* 53–55.

22. Heath, ed., *Mourt's Relation,* 55 ("speak a little," "could not"), 56 ("the interpreters").

23. Heath, ed., *Mourt's Relation,* 55–56 (the Massasoit/Winslow meeting); 57–58 (the Massasoit's face paint, dress, tobacco bag, beaded necklace, and knife).

24. Heath, ed., *Mourt's Relation,* 54–56; Bradford, *OPP,* 120–21.

25. Heath, ed., *Mourt's Relation,* 56.

26. Heath, ed., *Mourt's Relation,* 55–58, 56 (treaty text, "King James").

27. On the Julian calendar which the English still used, the new year began on March 25, and the days were ten days behind the modern Gregorian calendar. So while we would say the summit with the Massasoit happened on April 1, 1621, in the colonists' view, it happened in the previous month and year on March 22, 1620.

28. Heath, ed., *Mourt's Relation,* 57–58.

29. Heath, ed., *Mourt's Relation,* 58–59.

30. Heath, ed., *Mourt's Relation,* 58 ("would come and set corn").

31. Bradford, *OPP,* 118; Morton, *New English Canaan,* 23–24; Johnson, *Wonder-Working Providence,* 40–43.

32. James Deetz and Patricia Scott Deetz, *The Times of Their Lives: Life, Love, and Death in Plymouth Colony* (New York: Anchor Books, 2000), 28–29.

33. Seelye, *Memory's Nation,* 293, 592.

34. Bradford, *OPP,* 111 ("spetiall instrument").

Chapter 12. Patuxet Reborn

1. Heath, ed., *Mourt's Relation,* 59 ("sweet and fat").

2. Heath, ed., *Mourt's Relation,* 61–62 ("came very often . . . wives and children").

3. Bradford, *OPP,* 115–16 ("showing them").

4. Williams, *Key,* 99 ("out of love," "very loving . . . friendly joyning"); a Dutch writer observing his culturally similar Munsee neighbors concurred with Williams's observation that men did not particularly like to help with planting. See Van der Donck, *Description of New Netherland,* 97–98. ("The men are hardly concerned with it, unless they are very young or very old," and all who help worked "under the direction of the women.")

5. Bradford, *OPP,* 115–16; Heath, ed., *Mourt's Relation,* 82–83, 82 ("with great ease"); Nanepashemet, "It Smells Fishy to Me," 42–50; Mrozowski, "Native American Cornfield on Cape Cod," 57–58 (fish fertilizer).

6. Winslow, *Good News,* 113 ("be watched by night"); Roberts, "That's Not a Wolf," 357–92.

7. Heath, ed., *Mourt's Relation,* 62 ("some ten or twelve . . . weary of them").

8. Heath, ed., *Mourt's Relation,* 62.

9. Heath, ed., *Mourt's Relation,* 61–62; Lisa Brooks, *The Common Pot: The Recovery of Native Space in the Northeast* (Minneapolis: University of Minnesota Press, 2008), 3–8.

10. Christa M. Beranek, David B. Landon, John M. Steinberg, and Brian Damiata, eds.,

"Project 400: The Plymouth Colony Archaeological Survey Public Summary Report on the 2015 Field Season Burial Hill, Plymouth, Massachusetts," Cultural Resources Management Study No. 75a (Boston: University of Massachusetts, 2016): 1–52; David N. Spidaliere and Alexander Patterson, "University of Massachusetts Summer Field School 2012, Plymouth," *Society for Historical Archaeology Newsletter* 54.4 (Winter 2021): 49–50. The lead archaeologist on the dig, David Landon, offers a lively and accessible summary of these finds on the YouTube MassArchaeology Channel, "Gene Winter Chapter Presents: Dr. David Landon," https://www.youtube.com/watch?v=go3gIn_hl1Y.

11. Beranek et al., "Project 400," 1–52.
12. Heath, ed., *Mourt's Relation*, 60 ("prevent abuses . . . might prosper").
13. Heath, ed., *Mourt's Relation*, 60 ("a horseman's coat") 60–64; Bradford, *OPP*, 127 ("a suite of cloaths").
14. Heath, ed., *Mourt's Relation*, 61–64.
15. Heath, ed., *Mourt's Relation*, 65–66.
16. Heath, ed., *Mourt's Relation*, 66–68.
17. Heath, ed., *Mourt's Relation*, 66–67, 67 ("King James his country").
18. Christopher Levett, "A Voyage into New England" (1628), in *Christopher Levett of York*, ed. James Phinney Baxter (Portland, ME: Gorges Society, 1893), 117 ("that they see"); Heath, ed., *Mourt's Relation*, 60 ("the great King"), 92 ("their greatest king," "many other kings"); Jenny Hale Pulsipher, *Subjects unto the Same King: Indians, English, and the Contest for Authority in Colonial New England* (Philadelphia: University of Pennsylvania Press, 2005), 1–36.
19. Wood, *New England's Prospect*, 103 ("not a little proud," "they love any man").
20. Heath, ed., *Mourt's Relation*, 67, 73 ("special and trusty man of Massasoit"); Bradford, *OPP*, 129 ("a proper lustie man").
21. Heath, ed., *Mourt's Relation*, 69–72.
22. Heath, ed., *Mourt's Relation*, 70 ("no less than . . . somewhat").
23. Bradford, *OPP*, 129 ("ther peace and aquaintance").

Chapter 13. Downfall

1. Heath, ed., *Mourt's Relation*, 73–74; Winslow, *Good News*, 86 (Corbitant's charisma).
2. Heath, ed., *Mourt's Relation*, 73–74, 74 ("held a knife"); on Corbitant's ambitions see also Bradford, *OPP*, 129.
3. Heath, ed., *Mourt's Relation*, 73–74; Bradford, *OPP*, 129.
4. Heath, ed., *Mourt's Relation*, 74–75, 75 ("hurly-burly," "Neen squares").
5. Heath, ed., *Mourt's Relation*, 75–76; Bradford, *OPP*, 129 ("came trembling," "their wounds drest").
6. Bradford, *OPP*, 129 ("much firmer peace"); Nathaniel Morton, *The New-England's Memoriall* (Plymouth, MA: Allen Danforth, 1826 [repr., 1st ed. 1663]), 44 (September 13/23, 1621, text).
7. Winslow to Anonymous, December 11, 1621, in Heath ed., *Mourt's Relation*, 8; on the larger mistranslations in this treaty and others between Plymouth and Wampanoags, see Jeffrey Glover, *Paper Sovereigns: Anglo-Native Treaties and the*

Law of Nations, 1604-1664 (Philadelphia: University of Pennsylvania Press, 2014), 118-57.

8. Bradford, *OPP,* 110-11.
9. Winslow to Anonymous, December 11, 1621, in Heath ed., *Mourt's Relation,* 81-82; James Deetz and Patricia Scott Deetz, *The Times of Their Lives: Life, Love, and Death in Plymouth Colony* (New York: Anchor Books, 2000), 42-43, 58-59.
10. Winslow to Anonymous, December 11, 1621, in Heath ed., *Mourt's Relation,* 82-83; Deetz and Deetz, *Times of Their Lives,* 2-10.
11. Winslow to Anonymous, December 11, 1621, in Heath ed., *Mourt's Relation,* 83 ("We entertain them").
12. Winslow to Anonymous, December 11, 1621, in Heath ed., *Mourt's Relation,* 82 ("it hath pleased").
13. Winslow, *Good News,* 59-60; Bradford, *OPP,* 135.
14. Winslow, *Good News,* 60 ("enmity," "challenge"); Bradford, *OPP,* 135.
15. Winslow, *Good News,* 61, 66 (gunpowder); Bradford, *OPP,* 135-36.
16. Winslow, *Good News,* 64 ("ends were only"); Bradford, *OPP,* 137 ("plaid his own game").
17. For material evidence corresponding with political shifts, see Eric S. Johnson, "Community and Confederation: A Political Geography of Contact-Period Southern New England," in *The Archaeological Northeast,* ed. Mary Ann Levine, Michael S. Nassaney, and Kenneth E. Sassaman (Westport, CT: Bergin and Garvey, 1999), 155-68; Johnson, "The Politics of Pottery: Material Culture and Political Process among Algonquians of Seventeenth-Century Southern New England," *Interpretations of Native North American Life: Material Contributions to Ethnohistory,* ed. Michael S. Nassaney and Eric S. Johnson (Gainesville: University Press of Florida and the Society for Historical Archaeology, 2000), 118-45.
18. Winslow, *Good News,* 64 ("greater esteem"); Bradford, *OPP,* 137 ("gifts").
19. Winslow, *Good News,* 62-65, 64 ("lead us to peace or war," "sending them word"); Bradford, *OPP,* 137.
20. Winslow, *Good News,* 59-60; Bradford, *OPP,* 135-36.
21. Winslow, *Good News,* 66; Bradford, *OPP,* 137.
22. Winslow, *Good News,* 61-63; Bradford, *OPP,* 137.
23. Winslow, *Good News,* 63 ("an Indian of Tisquantums . . . him in chase"), 64 ("he could not"); Bradford, *OPP,* 137.
24. Winslow, *Good News,* 59-60; Bradford, *OPP,* 135.
25. Winslow, *Good News,* 65 ("ready to deliver"), 66 ("mad with rage . . . great heat"); Bradford, *OPP,* 137.

Chapter 14. Death

1. Winslow, *Good News,* 68-70; Bradford, *OPP,* 130-40.
2. Bradford, *OPP,* 127 ("caused him to"); Winslow, *Good News,* 68 ("Massassowat . . . sent to us"), 70 ("was wrought).
3. Bradford, *OPP,* 128 ("emulation," "more squarely," "better intelligence").
4. Bradford, *OPP,* 140; Winslow, *Good News,* 70-71.
5. Bradford, *OPP,* 140; Winslow, *Good News,* 70 ("violent fever").

6. Bradford, *OPP*, 141; Winslow, *Good News*, 70–73.

7. Bradford, *OPP*, 141 ("in this place"); Winslow, *Good News*, 64 ("to make himself").

8. Bradford, *OPP*, 128 ("stick close to").

9. Studies that explore the additive rather than exclusive theology of Native converts include Romero, *Making War and Minting Christians*, and Silverman, *Faith and Boundaries*.

10. On the overall significance of reinterment and ossuaries among the Wendats/ Hurons, a different Eastern Woodlands Indigenous society, see Erik R. Seeman, *Death in the New World: Cross-Cultural Encounters, 1492–1800* (Philadelphia: University of Pennsylvania Press, 2010), 121–27; on evidence of the practice in the Dawnlands, see James W. Bradley, Francis P. McManamon, Thomas F. Mahlstedt, and Ann L. Magennis, "The Indian Neck Ossuary: A Preliminary Report," *Bulletin of the Massachusetts Archaeological Society* 43.2 (October 1982): 47–59.

11. Neal Salisbury, "Red Puritans: The 'Praying Indians' of Massachusetts Bay and John Eliot," *WMQ* 31.1 (January 1974): 27–54; Richter, *Facing East*, 110–29 (communal sins); Seeman, *Death in the New World*, 162–69 (brushes with death).

12. Bradford, *OPP*, 141; Winslow, *Good News*, 70–73, 70 ("violent fever"), 73 ("found a great sickness").

13. Robert A. Caro, *The Passage of Power: The Years of Lyndon Johnson IV* (New York: Vintage Books, 2012), xiv ("although the cliché," emphasis in the original).

14. Winslow, *Good News* ("not caring . . . honour").

Chapter 15. Afterlives

1. Jean M. O'Brien, *Firsting and Lasting: Writing Indians Out of Existence in New England* (Minneapolis: University of Minnesota Press, 2010), 16–17.

2. O'Brien, *Firsting and Lasting*, 20–24, 108 ("the first last Indian"). These narratives of replacement are a central concept within the theory of "settler colonialism." Patrick Wolfe, "Settler Colonialism and the Elimination of the Native," *Journal of Genocide Research* 8:4 (2006): 387–409.

3. Seelye, *Memory's Nation*, 6–22; Deetz and Deetz, *Times of Their Lives*, 12–13.

4. Seelye, *Memory's Nation*, 641 ("fake"); "Stones Chipped; Canopy over Plymouth Rock Defaced," *Boston Globe*, December 12, 1900, 2; "Plymouth Rock Paint May Be Harvard Joke; Gov Hurley Directs Kirk to Offer Assistance in Tracking Down Vandals," *Boston Globe*, May 3, 1937, 7; Tom Coakley, "Swastika Found Spray-Painted on Plymouth Rock," *Boston Globe*, August 14, 1991, 21; Jon Auerbach, "Plymouth Vandals Mar a Piece of the Rock," *Boston Globe*, November 17, 1994, 42; "Intruders Paint 'Lies' on Plymouth Rock," *Boston Globe*, January 15, 2014; "Police Blotter: Vandalism Arrest," *Boston Globe*, February 28, 2020, B2.

5. Bob Lang, "I Don't Care If the Natives Do Seem Friendly . . . ," *Inside Politics*, February 12, 2004; Jeff Parker, "They Say They're Building a Wall . . . ," *Florida Today*, November 1, 2006; Etta Hulme, "Correction of History/Border Fenced at Plymouth Rock," *Fort Worth Star-Telegram*, November 22, 2005; Dana Summers, "We Better Not Issue Drivers' Licences to These Immigrants," *Orlando Sentinel*, November 21, 2007; Dana Summers, "They're Noisy, They Have No Jobs, and They Want What's Ours . . . ," *Orlando Sentinel*, 2011; David Sipress, "I'm Sorry, but This Beach Is for Residents Only," *New Yorker*, July 22, 2013; David Sipress,

Pilgrims at a Border Wall, *New Yorker,* February 19, 2016; Signe Wilkinson, "We Should Have Built a Wall!" *Mountain Mail,* January 14, 2018; Henry Wadsworth Longfellow, *The Courtship of Myles Standish* (Chicago: Thompson and Thomas, 1905 [1st ed., 1858]), 84 ("the corner-stone"). X's original quip about Plymouth Rock was a critique of false consciousness among Blacks who associated themselves with the *Mayflower* narrative of American origins, in the speech titled "Twenty Million Black People in a Political, Economic, and Mental Prison," January 23, 1963: "But this twentieth century Uncle Tom, he'll stand up in your face and tell you about when his fathers landed on Plymouth Rock. His father never landed on Plymouth Rock; the rock was dropped on him but he wasn't dropped on it." The more famous and pithy formulation quoted here comes from Alex Haley and Malcolm X, *The Autobiography of Malcolm X* (New York: Random House, 1964), 232.

6. Chester, ed., *Parish Registers of St. Michael,* 221.

7. Heath, "Introduction," Heath ed., *Mourt's Relation,* vii–xv; Kelly Wisecup, "Introduction," Winslow, *Good News,* 1–17.

8. Minkema, "Note on the Text," *OPP: 400th Anniversary Ed.,* 68–69.

9. Minkema, "Note on the Text," 68–69; Morton, *New English Canaan,* 104; Johnson, *Wonder-Working Providence,* 43.

10. John C. Kemp, "Introduction," *Governor William Bradford's Letter Book* (Bedford, MA: Applewood, 2002), v–viii; Minkema, "Note on the Text," 68–69.

11. Minkema, "Of Plimoth Plantation: An Overview," *OPP: 400th Anniversary Ed.,* 49–68.

12. The long debate about whether or not the Pequot War was a genocide is summarized and rather conclusively settled by Benjamin Madley in "'Too Furious': The Genocide of Connecticut's Pequot Indians, 1636–1640," in Ned Blackhawk, Ben Kiernan, Benjamin Madley, and Rebe Taylor, eds., *The Cambridge World History of Genocide: Volume 2, Genocide in the Indigenous, Early Modern and Imperial Worlds, from c. 1535 to World War One* (Cambridge: University of Cambridge Press, 2023), 215–42.

13. Silverman, *This Land Is Their Land,* 299–306.

14. Silverman, *This Land Is Their Land,* 319–22; DeLucia, *Memory Lands,* 289–324.

15. Silverman, *This Land Is Their Land,* 355–418.

16. Seelye, *Memory's Nation,* 23–40; Michael D. Hattem, *Past and Prologue: Politics and Memory in the American Revolution* (New Haven: Yale University Press, 2020), 56–58, 183–209.

17. Seelye, *Memory's Nation;* O'Brien, *Firsting and Lasting;* Joseph A. Conforti, *Imagining New England: Explorations of Regional Identity from the Pilgrims to the Mid-Twentieth Century* (Chapel Hill: University of North Carolina Press, 2001), 175–76; Deetz and Deetz, *Times of Their Lives,* 9–18; Pestana, *World of Plymouth Plantation,* 3–10.

18. Conforti, *Imagining New England,* 35–78.

19. Diana Karter Appelbaum, *Thanksgiving: An American Holiday, An American History* (New York: Facts on File Publications, 1984), 5–11, 26–30, 153–54; Sherbrooke Rogers, *Sarah Josepha Hale: A New England Pioneer, 1788–1879* (Grantham, NH: Tompson and Rutter, 1985), 15–27.

20. Richard Slotkin, *Regeneration through Violence: The Mythology of the American*

Frontier, 1600-1860 (Norman: University of Oklahoma Press, 1973), 369-568; Philip J. Deloria, *Playing Indian* (New Haven: Yale University Press, 1998), 10-70.

21. Brian Rouleau, *Empire's Nursery: Children's Literature and the Origins of the American Century* (New York: New York University Press, 2021), 21-54; Blee and O'Brien, *Monumental Mobility,* 31-63.

22. Deetz and Deetz, *Times of Their Lives;* Elizabeth Pleck, *Celebrating the Family: Ethnicity, Consumer Culture, and Family Rituals* (Cambridge, MA: Harvard University Press, 2000), 27-28.

23. Pleck, *Celebrating the Family,* 33-34.

24. Clyde Robert Bulla, *Squanto, Friend of the White Man* (New York: Scholastic, 1965; repr., 1982 as *Squanto, Friend of the Pilgrims*); Feenie Ziner, *Dark Pilgrim: The Story of Squanto* (Boston: Chilton Publishers, 1965; repr., 1988 as *Squanto,* Hamden, CT: Linnet Books); Stewart and Polly Anne Graff, *Squanto: Indian Adventurer* (Champlain, IL: Garland Publishing, 1965); Teresa Noel Celsi, *Squanto and the First Thanksgiving* (Milwaukee: Raintree Publishers, 1989); Cathy East Dubowski, *The Story of Squanto: First Friend to the Pilgrims* (Milwaukee : Gareth Stevens Publications, 1997); Eric Metaxas, *Squanto and the Miracle of Thanksgiving* (Nashville: Tommy Nelson, 1999); Joseph Bruchac, *Squanto's Journey: The Story of the First Thanksgiving* (Orlando, FL: Voyager Books, 2000); Arlene B. Hirschfelder, *Squanto, 1585?-1622* (Mankato, MN: Blue Earth Books, 2004); Joyce K. Kessel, *Squanto and the First Thanksgiving* (Minneapolis: Carolrhoda Books, 2004); Hannah Isbell, *Squanto: Native American Translator and Guide* (Buffalo, NY: Enslow Publishing, 2018); Ann Byers, *Squanto* (New York: Cavendish Square Publishing, 2018).

25. Kentley B. Page, "The Depiction of Squanto: Tisquantum's Portrayal in Children's Literature and the Connection to the American Civil Rights Movement" (master's thesis in history, Claremont Graduate University, 2011).

26. *Squanto: A Warrior's Tale,* dir. Xavier Koller (Walt Disney Pictures, 1994).

27. John Easton, *A Relation of the Indian War, by Mr. Easton, of Rhode Island, 1675* (digital repr., Lincoln: University of Nebraska Digital Commons, 2006), 10.

28. Silverman, *This Land Is Their Land,* 299-306.

29. O'Connell, "Introduction," *On Our Own Ground,* xiii-lxxvii.

30. Apess, "Eulogy on King Philip," in O'Connell, ed., *On Our Own Ground,* 281 ("young chiefs . . . savages were").

31. Silverman, *This Land Is Their Land,* 389-410; DeLucia, *Memory Lands,* 164-200; Judith A. Ranta, ed., *The Lives and Writings of Betsey Chamberlain: Native American Mill Worker* (Boston: Northeastern University Press, 2003), 3-14; Arnold Krupat, *"That the People Might Live": Loss and Renewal in Native American Elegy* (Ithaca: Cornell University Press, 2012), 122-25.

32. Silverman, *This Land Is Their Land,* 412-13. On Narragansett memorializing as a means of opposing their detribalization, see DeLucia, *Memory Lands,* 164-200.

33. Silverman, *This Land Is Their Land,* 2-18; Peters, "Of Patuxet," 45-47; Robert Carr and Andrew Blake, "Stage Plymouth Protest: Indians Take Over Mayflower II," *Boston Globe,* November 27, 1970, 1 (cool cloudy weather). Not all local activists were thrilled by these theatrics, which made the protest a national news story; they felt it distracted from the protest's main point—that Thanksgiving should be

remembered as National Day of Mourning. Carr and Blake, "Stage Plymouth Protest," *Boston Globe*, November 27, 1970, 28 ("Plymouth Rock is covered"); "Mourning Indians Dump Sand on Plymouth Rock," *New York Times*, November 27, 1970, 26 ("the start of everything bad," local misgivings).

34. Apess, "Eulogy on King Philip," in *On Our Own Ground*, ed. O'Connell, 286 ("of mourning"); Blee and O'Brien, *Monumental Mobility*, 132–35; DeLucia, *Memory Lands*, xii–xiv.

35. Blee and O'Brien, *Monumental Mobility*, 203–4; Meredith P. Luze, "Living the History: The Role of Archaeology in the Interpretation of the Wampanoag Homesite at Plimoth Plantation" (master's thesis in historical archaeology, University of Massachusetts Boston, 2015), 87–93.

36. Nanepashemet (Anthony Pollard), "Tisquantum: The Real Story of Squanto" (unpublished manuscript, 1988), 1–2, Plimoth Patuxet Museum Special Collections.

37. Luze, "Living the History," 92–105; "Mashpee Wampanoag Museum," https://mashpeewampanoagtribe-nsn.gov/museum; "The Cultural Center," https://www.aquinnah.org/cultural-center.

38. Rachel Devaney, "'Wampanoag Pilgrim Disney'?: Wampanoag Tribe Severs Ties with Plimoth Patuxet Museums," *Cape Cod Times*, August 19, 2022, https://www.capecodtimes.com/story/news/2022/08/19/wampanoag-tribe-scales-back-tribal-involvement-plimoth-patuxet/10326677002/; "Plimoth Patuxet Museums Statement," September 1, 2022, https://plimoth.org/news-press/plimoth-patuxet-museums-statement; Brian MacQuarrie, "Tensions Grow between Tribe, Museum: Apparent Rift between Plimoth Patuxet and Wampanoags Sparks Push for Boycott," *Boston Globe*, December 26, 2022, A1.

Epilogue

1. Anonymous, "Description of Cape Cod, and the County of Barnstable," *Massachusetts Magazine, or, Monthly Museum of Knowledge and Rational Entertainment* 3.2 (February 1, 1791): 73–76; William Cronon, *Changes in the Land: Indians, Colonists, and the Ecology of New England* (New York: Hill and Wang, 1983), 159–60; Glenn Motzkin and David R. Foster, "Grasslands, Heathlands and Shrublands in Coastal New England: Historical Interpretations and Approaches to Conservation," *Journal of Biogeography* 29 (October 2002): 1569–90.

2. "Description of Cape Cod," *Massachusetts Magazine*, 75.

3. "Description of Cape Cod," *Massachusetts Magazine*, 75 ("would be of use," skeleton height, "that this person").

4. W. Sears Nickerson, "The Old Sagamore: Mattaquason of Monomoyick," *Bulletin of the Massachusetts Archaeological Society, Inc.* 19.4 (July 1958): 58 ("bore every evidence"); on his further claims the grave was Tisquantum's, see also Delores Bird Carpenter, ed., *Early Encounters: Native Americans and Europeans in New England: From the Papers of W. Sears Nickerson* (East Lansing: Michigan State University Press, 1994), 146, 238.

5. Carpenter, ed., *Early Encounters*, 31 (golf course); See the tab "History" on the "General Information" for the Eastward Ho! Country Club (formerly the Chatham Country Club), https://www.eastwardho.org/.

6. Frank Falacci, "History's Riddles Stir Winter Fires," *Boston Globe,* December 6, 1959, 40 (road gang gravestone); Nickerson Family Association website, "Where in the World Is Squanto," https://nickersonassoc.com/2015/06/01/104/ ("buried somewhere"); Susan Milton, "Are Chatham Remains Those of Squanto?" *Cape Cod Times* (March 9, 2011) (North Chatham grave).

7. Heath ed., *Mourt's Relation,* 27 (boards in grave); Thomas Morton, *New English Canaan, or New Canaan Containing an Abstract of New England, Composed in Three bookes* (London, 1637; repr., Boston, 1883), 170 ("put a planck"). Historian Erik Seeman also notes this quotation and points out that coffin burials were only just catching on with the English in the seventeenth century, and plenty of dead colonists were interred without them. Seeman, *Death in the New World,* 8, 16, 100.

8. See 25 U.S. Code c. 32 § 3003–3005 (NAGPRA); Mass. Gen. Laws c. 38 § 6, MGL c. 114, § 17 (Mass. Unmarked Burial laws); Valerie A. Talmage, "Massachusetts General Laws and Human Burials," *Bulletin of the Massachusetts Archaeological Society* 43.2 (October 1982): 60–65; Simon, "Collaboration between Archaeologists and Native Americans in Massachusetts," in Kerber, ed., *Cross-Cultural Collaboration,* 44–58.

9. Peters, "Consulting with the Bone Keepers," 32–43.

10. Winslow, *Good News,* 111; This focus on memorials was hardly unique to the man from Patuxet. The colonist Thomas Morton, who probably never met Tisquantum, recalled numerous Native people who had a similar relationship with the landscape, writing, "I have bin shewed the places, where such duels have bin performed, and have found the trees marked for a memoriall of the Combat." Morton, *New English Canaan,* 37.

11. Winslow, *Good News,* 111.

Acknowledgments

NO BOOK IS WRITTEN ALONE AND this one certainly needed a lot of help. From the beginning, I was aided by librarians and archivists at the American Antiquarian Society, Bodleian Libraries Special Collections at Oxford University, the British National Archives, the British Library, Columbia University Libraries, the Huntington Library, the John Carter Brown and John Hay Libraries at Brown University, the Massachusetts Historical Society, and Plimoth Patuxet Special Collections. My research was largely supported by funds from Barnard College and a yearlong fellowship from the National Endowment for the Humanities at the Huntington in San Marino, California. My time there was genial and generative thanks to director of research Steve Hindle and all the members of the Long-Term Fellows Working Group.

Adina Popescu shepherded this slow-moving project to a conclusion with her enthusiasm and patience. I owe a great debt to the scholars who read full manuscript drafts and offered trenchant criticisms and suggestions that I took to heart: Robert McCaughey, Jim Merrell, Paula Peters, Dan Richter, and the readers for Yale University Press. A few more historians offered particularly helpful tips, critiques, and cautions at various stages in the project's evolution that all improved the book: Francis Bremer, Timothy Lindberg, Peter Murkett, John Paul Paniagua, Caroline Dodds Peddock, Josh Reid, Alden Vaughan, Richard White, and the late Neal Salisbury. Paul Schneider offered thoughtful edits when he published an offshoot of this book in *Martha's Vineyard Magazine* in winter 2022. Purificación Ruiz García and Antonio Giron got in touch when the manuscript was in copyedits to alert me of Puri's new scholarship on the sale of the Wampanoag captives in Spain and to share Antonio's translations of the sources: they have my most heartfelt *muchas gracias.* I also want to thank Erin Greb for making the maps, Eliza Childs for copyediting, and Sandy Sadow for indexing.

The biggest breakthroughs in my thinking came through engaging with public historians who have been retelling Squanto's story for far longer than I have. I owe a special thanks to Richard Pickering of Plimoth Patuxet Museums, who has shared countless bits of wisdom with me and has been a champion of this project for years. I'm similarly indebted to the former head of Wampanoag education at the museum, Darius Coombs. Darius generously invited me to paddle up the Eel River with him in a *mishoon* (canoe) and gave me an eye-opening tour of the Plymouth waterfront in July 2017; later he joined me for a panel discussion on the *Mayflower* and memory in Los Angeles in 2018. Other experts at the museum— especially Malka Benjamin, Fred Dunford, Hillary Goodnow, Annie Greco, Brad Lopes, Daniel Rosen, and Emma Weber—have vastly improved my understanding of life in Patuxet and Plymouth. I'm grateful as well for my correspondence and conversations with staff members from the Aquinnah Cultural Center, the Mashpee Wampanoag Indian Museum, and the Smithsonian Institution's National Museum of the American Indian in New York City and National Museum of American History in Washington. Although I never had the pleasure of meeting him, I am thankful as well for the scholarship of the late Nanepashemet.

I got welcome critical feedback from audiences in several scholarly venues, including conferences held by the American Society for Ethnohistory, the Forum on European Expansion and Global Interaction, and the Native American and Indigenous Studies Association, plus talks at Brandeis University; California State University, Channel Islands; California State University, Fullerton; the Center for Seventeenth- and Eighteenth-Century Studies at the University of California, Los Angeles; Syracuse University; and the Truro Historical Society. The same goes for participants who workshopped chapter drafts at the Columbia Seminar in Early American History and Culture, the History Department at Johns Hopkins University, and the City University of New York's Early American Republic Seminar.

Many individuals at Barnard and Columbia were model colleagues who inspired me with their brilliant scholarship, kind words, and astute suggestions: Gergely Baics, Christopher Brown, Angelo Caglioti, Mark Carnes, Hannah Farber, Severin Fowles, Abosede George, Yoav Hamdani, Martha Howell, Karl Jacoby, Richard John, Thai Jones, Joel Kaye, Dorothy Ko, Stephanie McCurry, Justine Meberg, Anne Mesquita, Nara Milanich, Monica Miller, José Moya, Premilla Nadasen, Celia Naylor, Mae Ngai, Sully Rios, Ann Thornton, Lisa Tiersten, Deborah Valenze, Carl Wennerlind, Michael Witgen, and the late Herb Sloan. I'm especially grateful to my current and former students who expressed an interest in this book; I tried to write with them in mind as readers.

Quite a few more folks not yet named—some academics, some not—helped make this book a reality with their insights, encouragement, and most of all, their friendship: Leah Astbury, Zach Bennett, Daya Wolterstorff Berger, Spencer Berger, Ben Bernard, Andrew Berns, John Blanton, Molly Bloom, Tanya Both, Rainer Buschmann, Isaac Butler, Josh Chafetz, Adrienne Phelps Coco, Pete Coco, Andrew Wender Cohen, Jo Cohen, Kate Cuno, Alejandra Dubcovsky, Simon Finger, Julie Fisher, Claire Gherini, Rob Goldberg, Glenn Gordinier, Andrew Gottleib, Kate Grandjean, Fanny Gribenski, Aida Gureghian, Andrew Heath, Marilee Herring, Rachel Herrmann, Katherine Hill, Danny Jensen, Cole Jones, Matt Karp, John Kenney, Osamah Khalil, Sara Kriegel, Benjamin Madely, Peter Mancall, Kate Marshall, Erik Mathisen, Cara Murray, John O'Hara, Jaffa Panken, Chris Pastore, Clara Platter, Nick Radburn, Sharon Richter, Kate Roach, Jessica Roney, Mark Rose, Brian Rouleau, Mark Schmeller, Jonathan Schultz, Pauline Shapiro, David Silverman, Rusty Singletary, Lauren Steffel, Jessica Yirush Stern, Junko Takeda, and Pete Wagner.

None of this would be possible without the love of my mishpocha: Roger, Jasmine, Jake, Philip, Kate, Frankie, Amelia, Maxx, Elisa, Meghan, and Willa. Lastly, I need to thank two people who are not here to read these words but nonetheless are with me every day: my parents, Margie and Steve.

Index

Italicized page numbers indicate illustrations.